Heroes in Dungarees

Heroes in Dungarees

THE STORY OF THE AMERICAN MERCHANT MARINE IN WORLD WAR II

John Bunker

Naval Institute Press
Annapolis, Maryland

Library of Congress Cataloging-in-Publication Data

Bunker, John, 1913–
    Heroes in dungarees : the story of the American merchant
    marine in World War II / John Bunker.
        p.   cm.
    Includes bibliographical references and index.
    ISBN 1-55750-093-2 (acid-free paper)
    1. Merchant marine—United States—History—20th
    century.   2. World War, 1939–1945—Naval operations—
    United States.   3. Merchant mariners—United States—
    Interviews.   I. Title.
    D810.T8B79   1995
    940.54'5973—dc20   95-6785

Printed in the United States of America on acid-free paper ∞

02 01 00 99 98 97 96 95   9 8 7 6 5 4 3 2

First printing

*To the ships
and the men
who sailed them*

Contents

Preface

HIS IS THE STORY OF THE U.S. MERCHANT MARINE during World War II—the freighters and tankers and the men who sailed them to invasion beaches and battlefronts all over the world. The Merchant Marine was in the forefront of battle from Pearl Harbor until the end of the war. It transported the steel, fuel, and food, as well as the guns, tanks, and ammunition, that kept Britain and Russia in the war. It carried rubber, oil, ores, and other raw materials for the American war arsenal. The Merchant Marine took the soldiers to war, too. Merchant seamen braved bombs, torpedoes, kamikazes, and the hazards of storm, ice, and collision in convoy, from the icy Barents Sea to Pacific invasion beaches. Shells from the guns of merchant ships streaked through many foreign skies. Wherever the freights of war were needed, the cargo ships were ready to deliver.

Hundreds of ships were sunk by bombs, torpedoes, and gunfire; by storms; or by collisions in thick fogs and blanketing snow. Thousands of seamen went down with their ships or were killed or wounded in action. For some, there are names to mark their passing—Bari, Leyte, Mindanao, Anzio, Bizerte, Okinawa, Avola, Normandy, the Bay of Bengal. For others, there are only the restless, rolling waves, whispering a requiem across the ocean deeps.

The author wishes to express appreciation for the help of the following individuals and organizations:

Richard A. von Doenhoff and associate staff members of the Military Reference Branch, National Archives, Washington, D.C.

Angie Spicer VanDereedt, Archivist, Civil Reference Branch, National Archives.

Public Affairs Office, U.S. Coast Guard, Washington, D.C.

Public Affairs Office, U.S. Maritime Administration, Washington, D.C.

Photographic Section, Curator Branch, Naval Historical Center, Washington, D.C.

Public Information Office, U.S. Merchant Marine Academy, King's Point, New York.

The libraries of the South Street Seaport Museum, New York, New York; the Mariners Museum, Newport News, Virginia; and the Peabody-Essex Museum, Salem, Massachusetts.

The author is also indebted to the many seamen, some of them his shipmates, who, over the years, have recounted their wartime adventures in the hope of contributing to an appreciation of the Merchant Marine's vital role in World War II.

Introduction

IN PEACETIME, the U.S. Merchant Marine includes all of the privately owned and operated vessels flying the American flag—passenger ships, freighters, tankers, tugs, and a wide miscellany of other craft. Merchant Marine vessels ply the high seas, the Great Lakes, and the inland waters, such as the Chesapeake Bay and navigable rivers.

Prior to U.S. entry into World War II, the deep-sea and coastwise segments of the Merchant Marine, the part that could be immediately enlisted for war service, consisted of about 1,400 ships, including a sizable fleet of passenger vessels, mostly in the coastal, intercoastal, and Caribbean trades. Many ships of the prewar dry cargo fleet were products of the huge World War I emergency shipbuilding program that launched hundreds of ships. Except for a few, these ships were completed too late to take part in the war effort, but they served the Merchant Marine well during the 1920s and 1930s. In 1941, they comprised a large part of our deep-sea dry cargo fleet. Many of them were sunk during World War II.

When we entered the war, the Merchant Marine, although still privately owned, came under government control. The men who sailed the ships were civilians, but they also were under government control and subject to disciplinary action by the U.S. Coast Guard and, when overseas, by local U.S. military authorities.

Compared with soldiers and sailors, merchant seamen had much more freedom of movement. After completing a voyage, they could usually leave a ship but had to join another vessel within a reasonable period of time or be drafted into the U.S. Armed Forces. There was no uniform required for merchant seamen. Some officers wore uniforms; many did not.

During the war, merchant ships were operated by some forty steamship companies, and the War Shipping Administration assigned new ships to them as they were completed.

A total of 733 U.S.–flag merchant ships were lost during World War II.

More then 6,000 merchant seamen died as the result of enemy action.

Glossary of Merchant Marine Terms

Able seaman   The next grade above the beginning grade of ordinary seaman in the deck crew.

Black gang   Term used for the engine room force, which included the engineers, firemen, oilers, and wipers.

Bos'n   Shortening of the old term "boatswain": an unlicensed member of the crew who supervised the work of the deck men under direction of the first mate.

Chief   The crew's term for the chief engineer.

Chief mate   Another term for first mate.

Fo'c'sle   A modern version of the old term "forecastle," or bow section of the ship, where the crew lived. Today, as generally they did during World War II, the crew lives amidships or aft in cabins allotted for one or more men.

Freighter   A ship designed to carry all types of general cargo, or "dry cargo."

Head   Sailors' term for the toilet.

Ladder   Sea term for stairs.

"Lame duck"   Term for disabled vessel that had to fall out of a convoy and thus became easy prey for submarines.

Master   A term for the captain, a holdover from the days when the captain was literally, and legally, the "master" of the ship and crew. His word was law.

"Nantucket sleigh ride"   A term for what frequently happened to Nantucket whalers when they left the whaling ship in a small boat to go after a whale. If they harpooned the whale without mortally wounding it, the animal took off with the whaleboat in tow. The whalers referred to their resulting wild ride as a Nantucket sleigh ride.

Messman   A member of the steward's department who served meals to officers and crew.

Ordinary seaman The beginning grade for members of the deck department. The next step is able seaman.

Port The left side of the ship.

Rustbucket Sailors' term for an old ship that needed a lot of paint and repairs.

Ships time Ships time was reckoned by the half hour, starting at midnight. A half hour after twelve was one bell; one o'clock, two bells; and so on until four o'clock, which was eight bells. The reckoning then started over again, with 4:30 being one bell. It has been customary in the Merchant Marine, probably for hundreds of years, to strike the time on a bell placed by the wheel on sailing ships and over the wheel in the pilothouse on steamships. On some ships, the lookout in the bow also struck the time on a large bell on the fo'c'sle head. The watches, which were four hours each, ended at eight bells. A crewman stood two watches during the twenty-four hours.

Sparks The radio operator.

Stack The ship's funnel or smokestack.

Starboard The right side of the ship.

Tanker A ship designed to carry various types of liquid cargo, from oil and gasoline to molasses, water, and vegetable oil.

Wiper A general handyman in the engine room.

Heroes in Dungarees

1
Prelude to War

World War II began for the U.S. Merchant Marine long before the Japanese attack on Pearl Harbor, 7 December 1941. It started on 9 October 1939, when the freighter *City of Flint*, about 1,500 miles east of New York, was bound for England with general cargo. Captain Joseph Gainard and his first mate were on the bridge in the late afternoon when they spotted an indistinct shape on the horizon off the starboard bow. At first it looked more like a rain cloud than a ship, but in a few minutes they identified a large vessel and could tell through the binoculars that she was a warship with many guns.

"She's a big one," said the mate. "A cruiser at least."

"Or even bigger," said Gainard. "My guess is a battle-wagon."

As Gainard recounted later: "We could see that it had big guns—I mean *big* guns—and they were trained on us. Those guns could have blown us to 'kingdom come' in one blast. We didn't know whether it was French or English or German. We just hoped that nobody on board of her was trigger happy. It was doing a good twenty-five knots."[1]

By then, the officers on the warship, with their high-power glasses, could see the American flag painted on the side of the *City of Flint*. They altered course, brought the guns inboard, and closed at high speed.

"It sure was good to watch those big guns turn around," Gainard said. "Even then I'm sure there were five-inchers and small stuff trained on us." The stranger then sent up a flag hoist. The flags were whipping in the wind and were difficult to read at a distance, but the freighter's crew were finally able to spell them out by referring to the international code book of signals.[2] The message said, "Do not use your radio or we will sink you. Stop. We are sending over a boat." They could now see the German flag.

Gainard rang for "stop" on the engine room telegraph. As the *City of Flint* lost way, he and the mate watched a motorboat, chock full of armed men, swing over the side of the warship and head their way. A young lieutenant in charge of the boarding party apologized to Captain Gainard for stopping his ship but said he would have to inspect the ship's papers and the manifest, which listed all items of cargo. He was obviously looking for cargo that the Germans considered contraband material especially useful to the enemy. The manifest listed such things as lumber, machinery, flour, lard, and canned foods, but then the officer came to 26,000 drums of lubricating oil. He grunted in satisfaction.

"You are guilty of carrying contraband to the enemy," he said triumphantly, and his signalman passed on this information to the warship by blinker. A return message said that a prize crew was being sent to take over the *City of Flint,* along with thirty-eight prisoners from the British freighter *Stonegate,* which the Germans had sunk. After the prize crew of eighteen had taken over, the battleship resumed her course and was soon lost to sight over the horizon. A not unfriendly Lt. Hans Pushbach told Captain Gainard that the ship would be taken to Germany by a circuitous route far north of the British Isles. This plan became uncertain soon afterward, however, when the freighter's radio went on the blink and it was impossible for the Germans to communicate with their naval headquarters. The German officer was now in a most delicate situation—in charge of an unarmed American merchant ship taken on the high seas while the United States was ostensibly a neutral nation. He wasn't sure what higher authorities in Germany would want done with the *City of Flint*, so he told Gainard to head for Tromsö on the northern coast of Norway above the Arctic Circle.

The vessel skirted ice fields, and the Germans kept a nervous lookout for British patrols. Meanwhile, the prize crew and the British prisoners all but finished off the freighter's food supply. Eggs and bacon were delicacies that disappeared like bonbons. "They all ate like they hadn't had a good meal for months," said Gainard.

The ship reached the mountain-girded, isolated port of Tromsö without being spotted by British patrols and, after a brief stay there, steamed up the coast. Hugging mountains and fjords, the *City of Flint* rounded the tip of Europe and reached the Russian port of Murmansk on the White Sea through channels kept open by icebreakers. In a harbor crowded with ships of many nations were the famous German liners *Bremen* and *St. Louis.* Gainard had no idea what would happen to his ship and crew, for the Russians and Germans at this point were uneasy allies, playing a cat-and-mouse game with each other through the Hitler-Stalin nonaggression pact. The Russians were cold and indifferent, but they were not hostile. Although the crew were not allowed on shore, the Russians told Gainard after a week or so that he could leave at any time.

The German prize crew came back on board, and the strange peregrination of the *City of Flint* continued, with Gainard obeying orders to skirt the coast and return to Tromsö. On the way, they met the German ship *Schwaban*, which relayed orders for the *City of Flint* to put in at Haugesund, Norway, where they arrived on 3 November. While at anchor there and with the German prize crew peacefully asleep at night, a boarding party of armed Norwegians, in the best tradition of a James Bond movie, came quietly on board, roused the unsuspecting Germans, and hustled them ashore for internment. Gainard then steamed on to Bergen, Norway, where the cargo was finally discharged, except for thousands of apples, which had rotted in the hold during the ship's unwonted wandering. When the cargo was discharged, the *City of Flint* finally headed for home. She arrived at Baltimore, Maryland, on 27 January.

The capture of the *City of Flint* sparked some indignation and allegations of piracy on the high seas but did not cause the outrage that one might expect, probably because the ship did come safely home and no one was killed or hurt in the episode.[3]

There was also strong sentiment at the time against U.S. involvement in the war.

The first American Merchant Marine casualty of World War II occurred on the freighter *City of Rayville* of the American Pioneer Line, when she struck a mine near the coast off Cape Otway, about 120 miles from Melbourne, Australia, on 8 November 1940. People on shore heard the explosion and saw the flash of fire that followed. They put off in small boats to rescue survivors; one seaman was killed.

Just a few hours before, a British ship had hit a mine in that same area.

It was the sinking of the American freighter *Robin Moor* on 21 May 1941, however, that brought a denunciation of Germany from President Franklin D. Roosevelt, spurred a call for the arming of American merchant ships, and moved the United States a step closer to war. This ship was bound from the United States toward South Africa with general cargo and eight passengers, including a woman and a child. A total of forty-five people were on board.

Chief Officer Melvin Mundy was on the bridge at about 0400 when he was startled to see a blinker light on the horizon that was flashing a message in international code: "What ship is that?" Using a signal lamp kept handy in the wheelhouse, Mundy stepped out on a wing of the bridge and flashed back: "American steamship *Robin Moor*." By this time, Captain William Myers had come on the bridge and told Mundy to ask, "What ship are you?" The answer came quickly: "submarine." This was followed in a few seconds by the international code letters LRL (do not use your wireless). The next message ordered the *Robin Moor* to send over a boat. With Mundy in charge, a boat was launched, and it headed toward the pinpoint of light from the U-boat, which was moving closer. Mundy was interrogated by the submarine's youthful commander: "What is the name of your ship? Where do you sail from? What is your destination? What is your cargo?"

Mundy had the feeling that the Germans knew all about the ship and had the answer to these questions without having to ask them.

When he said that the ship was carrying a general cargo and that none of it could be considered contraband, the officer replied sharply, "Our information is different. You are carrying a contraband cargo of war supplies. I will give you twenty minutes to abandon ship. I remind you not to use your radio. Do not send an SOS."

Mundy and his men returned hurriedly to the ship. After the passengers and crew had been alerted, the captain gave the order to abandon ship. As soon as all hands were safely away in four lifeboats, the *Robin Moor* was torpedoed. Not wanting to expend any more torpedoes on such a vulnerable target, the U-boat opened fire with her deck gun and put some thirty shells into the vessel before she went down. Fortunately, only a light sea was running. The sinking had occurred about four hundred miles south of the Cape Verde Islands and nine hundred miles west of Liberia.

Three of the boats, with thirty-five survivors, were found by an English ship after being adrift for thirteen days, and the survivors were taken to Cape Town, South Africa. Among the castaways was two-year-old Robin McCullough, along with his parents, Mr. and Mrs. Robert McCullough. Despite a hot sun and the

An American flag painted on the hull of the Robin Moor *proclaims her status as a neutral ship, but it did not keep her from being torpedoed by a U-boat before the United States entered the war. (The Mariners Museum, Newport News, Virginia, PB 9669)*

rigors of exposure in open boats, all hands were landed in good shape, including Robin, who had amused himself by watching the "pretty fishes." The others didn't think Robin's fishes were so pretty, for they were big sharks that followed the boats until porpoises came along and drove them away. It had rained several times during the thirteen days, and there had been no lack of water. After the *Robin Moor* went down, the submarine had come up to the lifeboats and given them several tins of bread, butter, and biscuits, which helped somewhat with the diet of lifeboat hardtack.

The fourth lifeboat was found by the Brazilian freighter *Osorio* after it had covered one thousand miles in eighteen days.

Although there were no casualties in the sinking of the *Robin Moor* and all hands came through the ordeal without injuries, the incident was a setback for the strong isolationist movement in Congress. At the same time, it provided ammunition for those who favored more aid to Britain and an end to the Neutrality Act, which forbade American ships to travel in war zones.[4]

The *Steel Seafarer*, another product of the World War I "bridge of ships," was bombed and sunk in the Red Sea near Suez on 7 September 1941, probably by an Italian plane during one of the numerous Italian bombing raids over and near the Suez Canal.

The American-owned tanker *I. C. White*, flying the Panamanian flag, was torpedoed on 27 September 1941, four hundred miles east of Pernambuco, Brazil, while en route to Cape Town with 76,000 barrels of fuel oil. All but three of the crew were picked up by the American freighters *Del Norte* and *West Nilus;* the latter would become one of the block ships off the Normandy beachhead in 1944.

Another American-flag sinking, that of the *Lehigh*, appeared to be intentional. After discharging a cargo in Bilbao, Spain, the *Lehigh* was proceeding to Takoradi on the Gold Coast of Africa to load manganese ore. German agents at Bilbao had probably learned about the ship's itinerary. She was torpedoed on 19 October 1941, without warning, seventy-five miles west of Sierra Leone, West Africa.

According to Captain Vincent Arkins, nothing was seen of the submarine either before or after the ship was hit. All four lifeboats got away safely with thirty-nine crewman and five stowaways.

Survivors spent seven days in lifeboats after the American-flag freighter *Sagadahoc* was torpedoed on 3 December 1941 in the South Atlantic en route to Africa. The ship sank in twenty minutes, after which the submarine surfaced and asked questions about the cargo and destination. One lifeboat was in charge of Captain Frederick Evans, with the other under First Mate Norris Chadbourne. One man in the engine room was killed in the blast.

While in convoy in the North Atlantic several more American-owned ships with Panamanian registry were sunk in 1941. An American-owned tanker under the flag of Panama, the *Stanvac Calcutta*, would later add her name to the role call of heroic ships in one of the great sea fights of World War II.

The sinkings in 1941 were the prelude to what would become the U.S. Merchant Marine's full-scale participation in the great "Battle of the Atlantic," the longest, costliest, and most crucial battle of the war, ranging from the frigid Barents Sea to the palm-fringed Caribbean and the coastal waters of America.

Already, during two years of war, this battle had produced a terrible toll—hundreds of ships sunk and thousands of men lost. Soon, the names of many American ships and seamen would be added to the long roll of casualties in the Battle of the Atlantic.

2

The Ships and Men of the Merchant Marine

T HE HUGE U.S. MERCHANT MARINE of World War II had its genesis during World War I when Congress created the Emergency Fleet Corporation to build shipyards and ships for a "bridge of ships" to Europe. This program produced hundreds of cargo carriers that were the backbone of the dry cargo fleet when the United States entered World War II. It also pioneered new concepts in shipbuilding: using prefabrication to speed up construction and utilizing the facilities of factories far from shipyards to cut and shape steel parts for the ships.[1]

Prefabrication was employed during World War II to the extent that parts of the ship were built in various places within the yard, then lifted by cranes into place on the shipways, thus greatly reducing the time that a vessel occupied a shipway. A hull could be completed, from keel laying to launching, within a matter of weeks or even days. Also, most of the ships in the emergency fleet were welded, which saved both time and steel over the World War I method of using rivets to hold ships together.

The World War I program had concentrated on several standard designs, with the best known being the "Hog Islander," so called because the ships were built at Hog Island near Philadelphia, Pennsylvania. This war-built yard, with fifty shipways, was the largest the world had ever seen. A Hog Islander could be quickly recognized by any seaman. The design incorporated a great number of straight-line hull parts that could be made by workers with no experience in shipbuilding and the ship could be assembled at the yard with little shaping and fitting. The product was a vessel with a flat deck, flat bottom, and straight sides and with a minimum amount of bends at bow or stern. Hog Islanders, powered by steam turbines, proved to be good ships and were popular with shipowners. A total of 122 were built at Hog Island. Of these, 55 were lost during World War II.

When the World War I shipbuilding program began, an early end to the war was not anticipated. Because contracts and construction could not be quickly terminated, shipbuilding continued until the summer of 1920. Many of these emergency ships, especially the wooden steamers and schooners, never made more than a few trips, if any. A large number of small steel steamers were sold to Henry Ford to be made into "tin lizzies." Others were tied up in reserve fleets, many to be purchased by the British at the outbreak of World War II.

The massive World War II production of ships was made possible when Congress created the U.S. Maritime Commission in June 1936 "to provide the nation with a modern merchant marine, which would also serve as a naval auxiliary in time of war."[2]

The Maritime Commission lost no time in developing plans for a complete rebirth of the Merchant Marine. It envisioned the production of five hundred ships over a period of ten years and the rejuvenation of idle shipyards on all coasts. The nation's new Merchant Marine was to be based on several standard types designed for mass production, C-1, C-2, and C-3, and on several types of tankers.

The C-1 was 417 feet long, with a beam of 60 feet; of 9,075 deadweight tons (dwt); and speed of 14 knots.

The C-2 was 459 feet long, with a 63-foot beam; of 8,794 dwt; and speed of 15.5 knots.

The C-3 was 492 feet long, with a beam of 69 feet; of 12,500 dwt, and speed of 16.5 knots.

The "birthday" of this ambitious nautical renaissance came with the launching of the *Donald McKay*, a C-2, on 22 April 1939. The name was appropriate, for Donald McKay had designed and built clipper ships that made the U.S. Merchant Marine preeminent on the seas during the 1850s.

A number of big, fast tankers, however, had preceded the *Donald McKay*. These 553-foot, 19-knot ships were intended for naval use in time of war.

The *Donald McKay's* sister ships, named for famous American clippers, were launched in May 1939.

On 14 September 1939, the *Sea Arrow*, a C-3, was launched in Oakland, California. She was the first oceangoing freighter to be built on the Pacific coast since World War I.

Realizing that the war in Europe might exert tremendous demands on American shipping, the Maritime Commission looked at various plans for a standardized type of freighter suited for mass production. Its choice became the famous "Liberty." Classified as EC-2 (emergency cargo 2) by the Maritime Commission, the Liberty was an adaptation of a British tramp ship design.

The EC-2 was 441 feet long, with a 57-foot beam, and could carry 9,146 tons of cargo. Actually, she usually carried more; few Liberty ships left port without some tanks, planes, or trucks on deck. The ship was powered by a 2,500-HP reciprocating steam engine for a speed of 11 knots. A Liberty had five holds, three forward of the deckhouse and two aft.

Eighteen shipyards were set up just to build Liberty ships. The first was the *Patrick Henry*, launched by the Bethlehem-Fairfield Shipyard in Baltimore, Maryland, on 27 September 1941, as a band played "The Star Spangled Banner." Mrs. Henry A. Wallace, the wife of the vice president of the United States, christened the *Patrick Henry,* the first of 2,751 sister ships. This yard alone launched 312 of them.

The day was proclaimed "Liberty Fleet Day," with the public invited to visit yards where Liberty ships were being built. The *Star of Oregon* was launched at Portland, Oregon, and the *John C. Fremont,* named for an early California explorer, at Los Angeles, California.

The *Patrick Henry* sailed throughout the war. She made thirteen voyages and steamed 175,000 miles.

Except for a few, such as the *Houston Volunteers* and the *Stage Door Canteen,* Liberty ships were named for men and women who had made significant contributions to the country. A few were named for merchant seamen who had performed acts of heroism. The *Houston Volunteers* honored the hundreds of young men from Houston, Texas, who volunteered for the navy after the

The famous Patrick Henry, *the first Liberty ship, is framed between the antiaircraft guns of another Liberty in 1944, three years after she was placed in service. A veteran of many voyages and battles, the* Henry *was a proud "heroine" of the wartime merchant fleet. (U.S. Maritime Administration, 3980)*

cruiser *Houston* was sunk in the Pacific. *Stage Door Canteen* was named for the famous hospitality center in New York that entertained men of the armed forces. Ironically, men of the Merchant Marine were not admitted.

The basic construction cost of a Liberty was $1½ million. A measure of the task involved in producing hundreds of such ships, called for by the president, can be seen in these figures: 100 EC-2s required 100 main engines, 200 boilers, 100 steering engines, 200 condensers, 400 lifeboats, 600 generators, and 600 steam pumps, plus hundreds of anchors, windlasses, and other equipment.

Peak production came in July 1943 when 158 cargo vessels were delivered, including 109 Liberty ships. Some newspaper stories about Liberty ships cracking and sinking gave rise to a popular misconception that these vessels were coming apart and going down all over the oceans. Several ships were lost because of hull fractures, but the news stories were greatly exaggerated.

A number of U.S. and Allied ships suffered serious cracks in the hulls and had to be abandoned.

When the hull fractures were reported by the captains of Liberty ships and other warbuilt welded types, the War Shipping Administration and the U.S. Maritime Commission initiated an intensive study of their construction. The causes were quickly discovered, and measures were taken to improve welding techniques and to make structural changes in the hulls to limit welding failures.

Ship welding was a new technique in World War II and was adopted to speed up construction and to save steel. A large amount of steel was needed for rivets in the old style of shipbuilding, in which riveting was used to join hulls and superstructures. The speedy construction of the wartime armada of cargo ships and warships would have been impossible without the use of welding.

Also, most welders had never been on a ship or even in a shipyard. They had to be trained from the ground up in the skills of shipbuilding. Welding methods were constantly being refined and improved to get better welds and to increase production rates.

Two Liberty ships have been preserved as living memorials to the great wartime Liberty ship production program and to the nation's prodigious overall wartime shipbuilding record in general.

The *John W. Brown,* used as a New York City maritime schoolship for some years after the war, was saved from destruction by an organizarion of World War II Merchant Marine veterans and commercial maritime interests. Restored to operating condition and docked at Baltimore, she is open for public visiting and occasionally takes trips on Chesapeake Bay.

The *Jeremiah O'Brien,* also saved from the wreckers and restored by volunteer workers, is open for public visiting in San Francisco. This ship made world news in May 1994 when, manned by a crew of Merchant Marine veterans, she steamed from San Francisco to England to take part in ceremonies marking the fiftieth anniversary of the Allied invasion of France on 6 June. A public fund drive raised money to finance the trip.

From January 1942 to September 1945, U.S. shipyards delivered 5,304 ships of all types, probably the greatest achievement of industrial production that the world has ever seen. For example, a total of 1,677 deep-sea ships were launched in 1944, compared with 9 in 1936. Contributors to this massive industrial effort included steel mills, railroads, engine makers, and manufacturers of the thousands of parts and pieces of equipment that a ship required before she was ready for sea.

The need for a faster cargo ship resulted in the design and production of the Victory. She carried the same amount of cargo as the Liberty but, in each of two versions, was several knots faster and better suited for the long haul in the Pacific.

The Victory ship was 455 feet long, with a 62-foot beam and 10,800 dwt. Compared with the Liberty's 2,500-HP reciprocating steam engine, the Victory had a steam turbine of 6,000 HP for a speed of 15 knots plus.

A total of 414 Victory cargo ships were built, plus 117 Victory-type transports for the navy. Used only in the Pacific, the Victorys played no part in the Battle of the Atlantic or in European operations.

The *Lane Victory*, a World War II veteran of action in the Pacific, steamed from San Pedro, California, to participate in the D-day anniversary ceremonies in 1994. Many of her crew had manned Victory ships during the war. Chief Mate Bill Skinner was seventy-six years old at the time, and Chief Engineer Peter Jacobelly was seventy-two. Almost all of the crew were in their seventies. The government gave the ship to the U.S. Merchant Marine Veterans of World War II, who raised more than $1 million to pay for the trip. When the ship arrived in Panama, she encountered mechanical difficulties and was unable to complete the voyage.

A large type of ship with engines aft, called C-4, was designed for use as a freighter, but most of the C-4s were converted to troop ships. The C-4 was 522 feet long, with a 71-foot beam, and she had six holds. Speed was 21 knots.

In addition to its C-type cargo ships, the Maritime Commission built 218 coastal cargo ships, plus hundreds of tugs, concrete freighters, wooden and concrete barges, and other types of vessels. It also built hundreds of vessels for the navy, including escort carriers, frigates (also known as corvettes), and LSTs (landing ships, tank).

After a cargo ship was completed, she was assigned to a private steamship company for operation. The company arranged for a stevedoring firm to load the ship; called the union hiring hall for a crew; and, most important, saw that the ship was properly fueled and provisioned for the voyage. The logistics of supplying the ships was no small part of the wartime transport saga. A Liberty could burn one hundred barrels of fuel oil every day and use many gallons of lubricating oil for the main engine and bearings.

On a typical voyage from New York to the Persian Gulf by way of Cape Horn, the Liberty ship *Daniel Webster* logged 17,598 miles by the time she arrived at her destination and then spent fifty-two days waiting to discharge. The boilers were burning oil during the layover, and the crew had to eat.

The War Shipping Administration set up a network of steamship agents in most areas of operation to meet the supply needs of ships. The round trip of the *Daniel Webster* covered 32,528 miles. The ship logged 243 days steaming and 97 days in port. Before sailing from New York, the vessel was stored with 9,402 pounds of flour, bread, and cereals; 8,409 pounds of miscellaneous groceries; 15,000 pounds of canned fruit; 29,947 pounds of fresh and canned vegetables; 12,000 pounds of lard and dairy products; 22,384 pounds of fresh, canned, salted, and smoked meat; 3,881 pounds of poultry; and 1,726 pounds of fish. Perishables were stored in large refrigerators. All provisioning was arranged by the port steward of the operating company and his staff.

Prodigious amounts of coffee were consumed on merchant ships during the war. Fresh coffee was always on tap in the mess room percolator, as well as in the gun crew quarters and saloon. The custom of midwatch coffee was also dear to the hearts of the men below, and every well-found engine room had its percolator, a can of coffee, and a row of cups generally hanging somewhere near the log desk. It is traditional for the oiler leaving the watch to brew a pot of "jamoke" for the watch coming down.

The following was a typical weekday menu on a merchant ship at sea:

Breakfast

Fruit juice — Prunes
Eggs to order — Bacon
Home-fried potatoes — Biscuits
Hot cakes and syrup
Coffee — Tea

Dinner

Pea Soup — Crackers
Iced tea — Coffee
Yankee pot roast — Liver and onions
Boiled potatoes
Green peas — Vegetable salad
Fresh fruit

Supper

Cold cuts — Frankfurters
Baked beans — Beets
Potato salad
Tea — Coffee
Canned fruit — Cake

Ice cream was almost always taken on board before a ship left the States. It was on the menu about twice a week until the supply ran out.

Crews were well fed except during long trips when it was impossible to restock the larder or on ships with incapable cooks. Poor cooks and poor food made for an unhappy ship, and griping and friction inevitably resulted. The voyage report of one Liberty ship told of the steward being demoted to galley boy scrubbing pots and pans.

"This man," the captain said, "was completely incompetent. He knew nothing about preparing menus or supervising his staff."

Fortunately, this kind was rare, and the difficult task of feeding a "happy" ship was in the hands of capable men. The steward's department was a very important, and mostly unappreciated, part of the ship's company.

The hundreds of new ships needed crews: about forty-two men for a Liberty and slightly more for a C-3. When the war started, American ships were manned mostly by professional seamen for whom seafaring was a way of life. In addition to American-born seamen, ships' crews included thousands of Scandinavians, Germans, and men of other nationalities who had become American citizens. Also, many Puerto Ricans worked on ships running from U.S. ports to the Caribbean.

Many officers, including captains, mates, and engineers, had, as old sailors would say, "come up through the hawse pipes," that is, without benefit of much formal education. They had advanced themselves by self-study and by preparing for advancement in grade at one of the many small navigation and engineering preparatory schools at the big seaports.

The state maritime academies of Maine, Massachusetts, New York, Pennsylvania, and California also contributed officers to the merchant service. These schools had practical two-year courses that included much "hands-on" learning on board training ships. The New York, Massachusetts, and Pennsylvania schools had been turning out deck and engineering officers for more than half a century.

The National Merchant Marine Academy at Kings Point, New York, was established in 1941. Cadets had assignments on board ships during the war for practical experience in the deck and engine departments; some also acquired considerable battle experience. Most ships carried two or four of these young men, and they had stations at the guns along with the rest of the crew.

By December 1943, more than seven thousand cadets were enrolled at Kings Point. An honor roll there pays tribute to cadets who were lost in torpedoings, surface battles, and air attacks.

When the Liberty ship *John Drayton* was torpedoed 275 miles east of Durban, South Africa, on 21 April 1943, she had in her complement four cadet midshipmen: Morton Dietz, Thomas Kellegrew, Jack Stadstad, and Herman Rosen. Stadstad, an engineering cadet, was killed when, as so often happened, the torpedo exploded in the engine room. Kellegrew died just a few hours before the lifeboat, also containing Dietz and Rosen, was sighted and picked up by the *Mount Hodope*. The lifeboat had been adrift for thirty days.

Hundreds of newcomers went to sea by obtaining seamen's certificates, popularly known as "seamen's papers," from the office of a U.S. Shipping Commissioner and getting jobs through government shipping offices or union hiring halls. The War Shipping Administration created the Recruitment and Manning Organization in May 1942 to recruit young men and to contact men who had left the sea for shore jobs.

Schools were set up and operated by the U.S. Maritime Service to give a brief indoctrination for novice seamen and to qualify men with at least 18 months of sea experience as deck and engine officers. There were also schools for radio operators. Boys

Members of a merchant ship crew pose on deck with the traditional life ring showing the ship's name. Obviously, this photo was taken on a workday. A cook (front row, in white) has come from the galley to be included. (Author's Collection)

age sixteen and older were eligible to train for beginning jobs in the deck, engine, and steward departments. Post offices displayed enlistment posters. Radio announcements proclaimed the need for men to "Keep 'em sailing."

Not a few old-timers returned to sea; some were in their seventies. The author served wartime duty on a ship whose chief engineer had held the same position on a battleship during the 1920s. Men who had been honorably discharged from the armed forces because of wounds were also recruited.

Few ships were held up for lack of crews. In the few cases when this did occur, the need was usually for a mate, radio operator, or engineer. By August 1944, approximately 160,000 men were serving on U.S. merchant ships. The prewar shipboard labor force had been about 55,000.

The manning requirements for a Liberty ship were as follows:

Captain	Chief engineer
First mate	First assistant engineer
Second mate	Second assistant engineer
Third mate	Third assistant engineer
Purser	Deck engineer
Radio operator	Three oilers
Deck maintenance man	Three firemen
Boatswain (bos'n)	Two wipers
Six able seamen	
Three ordinary seamen	

Steward Department

Chief steward	Saloon messman
Chief cook	Pantry messman
Second cook	Crew messman
Baker	Two utilitymen

Ships sailing under contract with West Coast unions also carried a carpenter. There were various other ratings on tankers, refrigerated ships, and ships with turboelectric drive.

In 1942, there was a serious shortage of crews on foreign ships ready to sail from American ports. More than 6,000 men had deserted foreign-flag ships to get jobs on shore or on American ships,[3] or to escape the dangers of life at sea. These deserters came from British, Dutch, Norwegian, Greek, Polish, Yugoslav, and Belgian ships. This problem, plus the need for a central organization to mobilize and coordinate the nation's marine manpower, resulted in the creation of the Recruitment and Manning Organization (RMO) "to insure a steady flow of deep sea traffic, so far as this depends upon the efficient use of seagoing manpower."

One method that the RMO used to achieve this goal was to check the files of men who were draft-deferred because of service in the Merchant Marine and determine if they were actively sailing. Men who had left their ships for jobs ashore often discovered that they were now eligible for army service.

The RMO also initiated an intensive nationwide recruitment drive, not only to enlist young men but to tap a pool of men with sea experience who had left the sea for shore jobs. Especially needed were electricians, cooks, and practical engineers.

Many men of youthful years commanded ships during the war and proved themselves the equal of those adventurous young mariners who took American ships across the seven seas during the nation's glory days of trade and exploration.

The Liberty ship *James Ford Rhodes*, for instance, was skippered by William Travers, age twenty-two. His brother, the first mate, was twenty-one years old; Glen Hawkins, the third mate, was twenty. Some officials in foreign ports were reluctant to believe that Travers actually was the captain.

Captain Amos Beinhardt was twenty-seven years old when he took command of the *John C. Carlisle*. These young men were not intimidated by having a cargo worth millions of dollars in their charge and directing a ship and her crew under rigorous wartime conditions.

An additional responsibility of the RMO was the repatriation of American seamen from overseas. There were always several hundred seamen in foreign ports as a result of illness, arrest for deserting their ships, missing their ships at sailing time, or being signed off by mutual agreement with the captain because they were alcoholics, troublemakers, or incompetents.

The RMO set up a committee in 1943 to investigate and enforce crew discipline. The committee concluded that the principal trouble on shipboard was caused by "clashes of personalities, incompetence, and negligence." The Coast Guard also set up Merchant Marine hearing units to investigate complaints after a ship returned to an American port. These units had the authority to revoke or suspend licenses of officers and revoke seamen's papers for unlicensed personnel. Each ship was met by a Coast Guard boarding officer prior to crew payoff. If evidence of trouble was found, an investigation was conducted on shipboard before witnesses.

Insubordination and failure to turn to when ordered were considered serious offenses. On one ship loading tanks in Alexandria for the invasion of Sicily, several crewmen were influenced by a shipboard "sea lawyer" in refusing to rig the necessary heavy lifts and claiming that this should be done by the longshoremen. An army detachment was called, and the entire crew was assembled on deck to hear the Articles of War read by an army officer. The malcontents were then marched off to spend rigorous months in a military prison.

For willful disobedience on shipboard, an offender could be put in irons, confined, and subjected to forfeiture of wages of four to twelve days. Assault on an officer could be punishable with up to two years in prison.

When Congress approved the arming of merchant ships on 17 November 1941, the U.S. Navy searched naval shipyards and armories for weapons and ships were armed as quickly as guns could be obtained. Gun factories were pressed to produce new weapons, especially the efficient 20-millimeter Oerlikon, a Swedish antiaircraft gun.

Not only American vessels had to be equipped, but also the ships of Allied nations and American-owned vessels under the Panamanian flag. The navy armed Chinese, Dutch, Greek, Panamanian, Brazilian, Canadian, French, Polish, Honduran, Venezuelan, Soviet, and Belgian ships and furnished gun crews for some of them.

By war's end, 6,231 merchant vessels had been armed in American yards: 4,865 U.S. ships, 1,119 foreign ships, and 247 U.S. ships under foreign flags.

As ships were being armed, men had to be provided to serve the guns. The navy created a special branch of the service called the Merchant Marine Naval Armed Guard. Basic training schools were set up at Little Creek, Virginia; San Diego, California; and Gulfport, Mississippi. From there the men went to Armed Guard Centers in Brooklyn, New York; Treasure Island, San Francisco; and New Orleans, Louisiana. From these centers, which also served as training schools, the men were dispatched on board U.S. ships and many foreign-flag ships.[4]

It took many months for all U.S. merchant ships to obtain Armed Guards, partly because some had not been fitted with guns. Also, many ships on foreign voyages did not return home until after the United States entered the war.

In 1942, ships often sailed with such small Armed Guard detachments that the merchant crew served as gunners, too. In March, for instance, the *Vermar* had an Armed Guard of nine men and the *Klamath* had ten. Because of the dire shortage of naval officers, some units were commanded by cox'n's or bos'n's mates.

The freighter *Bacoi* left New Orleans for Puerto Rico in June 1942 with an Armed Guard consisting of one man, a navy cox'n who indoctrinated several of the merchant crew in the use of the vessel's newly acquired armament, an ancient four-inch gun mounted on the stern. The *Bacoi*'s novice gunners distrusted their weapon so much that they practiced firing it with a 30-foot lanyard. If it misfired, they wanted to be a safe distance away.

Throughout the war, men in the merchant crew served at the guns and passed ammunition. Many were caught in the ammunition magazines when they exploded.

The urgent need for gunners often meant that many men assigned to the Armed Guard received little training before being sent to a ship. The Armed Guard officer then had to complete the training.

In a letter to Secretary of the Navy Frank Knox in 1942, a distraught mother wrote that her son had been sent to a merchant ship and was serving in something called the Armed Guard. She was afraid he had not been properly trained for such dangerous duty and hoped he could be transferred to a battleship. Secretary Knox responded to her fears and assured her that her son was under the charge of a very competent officer and was serving his country as much as any sailor on a battleship. He did not deny that it was dangerous duty.

So great was the need for gunners in January 1943 that pressure was put on the Armed Guard schools to turn out "another 350 men per week," or 1,400 more men every four weeks. The quota of men from January 1943 to June 1943 was set at 32,724 enlisted men and 1,164 officers. Obviously, the Armed Guard was an important and sizable contingent in the Merchant Marine.

Officers were graduates of ninety-day training courses at various universities. Although many were disappointed at being assigned to duty on freighters and tankers, they took their assignments seriously and accredited themselves as well as any officer on a "spit-and-polish" cruiser or battleship. Many officers were killed while defending their ships, and several won the Navy Cross.

Hundreds of Armed Guard sailors were lost on the *Mary Luckenbach* during a Russian run, the *Timothy Pickering* in the Mediterranean, the *Jean Nicolet* in the Indian Ocean, the *John Burke* in the Pacific, and other merchant ships.

Armed Guard duty could be dangerous, but it also could be tedious and boring. Armed Guard units on tankers running between South Africa and the Persian Gulf could expect to be on a ship from six months to a year, with little chance to go ashore. When the tanker *Gulfcoast* sailed out for the Persian Gulf, she had an Armed Guard of fifteen. After six months, she had nine; six men had been put ashore because of illness.

The Naval Armed Guard on the Liberty ship William J. Worth *fires the four-inch stern gun during gunnery practice at sea, September 1943. (National Archives, 80-G-104069)*

Young men itching for action on ships hauling supplies on shuttle runs between island bases in the Pacific often encountered boredom in its place. An Armed Guard voyage report had this to say: "We were out seven months and never saw an enemy plane. My boys were very disappointed."

Mail was also a problem. One Armed Guard officer on a tanker complained that his men had not received mail for six months.

The record of most units of the Armed Guard could be exemplified by an Armed Guard officer's request to the Navy Department for letters of commendation for his men after they had shot down three planes during the invasion of Sicily. He wrote: "I am intensely proud of my men. They responded like veterans in every action. They performed their duties up to the highest traditions of the Navy."

In addition to guns, there were other ways of protecting ships and their cargoes. One method, which seems to be overlooked in books about the naval war, was the degaussing, or demagnetizing, of ships.

Hundreds of ships were sunk or badly damaged from mines planted by planes, minelayers, and submarines in restricted waters with heavy traffic, such as the North Sea, English Channel, and Mediterranean Sea. German submarines also laid a few mines at the entrance to Chesapeake Bay and the approaches to New York Harbor. The Germans counted on the submarine to win the war at sea, but they counted on the mine as an important "assist."

The magnetic mine was the most dangerous and destructive type. All steel ships have magnetism built into them. When a steel vessel passed over a magnetic mine, the magnetic forces in the ship triggered a mechanism in the mine that set off an explosion under the hull.

To counteract these powerful and destructive weapons, ships went through the process of degaussing. Bands of wire, aligned with the main deck, were fastened around the vessel from stem to stern. The wire was then energized with an electric current that neutralized the ship's magnetism. At one time during the war, the British used 1,200 miles of wire every week to protect ships against magnetic mines. This system saved countless numbers of ships from destruction.

Torpedo nets, a technique developed by the British in World War I, were used to protect ships from torpedoes.[5] Some 730 vessels, of which 305 were American, were fitted with nets. They were attached to the cargo booms, port and starboard, which were lowered to a 90-degree position once the vessel was at sea so that the net streamed out on each side of the ship. Many of these nets caught tin fish before they hit. It was impossible to protect the entire length of the vessel, so a torpedo could still strike forward or aft of the net.

Often, a deck cargo was loaded in such a way that the boom could not be lowered overside and the nets could not be used. The trouble involved in rigging the nets and streaming them out also discouraged many shipmasters from using them to advantage.

Several depots were set up at American ports to install and repair nets. The cost of installation was about $25,000 a ship.

The Liberty ship *James Fannin* had good fishing with her nets on a voyage to Malta in May 1943. Upon hauling in the net before entering harbor, the crew discovered a shiny tin fish. If the net hadn't snared the torpedo, it would have exploded in the engine room.

While the *Caxton* was eastbound in convoy ONS-45 on 22 March 1945, she streamed out the antisubmarine nets. Early the next day, Captain J. M. Cherry said there was a violent explosion close to his ship, the lead ship in the eighth column. On 24 March, the captain noticed that the net was badly torn and received permission from the convoy commodore to haul it on board. Much to the amazement and mystification of the crew, they found that the net had caught these items: an overall jacket with a German submarine service insignia on the sleeve, a German Navy life jacket, a notebook with personal photos, and a wristwatch.

What was the violent explosion on the 23rd? No depth charges had been dropped. How did the strange collection of items get into the net?

Had there been some internal explosion on board a U-boat under or near the *Caxton?* This remains a wartime mystery of the sea.

According to the Coordinator of Ship Defense Installations, of ships attacked while using nets in 1944, only one was sunk and one damaged. In two cases of torpedoes dropped by aircraft, two were caught in the nets of the *Kemp P. Battle* and the *Crosby Noyes,* both in the Mediterranean. The *Richmond Hobson* caught a torpedo that exploded in the net.

27

Captain E. W. MacLellan of the *José Navarro* was using a torpedo net en route from Calcutta, India, to Aden, Yemen, on 26 December 1943 when it caught a torpedo, but there was no sign of a submarine.

Balloons were used occasionally as a defensive measure against air attack. Most ships also carried canisters called "smoke floats." When dropped into the water, the chemical solution inside produced a dense cloud of smoke that helped to obscure the ship for a while from bombers or surface attackers.

Every American shipmaster was given these instructions by the Navy Department:

> It is the policy of the U.S. government that no U.S. flag merchant ship be permitted to fall into enemy hands. The ship shall be defended by her armament, by maneuver, and by every available means as long as possible. When, in the judgment of the Master, capture is inevitable, provision should be made to open sea valves and to flood holds and compartments adjacent to machinery spaces, start numerous fires and employ any additional measures available to insure certain scuttling of the vessel.

There is no record of an American ship having been captured by the enemy and taken to port as a prize. The *City of Flint* is rather a bizarre exception, especially as the United States and Germany were not at war at that time. Most of the sinkings of U.S. ships resulted from attacks by submarines or aircraft, which, of course, had no means of capturing them.

3
U-Boat Lane

EARLY IN THE MORNING of 19 January 1942, the *City of Atlanta*, captained by Lehman Urquart, was passing Diamond Shoals off the North Carolina coast on her usual run from Savannah to New York.

It was almost 0200. In the wheelhouse, the helmsman steered his course by the little binnacle lamp that lit the numbers on the compass card. He glanced at the clock on the bulkhead. In a minute, it would be time to reach for the cord overhead and strike four bells.

Second Mate George Tavelle had just stepped inside from the flying bridge. Perhaps he was looking at a faint light glimmering on the horizon, or he might have been watching the distant stars that seem so clear and intimate to ships at night.

Down below, some twenty feet under the water line, the *City of Atlanta*'s brawny, bare-chested firemen were working in front of the flaming fire doors beneath the boilers, their feet braced to the roll of the ship and their shovels moving in that almost effortless rhythm by which good "coal slingers" can feed the hungry fires hour after hour without tiring.

The water tender on the 12-to-4 watch studied the gauge glasses for a moment and watched the rise and fall of the boiler water as it shifted with each roll of the ship. Reaching up, he turned a check valve and stood for a few moments beneath the starboard ventilator. It was midwinter; a whipping breeze was shooting down the vent.

In the dusty dimness of the bunkers, grimy coal passers bit the ends of wetted rags between their teeth and shoved coal down chutes onto the fireroom's floor plates, where the firemen picked it up with their "banjos" and threw it onto the fires. The flames lit up the compartment in hot, red brilliance, with sharp tongues of orange light dancing along the bulkhead like wild, insouciant phantoms.

A portable electric light glowed dimly through the dust of the steel-cased bunker spaces, where the sounds of pounding engine cranks, the banging fire doors, and the firemen's shovels scraping on steel plates were almost muted. As the coal passers bent to their work, they tried not to think about what would happen if a torpedo smashed through the hull beside them. Being trapped in the bunkers without a chance of escape wasn't a pleasant thing to contemplate.

While the water tender was breathing in the cool night air and the helmsman was reaching for the cord to strike four bells, the *City of Atlanta* was convulsed by an explosion that all but lifted her out of the water.

A torpedo had streaked to its mark from a lurking submarine. Crashing through the hull plates into the fireroom, it turned the engine spaces into a hell of roaring steam. The coal passers never had a chance to get out of the bunkers. The firemen and the water tender probably never realized what happened in that wild, bewildering moment when the thundering blast tore heavy steel plating as though it were paper, and cold, black water deluged the engine spaces.

Only three men of the crew of forty-three were able to relate what had happened during the terrible moments that followed. They were the only survivors.[1]

The old City of Atlanta *was one of the early victims of the German U-boat campaign in American waters. She was built in 1909 and owned by the Ocean Steamship Co. of Savannah. The high stack indicates that she was a coal burner. (The Mariners Museum, Newport News, Virginia, PB 14509)*

Oiler Robert Fennell, Jr., asleep in his bunk, awoke to see the entire side of the room blown away. He grabbed a life belt and was running up the passageway when he remembered that his wife's picture was hanging on the bulkhead in his room.

Motivated by one of those unexplainable impulses that, throughout the war, made men on sinking ships often go back to their lockers for mementos and knickknacks, Fennell returned to his room for the picture, carefully folded it, and put it into his pocket before hurrying topside to his lifeboat station.

At about this same moment, seaman Earl Dowdy was also running topside and pulling on a lifebelt as he went. He and Fennell arrived in the open to see their assigned lifeboat shattered and made completely useless by the blast. The ship was on fire. The only usable boat was already lowered over the side. The two men climbed over the rail, stared at the cold, flame-lit waters for a second or two, and then jumped.

They swam a safe distance away before looking back to see roaring tongues of flame lick the night sky above the wreck. Silhouetted against the flames, a lone lifeboat was bobbing against the vessel's side. There were several men in the boat and they seemed to be having trouble getting away. Perhaps the toggle was jammed in the block.

The men finally succeeded in freeing the boat from the falls and pulled frantically at the oars to get clear of the flaming hulk. But they had hardly taken a full stroke on the oars before the *City of Atlanta* shuddered from bow to stern, lurched precariously for one awful moment, and rolled over on top of them. As the big ship plunged below the surface, she whipped the sea into a froth, with the rush of air from the holds throwing planks, ship's gear, hatch covers, and broken lifeboats wildly into the air.

Less than ten minutes had passed from the time the torpedo hit before the *City of Atlanta* slipped beneath the waves.

While the churning waters calmed somewhat and the survivors groped for wreckage on which to cling, a searchlight probed the scene. The submarine then circled the area to inspect her kill.

After the U-boat disappeared, Dowdy and Fennell sought out the largest pieces of wreckage they could find and paddled toward others from the *Atlanta's* crew who had managed to clear the ship. At 0215 that morning, there were probably eight or ten of them hanging onto planks and hatchboards, singing for a while, joking about Bull Line Marie and the girls in Ybo City, vowing they would charge the company plenty of overtime for swimming around the Atlantic in the middle of the night.

Light-hearted banter was short-lived. The water was cold, and the night wind had a stinging bite. Several men had been injured—one by one, they let go their hold on the bits of wreckage and sank from sight. There were no dramatics, no heroics.

When the first streaks of dawn finally broke across the sky, only three men were left: oiler Fennell, seaman Dowdy, and Second Mate Tavelle. It looked as though another man was propped up on a mass of flotsam some distance away, but he didn't answer their shouts. After a while, the figure disappeared.

At about 0800, a lookout on the northbound *Seatrain Texas* spotted the *Atlanta*'s wreckage and Captain Albert Dalzell brought his ship alongside to pick up the survivors. The sea was calm, with an overcast sky and a light swell running, as a boat went overside to pluck the survivors out of the wreck-littered waters. The sea temperature was 47°F.

The boat crew found Dowdy clinging by one hand to a piece of box and gripping part of a shattered door with the other hand. A couple of hundred feet farther on, they found Fennell sitting atop an improvised raft with the lifeless body of George York, the second engineer.

"God!" Fennell said, "I'm sure glad to see you guys. I thought it was finished with engines for me this time."

Pulling about in the flotsam, the men from the *Seatrain Texas* saw several bodies bobbing in the long, lazy swells. These were men for whom there was no longer a frontier in Europe against the rising tide of fascism. They had died on a battlefront only a few miles off the East Coast of the United States.

The unarmed *Seatrain Texas* took the survivors aboard and left the area at top speed. The captain had taken a chance even to slow down and stop.

The scattered bits of wreckage soon blended in with the rolling waves. There was nothing else to mark the grave of those who went down on the *City of Atlanta,* one of the first ships to sink on U-Boat Lane.

The Atlantic coastal waters became known as U-Boat Lane. Submarines ambled down the seaboard on sinking sprees that cost hundreds of lives and sent scores of ships to the bottom, with a huge loss of valuable cargo.

The *City of Atlanta* was a victim of U-123 in Germany's Operation Paukenschlag (Operation Drumbeat), a submarine campaign against shipping in American coastal waters. In a modest experiment that could have been greatly more devastating if Hitler had permitted the use of more boats, five raiders arrived in coastal waters on 11 January 1942. They were U-123, U-130, U-66, U-109, and U-125.

Before returning to Germany in February, the U-boats had torpedoed twenty-two ships! They were succeeded by a second wave of five boats that sank nineteen ships.

This was the beginning of a tremendously successful campaign against Allied shipping along the East Coast and in the Caribbean and Gulf of Mexico. For a while, the U-boat crews must have felt like they were popping tin ducks in a shooting gallery. There was no opposition. As at Pearl Harbor, the U.S. Navy and Army coastal defense forces were taken by surprise. The military had made no plans for the protection of shipping, even though German submarines had raided U.S. waters during World War I.

In their reports to Adm. Karl Dönitz,[2] commander of submarines, the U-boat skippers exulted at the lack of defense. Spot a juicy target, fire torpedoes, and watch the sitting duck burst into flames or go down like a rock. It was a submariner's paradise, especially as many of their victims carried two of the most important cargoes in modern war, oil and bauxite (the ore used for making aluminum).

Through it all, the light of the coastal cities glared undimmed, as though there were no war within a thousand miles and the flaming decks of embattled ships were only part of an unreal fantasia that could not happen here. Submarines spotted their prey at night against this bright background, and it was not until May 1942 that the army established regulations for dimming the "great white way" that glowed like a specter of death along the coast. The lights of skyscrapers were then shaded at night and the lamps of seaside promenades screened for the protection of shipping.

As the rate of sinking increased, no seaman could be sure that his ship would reach its destination. Many didn't, but the tankers and the freighters kept sailing, with none of them idling in port for lack of crews. The merchant seamen manned their ships and kept the cargoes moving.

"Keep 'em sailing!" was more than a slogan of the citizen sailor. It was a battle cry.

The *City of Atlanta* was not the first victim of German submarines, but she typified the lack of plans for defense or counterattack against the U-boat menace along the American coast.

The infamous date of 7 December 1941, with our subsequent declaration of war on Japan and Germany, had caught the United States not only with an inadequate Merchant Marine for the enormous supply problem that confronted the nation, but it also found the navy unprepared to safeguard coastal shipping. As far as the Merchant Marine was concerned during the early period of conflict, there might as well have been no navy at all. No destroyers could be spared for Atlantic frontiers.

The U-boats did not take long to make the most of this situation. Following the torpedoing of several American ships by Japanese submarines off the California coast and in the Pacific during December, undersea warfare struck the U.S. East Coast in all its fury. On 14 January 1942, the 9,500-ton Panamanian tanker *Norness* was torpedoed and sunk not far off Long Island, New York.

Four days later, the 6,300-ton American tanker *Allan Jackson* went down in flames off the North Carolina coast sixty miles east-northeast of Diamond Shoals, with a toll of twenty-two dead from her crew of thirty-five. She was a fat prize to be had as she steered north from Cartagena, Colombia, with 73,000 barrels of crude oil in her tanks. Those who lived through this holocaust attributed their rescue to nothing less than a miracle. How else could one explain survival from the midst of a roaring furnace?

Two torpedoes from U-66 careened into the *Jackson* amidships, cutting her in half as neatly as though she had been sliced by acetylene torches and loosing a flaming flood of high–flash-point oil onto the sea around. Many of her crew were burned to death as they stood helpless on her deck, cut off from lifeboats and life preservers and faced with the sole alternative of diving into an oil-covered ocean swept by searing flames.

Bos'n Rolf Clausen was playing cards in the messroom aft with several others of the crew when the first torpedo hit on the starboard side forward, followed very closely by a second and greater explosion as the next torpedo broke the tanker's back and set her cargo afire.[3]

Rushing on deck, Clausen and his mates tried to launch the number four boat on the port side, but the flames, illuminating the ship and sea in a terrifying brilliance, were already so intense and enveloping the deck so fast that they had to abandon the attempt. Instead, they launched a starboard boat. Once over-side, they found themselves surrounded by an impasse of flaming oil that blanketed the water all around the wreck. They were saved from this inferno because the tanker's engines had not been stopped. The overboard discharge of cooling water from the engine condenser shot a heavy stream into the sea just ahead of them and forced the burning oil away from the lifeboat's side.

As they hurriedly cast off, the hulk of the broken stern section, listing precariously over the boat, threatened to topple onto it at any moment. They shipped the oars and pushed away from the tilting hull, but the wreck didn't capsize. The men found themselves fronted by a wall of fire fed by tons of crude oil pouring out of the shattered tanks.

Again they were saved from a fiery death, this time because the lifeboat was sucked toward the propeller, still thrashing out a few last revolutions before the boiler fires went out. While they narrowly escaped being sliced by the huge, revolving blades, the propeller wash pushed the flames away and provided a clear patch for them astern of the blazing ship. Like a path through the Red Sea, it seemed a miracle to them—salvation from the fiery furnace!

Clausen and his mates listened helplessly to anguished calls from men floundering in the oily inferno and heard a few agonized screams from shipmates trapped on board the tanker, but they could do nothing to help them. After a few minutes, they saw a white glow, which they supposed came from the submarine's conning tower. Hoisting sail, they steered from it as quickly as possible. At this stage of the war, seamen believed that German submarine skippers would order the machine-gunning of torpedoed men. This misconception was not to be dispelled for some months.

The men sighted the destroyer *Roe* two and one-half hours after the sinking and flashed a signal for help. Thinking the call for aid might be a U-boat trick in the darkness, the destroyer's commander circled them carefully several times. He had already picked up the *Jackson's* captain and several other survivors, and he ordered the men in the boat to give their names so that he could check them with those on board the *Roe*. As a double measure of safety, he told them to name other members of the crew before he stopped to pick them up. After six more hours of search, the *Roe* found no other survivors and left the scene. Five officers and seventeen unlicensed personnel had gone down with the ship.

More fortunate than the *Jackson* was the tanker *Malay*, a victim of U-123 the following day, 19 January, off the Virginia Capes, as she headed south in ballast for the Texas oil fields. Being empty, the old *Malay* was a poor target compared with the highly explosive *Allan Jackson*. Her holds had been subdivided into many watertight tanks for carrying oil, and she was able to defy the efforts of the exasperated U-boat captain to send her down.

In the early morning darkness, only the flashes from the U-boat's gun could be seen during the attack. As the shells crashed into the *Malay's* bridge, hull, and after quarters, Captain John Dodge swung the engine room telegraph to "Stop" and ordered the crew to abandon ship. The *Malay* had no guns for fighting back, and trying to run from the speedy U-boat was useless.

Seeing that the shells were doing no good except to pockmark the old ship with gaping holes, the submarine fired a torpedo that hit the tanker in her after bunkers just forward of the engine room, but which, fortunately, did not ignite the bunker oil.

For some reason, the U-boat then submerged, and the tanker's sixty-nine-year-old master led his men back on board. Despite a shattered bridge and a shell-torn hull, the crew got up steam, started the engines, and the *Malay* limped into Norfolk for repairs. Long after the war, the trim little *Malay* still continued her eventful career of sailing most of the "seven seas."

During this early phase of the war, American merchant seamen could not fight with guns or bullets, for they had none. "Fighting freighters," nonetheless, were the ships they sailed, their armament consisting of that unbeatable determination to get the cargoes through and "keep 'em sailing"—that refusal to be daunted by overwhelming odds that earned for the merchant mariner the right to be called "a hero in dungarees."

On 25 January, U-66 struck again and sank the *Venore* off Cape Hatteras, North Carolina, with a loss of eighteen men, including Captain Fritz Duurloo. The unseen submarine had signaled to the oncoming *Venore* that she was a lightship in need of assistance. The ore freighter had changed course and headed for what was supposed to be a disabled vessel. But when the *Venore* came close—too close for a miss—the U-boat's skipper fired two torpedoes and, almost immediately, opened up on the *Venore* with the deck gun.

The sinking of the *Venore* is partly told in the terse, dramatic calls for help sent out by radio operator Vernon Minsey.[4]

At 0047, he flashed this SOS: "Two crashes so far. Will keep informed. Think swimming soon."

This call came two minutes later: "Torpedoed twice. Ship still afloat, but listing badly. Captain requests assistance immediately." He then gave the ship's position a number of times.

The third and last message was heard at 0122: "Cannot stay afloat much longer."

No more reports came through. Soon after the radio operator had tapped out this message on his key, the *Venore* sank and Minsey went down with her.

Several lifeboats had been launched by the *Venore's* crew, and the survivors were picked up thirty-eight hours later.

When the tanker *W. D. Anderson,* with a crew of thirty-six, was torpedoed on 22 February, just fourteen miles off Stuart, Florida, only one man, wiper Frank Terry, escaped being trapped by the flames. Terry jumped overside and managed to stay afloat until he was picked up five hours later.

On the night of 11 March 1942, close to 2 months after the Panamanian tanker *Norness* was sent to the bottom off Long Island, the *Carib Sea* of the Stockard Line was proceeding alone and unarmed up the coast toward New York on her regular run from Trinidad, Jamaica, the Virgin Islands, Cuba, and other Caribbean points.

Captain Nicholas Manolis was leaning against the bridge rail as the *Carib Sea* pressed along on a course prescribed by the U.S. Navy at Key West, Florida. He had been on deck almost continuously for forty-eight hours when the second mate came over beside him and pointed out "what looks like a faint white light."[5]

"A light? What do you see . . . where is it?" That's as much as Captain Manolis was able to say before the ship was hit, for the white light the mate had seen in that pitch black night was the telltale wake of a speeding torpedo.

The captain shouted to the second mate to blow the whistle blasts for "abandon ship," but the *Carib Sea* sank so quickly that there was no time to blow the whistle, much less to launch the boats. Her cargo of manganese took her under almost immediately. Captain Manolis says it might have been one minute—two at the most—from the time the freighter was hit.

As his ship plunged beneath him, the skipper was swept off the bridge and drawn underwater in the suction. When he shot to the surface finally, choking for air, the sea was littered with hatch covers, potato crates, boards, and other debris. As he clung to a piece of wreckage, he could see the outline of a U-boat's conning tower. The raider scanned the wreckage for a few minutes and disappeared.

After a while, the survivors found one of the vessel's two life rafts, which had broken free and come to the surface. They were floating on this when they were picked up eight hours later by the *Norlandia*. Besides the captain, the raft held the third assistant engineer, two deckhands, a fireman, and an oiler.

Still the ships kept sailing. In the union halls and shipping offices up and down the coast, from Portland, Maine, to Corpus Christi, Texas, seamen signed on for the hazardous run down U-Boat Lane. The toll of sunken ships increased day by day, and more names were added to the roll of seamen who had made the last voyage.

Many were the incidents of quiet, spontaneous heroism and self-sacrifice, as the U-boats rolled up their deadly toll of coastal shipping. As a torpedo blasted the United Fruit Company's *Esparta* off the coast of Georgia on 9 April, the ammonia tanks for the freezing plant burst open.[6]

Fumes from the ruptured tanks overcame the first assistant engineer, and he slumped onto the deck unconscious. Although it was apparent that the ship would sink at any moment, able seaman Zack Williams picked up the stricken engineer, carried him to the main deck, and threw him over the side. Diving into the water after him, Williams helped him to safety on board a lifeboat.

And, grim as it was, the sea war was not without its humor.

On this same ship, able seaman Doroteo Villagarcia jumped over the rail even as the *Esparta* disappeared beneath the waves. While swimming about in the wreckage, he felt a sharp prick on his leg. A bite! Sharks! Like all good seamen, Villagarcia carried a sheath knife and he yanked it from his belt. Slicing in momentary terror at the water around him, he learned that he was carving harmlessly into a stick of floating bananas. The sharp stem of the bananas was the "shark" that had nibbled at his leg.

It was also on the *Esparta* that oiler Pedro Prondo was knocked out of his bunk by the explosion. He opened the door of his fo'c'sle to be swept down the alleyway by a roaring rush of water that threw him into the crew's toilet. To give his life for democracy while sailing a cargo of bananas was bad enough. But to depart this life from the inglorious bastion of a ship's toilet— that was too much! "It must not be!" yelled Pedro. Fighting with almost superhuman strength, he worked his way down the passageway to the open deck and literally walked off the ship as she went under.

On another luckless vessel, a youthful ordinary seaman was reading in his bunk on his first trip to sea when a torpedo hit. He had been relaxing in the nude because of the stifling heat inside the blacked-out ship. After recovering from the shock of the explosion, he ran for his boat station without stopping to don raiment. As the vessel was slowly going down, the crew suggested that his lifeboat ordeal would be more endurable if he paused long enough to borrow a pair of pants from the first assistant, whose room was close by. This he did, as the boat was being lowered over the side, but the "First" was a big man. When the youth slid down the falls into the boat, the pants slid off him into the water and sank. There was not an extra pair of pants to be had, so he stayed stark naked until a destroyer picked up the survivors the next day. The boy was grateful that the rescue ship had no women passengers on board.

During the last nineteen days of January 1942, U-boats had sunk shipping that totaled 250,000 tons along the East Coast of the United States. Long after the inauguration of coastal convoys on 14 May 1942, roving U-boats still tried their luck along the Atlantic seaboard from the Bahamas north to the Gulf of Maine. Not until VE-day in 1945 could antisubmarine vigilance be relaxed on U-Boat Lane.

Sinkings rapidly declined, however, when Vice Adm. Adolphus Andrews of the Eastern Sea Frontier was able to muster enough destroyers, corvettes, converted yachts, planes, and blimps to set up a convoy system from Maine to Key West.

A fitting close to this phase of the war is the story of convoy KS-520. Consisting of nineteen ships, the convoy left Lynnhaven Roads in Chesapeake Bay on 14 July 1942 under escort of the destroyers *Ellis* and *McCormick*, a corvette, a Coast Guard patrol vessel, a navy blimp, and several patrol bombers. This was a formidable escort under any conditions, and it was quite impressive in comparison with the hide-and-seek system prevailing heretofore. The weather was fine, the sky clear, and the sea moderate.

The Germans, however, were not deterred by the show of force. Shortly after 1600 on 15 July, when the convoy was about thirty-three miles south by east of Cape Hatteras, it suddenly ran into a flock of torpedoes.

Captain Harold Griffiths, of the Standard Oil Company tanker *Mowinckel*, later reported that no one on his ship saw any signs of a submarine until the *Chilore*, an ore carrier bound for Chile, was hit by a torpedo close by. Seconds later, the *Mowinckel* herself got hit, the ship shuddering violently as the "tin fish" blew a huge hole in her stern and injured those merchant men and navy gunners who were on the fantail and after gun platform at the time. Joseph Sokolowski, a wiper, was hit by a piece of flying steel and knocked overboard but was fortunately seen by another ship and picked up some twenty minutes later, dazed and winded but otherwise unhurt.

At about the same moment, the *Bluefields*, a small Nicaraguan freighter, was also struck, becoming almost instantly enveloped in a cloud of bluish white smoke and sinking in a matter of minutes.

Neither the *Mowinckel* nor the *Chilore* was fatally hit, but they both withdrew from the convoy while the destroyers rushed about dropping depth charges and U.S. Army planes peppered the area with bombs. Far different was U-Boat Lane now than it had been just a few weeks before. These ships were not sitting ducks to be slaughtered at a U-boat's leisure.

Captain Joseph Mulhe of the *Unicoi* rang the general alarm during all of this commotion, and his gunners were set and ready when the bow of a U-boat broke the water not more than two hundred yards away—so near they could read the numbers 576 on her conning tower. Unexpected as the U-boat was, the gunners were not too amazed to fire, and the first shot from their five-inch rifle on the stern hit the German just forward of and below the conning tower. Bombs from army planes cascaded onto the unfortunate raider seconds later. The U-boat opened up like a blossoming rose, split in two, and then plummeted to the ocean floor amid a boiling mass of debris and oil. Shooting her torpedoes from too near the surface, she had probably been blown to the top from their recoil, by the wash of the ships, or by the concussion from one of the explosions. At any rate, credit for the "kill" was shared officially by the planes and the *Unicoi*. The sharp-shooting Armed Guard on the *Unicoi* was commanded by Ens. M. K. Ames.

The *Mowinckel* headed for shore under her own power, only to run into a mine field and suffer a second explosion. She was salvaged soon after, but the crippled *Chilore*, which also collided with a mine while trying to make the beach, capsized and sank while being towed into Chesapeake Bay several days later.

The slaughter on U-Boat Lane was one of the great German submarine successes of the war. During the first three months of 1942 alone, a few German submarines had sunk more than forty American ships. The tragic toll of ships and men could have been greatly reduced if the top commanders of the U.S. Navy's and Army's continental defense had had enough foresight and imagination to realize that American and Caribbean waters would not be immune from submarine attack. British Prime Minister Winston Churchill was harshly critical of this total lack of defense for shipping, which, he said, resulted in "grievous losses" in ships, cargoes, and lives for ships of all the Allied nations. It was a negligence that bordered on incompetence and could well have been the subject of an investigation after the war.

Despite Britain's dire shortage of escort ships, Churchill authorized the dispatch of twenty-four antisubmarine trawlers and ten corvettes to help the U.S. Navy defend its home waters. The U.S. Navy, meanwhile, claimed to be sinking submarines, a fiction that fooled the public but did nothing to help the men who manned the ships.

In a communique issued 20 January 1942, the Navy Department proclaimed that it was taking "strong measures" against German submarines but offered no details. On 23 January, the navy said that a number of U-boats had been "liquidated" along the East Coast.

According to a U.S. Navy news release of 23 January: "Some of the recent visitors to our territorial waters will never enjoy the return portion of their voyage." The navy also stated that it would give no details of submarine sinkings "until such information is no longer of aid and comfort to the enemy. Secrecy surrounding the fate of their subs is a counterblow the American people can give them. Every American can regard silence and secrecy as his own personal anti-sub weapon."

This statement was almost humorously naive.

In its issue of 8 August 1942, *Life* magazine published a chart and list of ship losses along the Canadian / American East Coast, in the Gulf of Mexico and the Caribbean, and along the coast of South America from January to June. The total was 383. Of these, 154 ships were sunk along the American East Coast, 34 in the Gulf, and 133 in the Caribbean. (These figures included ships of all Allied nations.)

The *Life* article stated: "This chart bluntly contradicts assurances from responsible officials that things are getting better."

4
Caribbean Carnival

AFTER RUNNING UP A BIG SCORE along the Atlantic coast during the first few weeks of 1942, submarines moved south to the Caribbean and the Gulf of Mexico and their approaches. Seamen called those waters "the bloody sea." There was almost no naval protection for merchant shipping there during the first six months of the war. The crew of every vessel that coursed those waters did so knowing full well that the voyage could be a race with death in this uncontested carnival of destruction.

The worst of the U-boat campaign in the Caribbean and Gulf of Mexico was over before the new Liberty ships took to the sea in large numbers, so the brunt of the battle was borne by the older tankers and dry cargo ships. Their names were well known to prewar sailors: the *Ruth, Barbara, Catahoula, Alcoa Partner, Afoundria, City of Alma, Tillie Kykes,* and many others.

The *West Ivis,* a Liberty ship from the World War I emergency shipbuilding program, was the first victim, being sunk on 16 February 1942 with the loss of most of the crew. She was followed by more than 80 American ships before the year was half over and before the inauguration of convoys, plus increased antisubmarine protection, cut down on the U-boat depredations. Five American ships were bagged by U-boats during the last two months of 1943. Although these sinkings marked the end of the serious submarine offensive in these waters, the tanker *Esso Harrisburg* was sunk on 6 July 1944 and the American tanker *Oklahoma* in March 1945.

During the first two months of the war, six American ships were sunk in the Caribbean. From 16 February to 18 March 1942, six of Hitler's sea wolves, feasting on Caribbean shipping, sank 26 Allied freighters and tankers in what was called "Operation Neuland." Of 4 ships sunk by U-161, 2 were torpedoed inside the harbor of Castries on the island of Saint Lucia. In this group, U-129 sank 7 ships; U-156 and U-502 got 5 each.

Submarines were so audacious, with little to fear from air or surface forces, that they frequently attacked on the surface to save torpedoes and often stalked their prey within sight of land. For example, the American passenger liner *Robert E. Lee* was torpedoed close to the first sea buoy leading to the Mississippi River.

In April, 6 more American merchant ships were sent to the bottom. The Germans had a month-long spree during May and sank no less than 5 ships on the fourth, 2 on the sixth, and 3 on the twelfth. The total for the month of May in American vessels alone was 31 freighters and tankers.

The *Heredia* of the United Fruit Company felt the bold insolence of these tropic raiders. Shortly before she would have been safely inside the Mississippi River with a cargo of coffee and bananas, she was hit by three torpedoes. For two hours after the ship went down, one and possibly two U-boats cruised around the area and played searchlights over the wreckage. They dived only when the first streaks of dawn came fingering across the sea. The attack occurred so close to shore that, when morning came, the topmasts of the *Heredia* protruded above water, but she was sunk deep enough to claim a heavy toll. Thirty-six of the crew were lost.

The first Liberty ship to be sunk in the Caribbean was the *George Calvert* on her maiden voyage from Baltimore to Bandar Shapur in the Persian Gulf by way of Cape Town. She had been in convoy along the Atlantic coast as far as Guantánamo, where she had left convoy protection to strike out on her own across the South Atlantic. She was doing eleven knots and zigzagging when the first torpedo hit her at 1309 on 20 May 1942; a second torpedo followed, exploding at the stern. A third hit in the engine room broke the vessel's back, and she started to sink. Forty-seven of the crew of fifty survived and landed at Dimas, Cuba, the next day. The *Calvert* was carrying 9,116 tons of cargo for the Russians.

The *Sam Houston* was the next Liberty to be sunk. Her paint was still clean and bright; brasswork and steel gleamed and sparkled in the engine room; and pistons, pumps, and generators were not yet properly broken in before a U-boat torpedoed her on 28 June 1942. Except for three men in the engine room, who died in the first torpedo blast, the crew got away in the lifeboats. Four badly burned men died before the survivors were picked up by the minesweeper *Courier*.

From 12 April to 24 May, a single fleet of eight U-boats sank 48 ships in the bloody sea. U-507, U-125, and U-162 were especially productive, each of them sending 9 ships to the bottom. U-130 even shelled the oil installations on the Dutch island of Curaçao.

During a full moon on the night of 20 May 1942, the freighters *Elizabeth* and *Clare* of the Bull Line, deeply laden with steel, cotton prints, cigarettes and other merchandise for the island trade, plodded south along the southwest coast of Cuba. A torpedo sliced into the *Clare*, and the little ship quickly went down. A few minutes later, the same U-boat sank the *Elizabeth*, which was following a mile or so behind. Submarine warfare in the Caribbean for the U-boats was as easy as that—pick a ship, fire a torpedo, and chalk up another bottom lost to the Allied line of supply.

A group of four submarines operating in the Caribbean from 7 May to 28 June sank a total of 29 freighters and tankers.

Many small ships, such as these shown under the eyes of a U.S. Navy blimp, were victims of U-boats in the Caribbean. Neither of these freighters appears to have guns. (National Archives, 80-GK-13894)

Highest score went to U-156, which bagged 11 merchantmen and torpedoed the USS *Blakely*, a destroyer.

A submarine sounded a siren and fired a gun before she torpedoed the asphalt-laden tanker *Carrabulle* in the early morning hours of 26 May. Although most U-boats gave the crews time to abandon ship, this one poured shells and small-arms fire into the freighter while the boats were being launched. As the first boat pulled away from the ship's side, the U-boat captain hailed them from his conning tower.

"Are you all right?" he asked.

They shouted back that another boat had just been launched and had not yet pulled away, but the officer might not have heard them. At that moment, a torpedo streaked past their lifeboat and hit the *Carrabulle* at the exact position of the other lifeboat, as the men were trying to push off from the hull and shipping oars. The torpedo blew men and boat into a myriad of pieces.

Shortly after the *Carrabulle* was attacked, lookouts on the steamer *Atenas* saw a periscope at the mouth of the Mississippi, in the same area where the *Heredia* had been sunk a week before.[1] As the periscope approached at a 45-degree angle to its course, the captain swung his ship around so that the stern gun could bear on the U-boat, and the gunners opened fire. There were cheers as the first shell and then the second one sent up geysers of water near the enemy, but the submarine pulled in her periscope. When she again poked her eye above water, the gunners planted three more shells close by. Still not discouraged, the U-boat continued the chase as the *Atenas* dashed off at top speed. An hour later, the submarine surfaced and opened fire with tracer shells from a rapid-fire gun at about two thousand yards.

Lt. A. J. Powers, the officer in charge of the newly installed Armed Guard, sent his men to battle stations again as the captain once more swung the ship around so the stern gun could engage. Several shells hit the *Atenas* before her gunners bracketed the U-boat and followed up with what appeared to be a direct hit near the conning tower. The U-boat's gunners disappeared down the hatch, and the raider, probably meeting an armed ship for the first time, dived in a hurry. The *Atenas* escaped.

The next day, the *Atenas* met a freighter bound north and informed her of the submarine attack. After the stranger had cleared the horizon, the *Atenas* crew heard several deep, muffled explosions. The U-boat had probably made up for her unsuccessful encounter with *Atenas*.

An epic of survival followed the torpedoing of the *Jack* on 27 May 1942. Loaded with sugar and bound from Ponce, Puerto Rico, to New Orleans, Louisiana, this freighter ran afoul of U-55 near Haiti. The sixty-three men on board included a gun crew of eight navy and four army enlisted men under Lt. (jg) Albert Lind.

The ship sank too fast for the crew to launch lifeboats. A raft made of empty oil drums floated free and provided uncertain support for about thirty men, including gunner Westly McAlpine and Curtis Livingston.

After the *Jack* went down "with a loud gurggle and a whoosh," a lifeboat floated free and about half of the men chose to go in the boat with Lieutenant Lind. Two days later, the raft and the boat were separated. As the days went by, the men on the raft were dying one by one. Several became delirious and dropped off into the sea.

The crew saw a ship and shot flares, but the ship did not change course. When another ship turned toward them and then turned away, two more men gave up and died.

"We all prayed," said McAlpine. "There were several Negro crewmen and they sang spirituals. We all sang 'The Old Rugged Cross,' 'Onward Christian Soldiers,' and other songs we knew from Sunday school days."

Planes flew overhead but didn't spot them. The men thought they saw land several times, but the land and trees were mirages.

On the fifteenth day, they saw a ship less than a mile away. They waved shirts and oars and shouted, but the ship went on her way. Sharks, patiently waiting, kept them company. When sharks rubbed their snouts against the raft, the crew pushed them away with their oars.

Rations got so low that only two cans of pemmican a day were shared by the seven men who were left. Water was rationed, too.

On the thirty-second day, they saw a ship a mile or two away.

"By then," said McAlpine, "we were too exhausted to stand up and wave but they saw us, changed course, and came by."

The ship, a British freighter, hauled them on board, one by one—each gaunt, sunburned, tattered, and bearded. Two gunners and five merchant seamen were the determined survivors on the raft.[2]

Bound to Baltimore from Trinidad, the *City of Alma* was almost blown in half by a torpedo on 2 June. Ten of the crew survived because they jumped clear of the ship before she plunged and later climbed onto a life raft that had floated free. There had been no time to launch the boats.

Because a ship sank so fast, the crew were often unable to launch lifeboats in time and jumped overside to avoid going down with the ship. Most ships carried life rafts that could be released quickly, and these were the means of saving more men than lifeboats.

When the freighter *Suwied* was hit on 7 June 1942, there was no time to launch boats and hardly time enough for Captain Bernard David to pull the whistle cord to abandon ship. "I just walked off the bridge into the water," he recalled later. "When I looked around the topmasts of the old girl were just disappearing under the waves."[3]

Within two minutes, the *Suwied* was gone, along with her cargo of bauxite, so vital to the production of aircraft. The submarine surfaced, and her crew watched the survivors climb onto rafts but did nothing to interfere. The men were picked up the next day by a U.S. Navy patrol boat. That they were saved could be credited to the quick thinking of First Mate John Hume, who ran along the deck to release the life rafts until the deck was awash and the ship was going under.

Seamen coursing the bloody sea took a long chance with the U-boats. Most of the ships sunk during this period were only lightly armed, and some, like the little *Suwied*, had no guns at all. In most cases, guns would not have helped much anyway. The U.S. Army transport *Sicilian*, for instance, was torpedoed on the dark and cloudy night of 7 June near Puerto Rico. The submarine was never seen by the crew until she surfaced after the ship had gone down. Forty-six men were lost.

On the night of 9 June, a submarine bagged the little *Merrimack* as she zigzagged toward Panama with holds full of Army supplies. A lookout saw the lacy track of the tin fish off the beam and yelled, "Torpedo," but the speeding bomb hit and exploded just forward of the bridge; the hold was flooded in a matter of seconds. Two rafts were cut loose by crewmen who neglected to secure the painters (tow lines). As the ship was still under way, the rafts were soon lost astern. Two boats were launched, but one drifted under the stern and its occupants were cut to pieces by the propeller, which was still turning.

Nine of the crew managed to struggle onto a raft. During the night, they saw life belt lights and heard the emergency life belt whistles of their companions who were floating in the sea, but the sea was choppy and they couldn't paddle the clumsy raft well enough to reach any of them. By daylight, those in the water had disappeared. Forty-one men went down with the *Merrimack*.

The *Warrior* left Port of Spain, Trinidad, at 0600 on 1 July 1942. By 1240, she was on her way to the bottom. Smashing into the stern, a torpedo set off an explosion in the ammunition magazine and killed a number of crewmen in their quarters aft. The survivors were picked up by a U.S. destroyer.

The *Stanvac Palambang*, a Socony-Vacuum tanker sunk on 10 July 42, had a three-time loser on board. Zosimo Tabudlong, an ordinary seaman for whom torpedoings had become routine, had survived two sinkings while on English ships and one on a Dutchman. Zosimo was credited with saving the life of the *Stanvac*'s radio operator. Along with the other survivors, he was picked up by a patrol boat and taken to Port of Spain, Trinidad. Shortly afterward, he shipped for New Orleans on the American passenger ship *Robert E. Lee*, which was returning workers and their families from construction sites in the islands. They received a violent homecoming—the ship was torpedoed when she was almost inside the Mississippi River. Zosimo was lauded for helping to save several people in his fifth dunking by tin fish.

When the *Robert E. Lee* was hit, fireman Robert Burton was below. Burton also had been on the *Robin Moor* when she was sunk by a U-boat in the South Atlantic.

"I was talking to the engineer [on the *Robert E. Lee*] when there was a terrific crash," Burton recalled. "I was thrown off my feet onto some machinery. It knocked me out. The next thing I knew I was in the water. The engineer was killed. So was the engine cadet who was standing at the log desk near us. I don't know how I got out of that fireroom. I was just blown out into the sea."[4]

Survivors reported that the boilers exploded, blasting a big hole in the ship's side, through which Burton must have been shot into the water. He escaped the experience with only scratches and nervous shock. A year later, he had another seemingly miraculous escape from the fireroom of a Liberty ship torpedoed in the Atlantic.

The waters around Guantánamo probably had a sweet taste in August 1942, when a submarine sank the *John Hancock* just ninety-six miles offshore and sent her down with 10,517 tons of sugar destined for a refinery in Philadelphia. The entire crew of forty-nine were rescued by a British corvette.

A raid in the Caribbean by ten U-boats during August and September 1942 was not very productive, accounting for only fourteen victims, one of them a small sailing ship. U-654 ventured too near the Panama Canal and was sunk by U.S. Army aircraft.

By August 1942, Nazi subs had sunk a total of 222 Allied ships in the Caribbean Sea and Gulf of Mexico and along the northeast coast of South America.[5] Another 44 American ships were sunk before the end of the war in those waters.

The *Nathaniel Hawthorne* was attacked early in the morning of 7 November 1942, while bound in convoy from Trinidad to New York with 7,576 tons of bauxite. After being hit by two torpedoes in quick succession, the *Hawthorne* plunged to the bottom, bow first. With no time to launch the lifeboats, the crew jumped overboard and swam to three rafts that had been blown free of the ship. The few who managed to hold onto the rafts for thirty-nine hours were found by the destroyer *Biddle* and taken to Trinidad. There were only thirteen survivors out of the crew of fifty-two merchant seamen and Armed Guard gunners.

Another vessel in the convoy, the British freighter *Lindenhall*, was lost because her Lascar (Indian) firemen had seen what happened to the *Hawthorne* and refused to go on watch. As a result, steam pressure dropped and the vessel could not keep up with the convoy. Although the third engineer, the second cook, and a messboy volunteered to shovel coal and keep the fires going, they could not make up for lost time and the ship fell far behind the escorts. She was hit just two hours after the *Hawthorne* went down. Loaded with 4,000 tons of Brazilian iron ore, the *Lindenhall* sank in less than a minute. The only survivors were those who were on deck and able to jump overboard. Forty-three were lost, including the brave trio who had volunteered for hazardous duty beyond the routine demands of their jobs.[6] Ironically, had the cowardly Lascars stood their watch below, the ship probably would have stayed in convoy and made it safely to port.

Another story of survival occurred in the fall of 1942 when the foreign-flag *Pompoon*, one of many freighters named for fa-

A Coast Guard seaplane, with a bomb slung under a wing, shepherds a convoy in the Caribbean. This photo shows the spacing between ships in a convoy. (National Archives, 80-G-457809)

mous winners of the Kentucky Derby, was torpedoed at midnight about ninety miles from Cartagena. She was en route from the Canal Zone to Barranquilla, Columbia, with steel pipe, concrete reinforcing rods, and other materials for enlarging a refinery. The torpedo blast broke the ship in two, and the only survivors were five men who jumped overboard and climbed onto a raft. They spent twenty-one days on the raft until their rescue by a Panamanian freighter. Their provisions consisted of six gallons of water, eight bottles of malted milk tablets, three pounds of chocolate, and ten pounds of hardtack. They supplemented their stores by catching rainwater in a piece of canvas and catching fish with a hook and line from the raft's emergency kit.[7]

Sailors in dungarees performed many acts of heroism as freighters and tankers ran the U-boat gauntlet in the bloody sea. One of these took place on the ore-laden *Melville Stone* when she was torpedoed seventy-five miles from the Panama Canal on 24 November 1942. The torpedo, exploding in the engine room, destroyed the dynamo and cut off the electricity. The radio transmitter had emergency power, so radio operator Peter Carrier was able to send out an SOS asking for help and alerting other ships about the presence of a submarine. Captain Laurence Gallagher held a flashlight for him as he tapped out the distress calls. The ship's cargo of iron ore took her down so quickly that neither man had a chance to run for the open deck before the ship sank. After she went down, fireman William Wehrman swam around the wreckage and helped men to find hatchboards and other flotsam on which to cling.

When the tanker *Scottsburg* was torpedoed, Charles Drake, Jr., single-handedly launched a lifeboat and then pulled twelve exhausted shipmates from the water into the boat, a feat of determination and strength that few men would have been able to accomplish. He again exhibited these qualities after the *Kahuku* had picked up the tanker's survivors and then was torpedoed herself. This time, Drake supported a badly wounded seaman and swam with him to a raft more than a mile away. Later in the war, he was cited by the U.S. Maritime Commission for heroism when he saved three men from drowning after the *George Davis* collided with another ship in convoy.

Men such as these, and many more whose exploits went unpublicized, braved the U-boats and hauled the vital ore and bauxite through the bloody sea during World War II.

Submarine activity in the Caribbean became sporadic after 1942, but occasional sinkings took place until the end of the war. One of the most dramatic involved the new Liberty ship *James Sprunt* on her maiden voyage from Texas to India in convoy KG-123. At 0810 on 10 March 1943, she was just seven miles seaward of the U.S. naval base at Guantánamo, Cuba, when an unseen torpedo hit. An eyewitness on another ship in the convoy reported:

> "There was a tremendous explosion. There were violent tremors in the wind like a cyclone. The sky was lit with fire. Debris fell like hail on ships all around us. A few minutes later there wasn't much more than kindling to show where she had been." The ship was carrying explosives. There were no survivors.[8]

Just the previous day, convoy BT-6 had been bound from Bahia, Brazil, to Paramaribo, Suriname, when one or more U-boats attacked it during the dark, early-morning hours. Later, the British *Kelvinbank* was sunk and the American Liberty ships *James Polk*, *James Smith*, *Thomas Ruffin*, and *Mark Hanna*, were crippled.

The weather was clear and the sea choppy. The *James Smith* was the third ship in the starboard column of the convoy when a torpedo hit in number five hold, with a bright orange flash and a pervading odor of cordite. Eleven men, including five Armed Guard gunners, had been sleeping atop the hatch. All were mortally injured by flying hatch covers and steel hatch beams.[9]

After ordering most of his crew into the lifeboats in case a second torpedo should hit, Captain William Aguilar remained on board the *James Smith,* along with Lt. William Cashill of the Armed Guard and several navy gunners who hoped to get a shot at the submarine. But no U-boat showed herself, and before long the waves were washing over the after gun platform, the bow was out of the water, and the guns became canted at such an angle that they were almost useless. Aguilar ordered all hands off the ship, but they took the time to consign to the deep the mangled bodies of the men who had been killed in the torpedo blast.

Despite taking quick evasive action after the *Smith* was hit, the *James Polk* was torpedoed in the engine room. The explosion was described as "a dull, red momentary flash, followed by a sweetish, sickening odor similar to cordite with a slight tinge of ammonia." The ship settled by the stern until there were only three feet of freeboard, but she did not sink and was later towed to Port of Spain, Trinidad. The only man to be lost was killed by a lifeboat sent flying through the air by the force of the explosion just beneath it.

The *Thomas Ruffin* was hit in the engine room on the port side. Death from steam and flying steel fragments was the fate of the black gang, who, as so often was the case, had no chance to escape.[10] Three other crewmen later died of steam burns. Forty survivors were picked up by the USS *Courage,* and the ship was later towed into port. The *Mark Hanna* also stayed afloat and was towed to port. Thirty men were lost on the *Kelvinbank.*

Meanwhile, the crew of the *James Smith* had been picked up by a U.S. Navy patrol boat, whose commander decided that the *Smith* was too badly damaged to be of salvage value and she would certainly sink within a matter of hours. By radio, he ordered tugboats to assist the other damaged ships.

Aguilar, however, believed that his ship and the cargo were worth saving. He waited two days for a tug to reach the scene and then reboarded the hulk with some of his crew. They did everything they could to make the vessel more seaworthy. She was still floating on the sun-speckled sea as though to say: "No hurry. Take your time. It takes more than one tin fish to sink a Liberty."

A tugboat finally took the wreck in tow. Five days later, after traveling three hundred miles at the end of a towrope, the *James Smith* arrived in Trinidad. She was repaired and eventually went back to sea.

There is an interesting epilogue to the story of this tough "ugly duckling" that refused to go down. On a voyage across the Atlantic in the summer of 1943, the *Smith* claimed credit for helping to sink a U-boat that, a few minutes before, had hit and blown up HMS *Itchen,* one of the convoy escorts. Gunners on the *Smith* saw their shell hit the surfaced U-boat and, soon afterward the ship passed the crewmen of the sinking submarine as they struggled in the sea and watched their boat fill and plunge to the bottom.

Every day, thousands of vacationers ply the Caribbean on luxury cruise ships. Few of them probably know that scores of torpedoed ships carpet the bottom of the sea and that hundreds of their crewmen went down with the ships. It is hard to envision now that these placid azure waters were once called the bloody sea, a "happy hunting ground" for German U-boats intent on their prey.

5
Battle of the North Atlantic: Phase I

T HE GREAT BATTLE OF THE ATLANTIC, the longest and the most crucial battle of World War II, ranged over a vast expanse of oceans from the icy waters of the Barents Sea to the lonely latitudes of the South Atlantic. The main arena was the North Atlantic, along the shipping routes between the United States and Canada and Great Britain. Here, the great convoy battles were fought—German U-boats against Allied merchant ships and convoy escorts—while the fate of Britain hung in the balance.

Over these submarine-infested waters moved the oil, food, planes, tanks, ammunition, and a myriad of other materials of war. If this supply line could be cut, Hitler hoped to strangle the British into submission and then concentrate all his resources on the conquest of Russia. The U-boats came close to accomplishing this—they littered the floor of the Atlantic with hundreds of ships and their cargoes.

To paraphrase Winston Churchill's immortal tribute to the Royal Air Force in the Battle of Britain, it might be said of the U-boats that probably never in modern war was "so much done by so few." Had there been more U-boats, they could well have changed the course of history.

In 1940, German Admiral Dönitz had said, "I will show that the U-boat alone can win the war." It was not an idle boast.

Churchill summed up the importance of the ocean war in these words: "The Battle of the Atlantic was the dominating factor all through the war. Never for one moment could we forget that everything happening elsewhere, on land, sea or in the air, depended ultimately on its outcome, and amid all other cares, we viewed its changing fortunes day by day with hope and apprehension."[1]

American presidential advisor Harry Hopkins predicted that the Battle of the Atlantic would be "the final decisive battle of the war."

This great contest for the sea routes began on 3 September 1939, the first day of the war, when U-30 torpedoed the British passenger ship *Athenia* off the West Coast of Ireland in the belief that it was an auxiliary armed cruiser. Of the 112 people who lost their lives, 28 were Americans. U-boats accounted for forty-one of the fifty-three ships sunk that month. The rest were sunk by mines, which caused numerous sinkings in British home waters throughout the war.

At first, U-boats concentrated their efforts around the British Isles, where heavy traffic offered plenty of targets and submarine defenses were still being organized. Activity was gradually extended westward during July 1940, when the raiders sank thirty-eight ships, one of which was the *Arandora Star*, torpedoed off Iceland with the loss of 800 passengers and crew.

The period from July to October 1940 was known as "the happy time" to U-boat captains and crews. Convoy protection was inadequate, and U-boats sent hundreds of ships to the bottom. During the attack on one convoy in September, U-100 alone sank seven ships. One of the worst convoy disasters of the war occurred in October 1940, when eastbound convoy SC-7 from Halifax, Nova Scotia, lost twenty-one ships out of thirty-four.

Early in 1941, U-boats began wolf pack tactics against convoys, usually at night and on the surface, with several boats working together. Wolf packs were directed to a convoy after information about the fleet's movements had been received at Admiral Dönitz's headquarters at Lorient, France, either from reports by reconnaissance submarines or coded messages sent to the convoy by British naval headquarters that were decoded by the Germans.

The United States entered the battle of the Atlantic in July 1941, when President Franklin D. Roosevelt authorized the use of American warships to help protect convoys to Iceland. Roosevelt extended the U.S. role in September by approving the use of American warships in convoys from Halifax to England. This led to the torpedoing of the U.S. destroyer *Kearney* on 17 October 1941, with the loss of 11 men, and the torpedoing and sinking of the U.S. destroyer *Reuben James* in October, with the loss of 106 men.

No area of the Atlantic was immune from attack.

Two of the most dramatic sea fights of the war took place in the South Atlantic, when the tanker *Stanvac Calcutta* and the Liberty ship *Stephen Hopkins* dueled German raiders in a slugfest reminiscent of old-time sea fights in the days of "wooden ships and iron men." The engagements of these gallant ships were unexcelled in the annals of the Allied merchant marines in World War II. For details, see chapter 12 (*Stanvac Calcutta*) and chapter 13 (*Stephen Hopkins*).

Most of the North Atlantic convoys made up in Nova Scotia, at Halifax or Sydney on Cape Breton. In peacetime, the passage from Nova Scotia to ports in England was about 2,500 miles, but, in wartime, it covered a greater distance because the convoys had to be diverted from direct routes to avoid wolf packs and hopefully to confuse German intelligence. Moreover, the convoys had to proceed at the speed of the slowest ships, which was often six to eight knots.

A voyage across the Atlantic seldom avoided submarine alerts and was frequently spiced with actual attacks by the U-boats. Day or night, seamen never knew when a torpedo might hit.

In addition, storms battered and separated the convoys, so that stragglers had to be rounded up by the escorts and shepherded back to the flock. The winter of 1942 was especially cold, and the storms were severe. Fog, too, was a frequent hazard, especially on the Grand Banks, and collisions were not infrequent.

In broad daylight on 23 April 1942, the freighter *Lammot Du Pont*, bound from Buenos Aires to New York with 6,800 tons of linseed oil, caught a tin fish five hundred miles southeast of Bermuda. Within five minutes, the ship had gone under.

There were fifty-six men in the crew, including nine navy gunners. Except for four killed in the explosion, the rest were able to get away in a lifeboat and several rafts. Only one boat could be launched because the ship lay over on its side soon after being hit.

Captain Roger Gilman, then first mate on the *Du Pont*, described the experience:

> The captain and I jumped overside and were pulled under when the old girl sank. It seemed like we had gone down at least thirty feet or so till we fought our way out of the suction and came up in the midst of flotsam. Fortunately, the ship was a coal burner so there was no oil to contend with. The sub surfaced a few hundred yards away, hoisted the swastika, and then moved off. There was wreckage floating all around. I saw a raft and tried to swim to it but the wind kept taking it away. Even after I ditched my lifejacket I still couldn't make it. I was getting pretty exhausted when the lifeboat picked me up. It picked up the captain a little later. He had a gash in the head and soon became unconscious.
>
> After a while there were thirty-two men in the boat and seventeen on rafts. Several bodies were floating around, and as the captain was unconscious, I took command of the boat. I set a course for Bermuda, with the wind southwest.[2]

That night, they heaved to with a sea anchor and used some storm oil to break the waves. Two men had to work the steering oar to keep the boat from capsizing in a force seven wind. The crew pumped and bailed all night to stay afloat. There wasn't enough room for all hands to sit down at one time. The ones left standing had to maintain a precarious balance until their turns to sit on the thwarts. All of them were soaked clear through, and the wind was cold.

"After the storm blew over," Gilman said, "the wind turned northwest so we had to forget about making Bermuda and headed for the Caribbean, a long way to the south. Our only navigating instrument was a compass. At night we steered by the Pole star, sitting facing aft and keeping it on the starboard quarter about three points. We allowed a point for leeway and set."

They made a second sail by sewing two blankets together with sewing gear from the lifeboat's emergency kit and using an oar for a mast. Rationing began the first day: a cracker and a small piece of chocolate were a day's meal. The water ration was three ounces a day. Fortunately, there were several good rains.

On the fourteenth day, they sighted a ship but it was hull down. That same day, the first man died.

"He yelled out that we'd never make it so what was the use," Gilman said. "He just leaned against the gunwale and pretty soon he was gone."

Several more died in the week that followed.

On the twenty-third day, a plane sighted them and dropped a canteen with water and a note saying they would be reported. When a destroyer arrived a few hours later, they were only forty miles from San Juan, Puerto Rico: a magnificent job of navigation by dead reckoning.

"We all had lost about forty pounds and looked like a bunch of savages," Gilman commented, but he, the captain, and the chief engineer were back at sea on a new Liberty ship within a few weeks.

The men on the rafts had been picked up by a Swedish freighter after two days adrift.

As many more crews would learn, abandoning ship successfully was often only the prelude to a supreme test of men against the sea. At 0250 on the bright, moonlit night of 23 November 1942, a submarine targeted the oil tanker *Caddo,* loaded with navy fuel and three hundred drums of aviation gasoline. Most of the crew got away in boats.

After they had abandoned ship, the submarine surfaced. An officer asked for the captain, Paul Muller, and quizzed him about the ship and her destination. Muller was then ordered on board the submarine, along with First Mate Bendik Lande. Some weeks later, they were landed unharmed at a submarine base in Lorient, but Muller died later in a prisoner of war (POW) camp.

Meanwhile, on 7 December, a heavy sea had capsized the *Caddo*'s number three boat, which held seventeen men. They managed to right the boat and climb back in, but water beakers had been broken and some emergency food supplies lost. Within half an hour, the boat was capsized again. When the exhausted survivors managed to right the boat, there were only nine left. That night, two men became delirious and died. A third stood up and said, "The water is so beautiful." Then he jumped overboard.

Early the next morning, the men sighted a ship and shot off a flare. The Spanish tanker *Motomar* picked them up. The tanker had come along just in time. For the past twenty-four hours, they had been in water up to their waists as they tried desperately to stay afloat.

The sea war intensified during 1942 as more U-boats became operational. The Germans were determined to sever Britain's lifeline. Some convoys made it across with few losses, and others actually had no contacts with submarines. But rare was the crossing in which there was not at least one submarine alert or a signal from the convoy commodore: "Submarines in vicinity."

The battles were hard-fought and costly. The escorts tried to shepherd their flocks to safe haven, but some escorts were also torpedoed. More than 1,000 Allied merchant ships sank to the bottom of the Atlantic Ocean during 1942. Heaviest losses were in the North Atlantic, with its great concentration of Allied shipping and heavy deployment of German U-boats.

For the Merchant Marine crews and Armed Guard gunners, danger was always at hand. A seaman hit the sack in "abandon ship clothes"; there was seldom time to dress when a torpedo struck. His life belt or life jacket was always at hand. Even in the engine rooms, the men kept theirs close by.

In October 1942, westbound convoy SC-107 lost 15 ships totaling almost 90,000 tons. At about the same time, convoy SL-125, steaming eastward near Madeira, was attacked by a ten-boat wolf pack and lost 13 ships over a period of seven days as the raiders haunted the convoy's course. The worst month at sea for the Allies was November 1942, when 134 vessels were lost, mostly in the North Atlantic from submarine attacks.

Losses could depend on several factors: the number and skill of the escorts; the number, skill, and determination of the attackers; and, of course, the weather.

The latter part of 1942 and the first half of 1943 were the crucial period in the Battle of the Atlantic. It was touch-and-go between the convoys and the submarines. No ship that left port could be sure of arriving at her destination. Not until the summer of 1943 did the tide of battle turn.

There were countless heroes among the men who sailed the submarine-infested sea lanes of the North Atlantic, and many acts of heroism and self-sacrifice were unrecorded and unsung. But in all the annals of the sea, no man is more entitled to be called a hero than Gustave Alm, a carpenter on the freighter *Angelina*.

A terrific storm had separated this ship from the westbound convoy in the North Atlantic on 17 October 1942.[3] The ship plunged and rolled in seas thirty feet high and three hundred feet from crest to crest. Just before midnight, as the 8-to-12 oiler called the engine room watch and the third assistant engineer was making the last notations for the watch in the engine room log, a torpedo smashed into the *Angelina* amidships. It blew up the starboard boiler, released a cloud of scalding steam, and flooded the engine spaces and the dynamo platform. All the lights went out.

A typical winter storm in the North Atlantic. A lifeboat swung inboard and a life raft, just beyond it, are ready for instant launching. Open decks were dangerous for crewmen in this kind of weather, and ships had a hard time keeping their stations in convoy. (U.S. Maritime Administration, 3570).

The ship was soon abandoned. Forty-three men climbed over the side on the scramble nets into one lifeboat that was successfully launched on the leeward side. They expected momentarily to be caught up by one of the huge waves and smashed against the side.

Captain W. S. Goodman, along with the Armed Guard gunnery officer and several other men, climbed over the side into a raft because the lifeboat was already too full.

In the lifeboat, the oars were shipped and every man was designated to a place where he could be of some help, either pulling or bailing. The crew fended off and shipped oars but hadn't taken a dozen strokes before the boat broached and a mighty comber thundered toward them—a terrifying wall of water from which there was no escape. The wave towered over the tiny boat before it curled and crashed.

The lifeboat heeled over, hung on its keel for one awful moment, and then capsized. So quickly did it happen that there were only a few startled shouts. When the churning comber had swept on, fewer than half of the boat's crew were left to grope for a hold on the upturned hull. Coughing and cursing, they spat out the salt water, but there were a few prayers, too.

They called out the names of their shipmates to find out who was left.

"Is Blackie still here?"

"Where's the oiler?"

"Hey, Joe. You there, Joe?"

But there wasn't much talking. The waves drubbed them unmercifully as they clung to the grab rails attached to the underside of the boat. The water was cold. After a while, it began to numb their hands and feet, and then the numbness gave way to a pleasant drowsiness and feeling of peace and oblivion. They wanted to drop into the fathomless depths. A messboy went out of his mind. He babbled something about having to report to the galley. A few moments later, he disappeared.

Two Armed Guard gunners and one of the seamen struck out for the dark hulk of the half-submerged *Angelina*. They hoped to find a raft or climb on board and wait rescue by the convoy escort, which they thought would soon be answering the SOS. The helpless ship was a big, black blob in the dark, only a few hundred feet away, or so it seemed to those on the upturned boat. The three men were never seen again.

The tired, benumbed survivors were despairing of rescue. "It's no use to hang on any longer," someone said. "Nobody is going to find us out here. We might as well get it over with right now."

Gustave Alm, the carpenter, urged them to hang on. "Don't give up yet," he shouted. "There's always a chance. Somebody will find us when it gets light. Don't give up. Hang on."

During the cold, bitter hours of the night, a destroyer passed so close they could almost have reached out and touched the hull, but there were no answers to their shouts. Because of the huge troughs and the spindrift, no one on board the destroyer spotted the helpless men. One of the young navy gunners gave up after this and was swept away from his hold on the boat. Strong-armed Alm swam out and hauled him back through the black, tumbling seas and helped him keep a grip on the grab rail.

"Stick it out a few more hours," he kept telling them. "They're looking for us. They'll find us."

The young gunner was only one of the men saved from death by the carpenter that winter night. Every time a man was pummelled by a wave and lost his grip, Alm grabbed him by his arm or leg or wrapped a powerful arm around his waist until he could cough the water out of his lungs and breathe again.

He couldn't save them all. A sailor struck out for a piece of wreckage and was never seen again. One by one, others became delirious or unconscious or so numb with cold that their fingers could no longer grip the steel grab bars.

The British rescue ship *Bury*, one of the small vessels assigned to convoys for the express purpose of saving men from torpedoed ships, had responded to the *Angelina*'s SOS and picked up the men on the raft shortly after midnight. But the lookouts did not see the upturned boat until after dawn. By then, only a handful of survivors were clinging to the bottom. The men were too weak to wave or call out when the rescue ship approached.

Captain L. E. Brown of the *Bury* maneuvered his ship to within a few yards of the capsized lifeboat and dumped bunker oil to windward in order to break the heavy seas. He could count five men on the wallowing boat, but what amazed him was the superhuman exhibit of dogged stamina and courage by a man of broad shoulders and barrel chest: Gustave Alm, the carpenter.

One man after another was knocked off by the waves, but each time Alm hauled the man back to the boat and helped him regain a hold.

While the carpenter was trying to save his now completely exhausted shipmates, Captain Brown attempted to keep the *Bury* near enough that a line could be thrown to the men and they could be hauled on board. If the *Bury* rolled too close, she would smash the lifeboat and kill all the men on it with one slap of her ponderous steel hull.

As Alm tried to lift one of his helpless shipmates over the keel of the lifeboat, another man was washed away. With a deft turn of the helm, Brown swung his ship near enough that the third mate could reach over the side on an upcoming sea. He collared the drowning man as the wave surged and hauled him, unconscious but still alive, onto the deck.

Although the *Bury* was rolling and pitching and dipping her rail into the waves, first on one side and then on the other, Brown maneuvered the little ship to within a few feet of the upturned boat. It was a time for faultless judgment and iron nerve. A miscue at the *Bury*'s wheel; a roll of the ship at the wrong moment, and the *Angelina*'s survivors would have been ground beneath the sea. But Captain Brown handled his ship as though it were a dancing horse performing tricks in a show ring.

Alm raised himself on the bottom of the boat. He stretched out an arm to grab a line thrown from the *Bury*. Twice the line was thrown and twice he missed, but the carpenter grabbed the line on the third try and made it fast in a tight sailor's knot around a grab bar.

His half-conscious companions were too weak to know what was going on as Alm caught three more lines and secured each one in turn around the chest of a shipmate. One at a time, he freed each man and the crew of the *Bury* hauled him on board. When the last line was thrown, Alm was almost too exhausted to secure it around his waist. It was many minutes before he could summon enough strength to knot the line and wave to those on the rescue ship to haul him on board.

All this time, Captain Brown had kept the *Bury* within a few feet of the lifeboat—a masterful feat of seamanship and ship handling. Bobbing, pitching, and rolling, the *Bury* rode the huge waves like a cork. Brown reined in his vessel to perfection, as he gauged the wind and waves, so that the survivors were kept little more than an arm's length away from the hull.

Hauling in the line, the *Bury*'s men could see that Alm was exhausted and almost unconscious. Sailors reached over the side, ready to grab him and hoist him onto the vessel's deck. The little rescue ship rolled in a heavy sea and knocked the carpenter against the hull of the lifeboat. He went under, choking with salt water. The men above were sure that the blow must have killed him, but the sea would not now claim a man who had cheated it so often.

They finally fished Alm out of the water and onto the *Bury*'s deck. He was bruised, bleeding, covered with oil, and too exhausted to even raise his head, but he was still alive. When they gave him a swig of rum, he coughed, tried to say something, and then passed out.

Gustave Alm of the *Angelina* was awarded the Distinguished Service Medal of the Merchant Marine by the U.S. Maritime Commission. Several weeks later, he was back at sea on another ship sailing through "Torpedo Alley." Alm continued to serve throughout the war.

Captain Brown wrote to the U.S. Maritime Commission: "I feel honored to have played a part in the rescue of a man with such a wonderful spirit. He did credit to a great profession. He is a man that America can be proud of."

"A hero," said the poet Rupert Hughes, "is a man, plus."

Alm was "a man, plus."

The bitter year of 1942 in the North Atlantic ended with another display of heroism amid disaster. This is the story of a ship overcome by wind and waves, not by submarines. On New Year's Eve, the old freighter *Maiden Creek* was struggling for her life. Deeply laden with 6,700 tons of lead and copper concentrates in her holds, she was bound from Botwood, Newfoundland, to New York.

A series of tremendous seas smashed into the ship. Waves surging across the decks filled the forepeak and ripped up the steel guards over the steam lines, which ran from midships to the windlass and the winches on the foredeck. Curled into knives by the force of the waves, these strips of steel were forced upward until they cut through the heavy, protective tarpaulins over the hatches. Wind and waves then tore the tarpaulins away, and tons of water poured through the hatch boards into the holds.[4]

Water soaked the ore, and the laboring ship sank dangerously below her Plimsoll marks. Hour by hour, the storm increased in fury. Mile by tortuous mile, the ship lost speed. Finally, it was all the black gang could do even to raise steam for steerageway.

The lights were dimming because the fires were going out and there was no steam for the dynamos. The holds were flooding. Huddled in the shelter of the deckhouse, the crew prayed that a ship would come to their aid.

Captain G. R. Cook tried to bring the *Maiden Creek* about and run before the storm, but she was too heavy—too sluggish— to swing around against the pummeling seas.

The crew put on extra trousers, socks, and woolen shirts. They slept in the passageways and on the engine room gratings because it was too dangerous now to venture across the sea-swept decks to their quarters in the stern.

Their hopes soared for a few minutes around 1700 when lookouts spotted a westbound ship in the distance. They fired more than one hundred rounds from the Oerlikon guns to attract her attention. Flares were shot from the bridge. As the signals of distress bloomed out brightly against the bleak winter sky, the crew watched the distant vessel come about and head their way.

The good news sped from mouth to mouth throughout the ship: "Vessel off the port bow. They're turning and coming toward us."

Some of the men ventured onto the boat deck to watch the oncoming vessel. Not much could be seen of her through the dim light and the flying scud, but they could tell she was a big ship. The stranger made a wide sweep around the *Maiden Creek*. Then, despite more signals of distress fired into the gathering night, she turned away and disappeared into the mists.

The *Maiden Creek* was sinking by the head and no longer had steerageway. Spray drubbed like hail against the windows of the pilothouse. Waves clawed at the vessel's sides. Spumes of water shot higher than the masts each time a mighty comber broke against the weather side. The ship could plunge at any moment.

In the engine room, the black gang watched the steam steadily go down. They cleaned the burners, one by one, but it made no difference. The ship was filling as she labored under a double load of cargo and salt water. And water was getting into the oil. Fires sputtered and dimmed, and the steam gauge dropped five, ten, fifteen pounds.

At 1700, the radio operator sent out the SOS. He tapped out the ship's call number KIPX . . . KIPX. He gave her position. Again, KIPX. But there was no acknowledgment.

"Sinking by the head. Not long afloat. Request immediate assistance."

Still, no answer.

It was now getting impossible to steer the *Maiden Creek*. The chief engineer ordered his men on deck. The ship might take the final plunge at any time.

Captain Cook pulled the whistle cord and sounded the mournful call to abandon ship. The crew pulled on sweaters and oilskins as they left the shelter of the mess room for the open deck, their backs hunched against the bitter bite of wind and spray.

The captain gave the order to lower the boats.

"Make sure those plugs are in," the mate shouted. "Secure those painters.

"Away number one. Belay the falls. . . .

"Ready, three."

Huge seas clutched at the spray-swept boat deck. The ship wasn't rolling much now. She was too low in the water for that.

But the black, forbidding waves reached for men and boats and cascaded in showers of chilling spray as they smashed against the bulwarks.

Getting the boats lowered into those hungry, clamoring seas would take fine seamanship. Two of the crew would have to stay on board and tend the falls for each boat as it went over the side. It would be their job to lower the boats so they would hit the water just at the right moment to keep from being smashed to bits or swamped against the vessel's side. There was a good chance that the men who stayed on board would go down with the ship.

Able seamen Joseph Squires and Tom Crawford volunteered. No one asked them, but they knew the job required men with strong arms and experience in handling small boats. They were typical men of the sea—hard-muscled, broad-shouldered, with hands toughened and callused by years of chipping, painting, splicing, and other chores of a sailor's trade. Each had a wife and family back home, but they didn't think of this as they waved younger and less experienced men away from the falls.

When First Mate Charles Steiner tried to help with the after falls, Squires told him to get into the boat. "They're going to need someone who can pull an oar," he shouted. "Hurry up, or you'll be stuck here, too."

Per Lykke told what happened after that.

Lykke was a Norwegian-American. His father had been an owner of small ships in Norway, and Per had gone to sea almost as soon as he had learned to walk. Old-time "squarehead" sailors had taught him his trade—to splice and steer and point a lifeboat into a surging sea so that it would ride the waves and not broach.

Per was a thin, quiet man. He didn't talk much, but he possessed those qualities of a born seaman that were needed in emergencies. He had the instinct for command.

He was in the second boat that was launched. As soon as the boat touched the waves, he automatically took charge because he was the only one of the boat's crew who knew instinctively what to do.

"Free the falls," he yelled to the men. "Push her away."

Lykke continued with the story:

> The first boat had been swept more than one hundred feet away from the ship by one huge wave. It was the second mate's boat. Crawford and Squires couldn't possibly have reached it if they had jumped.
>
> That boat held engine gang men and stewards who had never handled an oar. They couldn't have pulled back to the ship if they wanted to. It was all they could do just to stay afloat.
>
> We intended to push away from the ship and then ride on the painter so Squires and Crawford could jump, grab the painter, and haul themselves toward our boat.
>
> But in the excitement, someone cast off the painter. It was a tragic mistake.
>
> A wave carried us away from the ship's side. We tried to get back. We shipped the oars and pulled like hell. The seas were so big they tossed us around like a chip o' wood. We pulled and pulled, but we were getting farther from the ship all the time.[5]

Squires and Crawford watched from the wind-whipped boat deck. They must have known that the bobbing lifeboat would never be able to get back to the ship and pick them up. Worst of all, they were probably losing sight of the boat in the dark. In a few more minutes, they would not be able to see it at all.

Crawford slid down the falls, hand over hand. He appeared to be gauging the moment when he could drop into the trough of a receding sea and strike out for the boat. Only a powerful and courageous man would have dared to pit his strength against such tremendous waves. The ocean was a mass of swirling whitecaps. While he was still hanging onto the ropes, a huge comber rolled up out of the darkness and smashed against the vessel's side. The water swallowed him up in a mass of foam. When the wave receded, he had disappeared.

74

Squires now stood alone on the slanting deck. For a few awful minutes, he waited by the empty davits. He must have been hoping that the boat would come close enough for him to make a jump for it, but the turbulent seas continued to carry it farther away.

The men in the boat watched as Squires jumped into the crest of a huge wave lapping the deck almost at his very feet. He had timed his jump perfectly, for the wave rolled back and carried him to within twenty or thirty feet of the lifeboat.

"We threw him a line," Lykke said. "He grabbed for it and missed. He couldn't have missed it by more than a foot or so. We pulled as hard as we could to reach him. For a moment we saw him struggling on top of a cresting sea."

Just then, another smashing comber almost overturned the boat. When the crew recovered from the impact, Squires was gone. The wave had carried him far beyond their reach in one powerful surge. They never saw him again.

At 1900, the *Maiden Creek* succumbed to the sea. Bow first, she plunged toward the bottom.

The other lifeboat, in charge of the second mate, shot two flares into the snow-blanketed sky shortly after midnight. These flares were probably their last desperate signals for help before foundering. Neither the boat nor its thirty-one occupants were ever found.

After three days of fighting the cold and the wind, Lykke's boat was picked up by the steamship *Staghound*, bound for England from New York. Another 48 hours adrift, according to the *Staghound*'s doctor, and the men probably would have frozen to death. For his outstanding abilities in boat handling and saving the boat and its crew, able seaman Per Lykke later received a naval commendation for "extraordinary courage and seamanship."

Those who survived owed their lives to Crawford and Squires, two valiant men of the sea. They died so that their shipmates might live. Truly "heroes in dungarees," they had lived up to the highest traditions of the Merchant Marine. Liberty ships were later named for them.

The tide of battle turned dramatically against the U-boats during the spring and summer of 1943. In large part, this was due to the advent of escort carriers, as well as to the development of long-range radar for aircraft by which a shore- or carrier-based plane could spot a surfaced submarine from many miles away. In numerous instances, the planes were able to pounce on submarines before they could submerge.

The escort carrier was a very effective member of the anti–U-boat "hunter-killer" team after 1943.

6
Sea Roads to Russia

AN IMPORTANT AND DRAMATIC PART of the Battle of the North Atlantic was fought along the convoy routes from Scotland and Iceland across the cold and stormy Arctic to the Russian ports of Archangel (Arkhangelsk) and Murmansk on the White Sea. These northern "sea roads to Russia" reached above the ice-fringed 70th parallel of latitude and were threatened by German bombers, battleships, destroyers, and submarines. The convoys setting out on what was popularly called the Murmansk run were vital to keeping the Soviet Union in the war.

Adolf Hitler's consuming passion was to crush the Soviet Union, take over its rich oil fields and other mineral resources, force its factories to support the German war machine, and turn its farms into a vast food basket for Germany and its satellites. Mad though this plan might have seemed, Hitler came close to achieving his goal. His hard-striking panzers reached points 1,000 miles inside the Russian border before being thrown back.

The only way to stop this maniacal march toward complete domination of Europe was to keep the Soviet Union in the war by

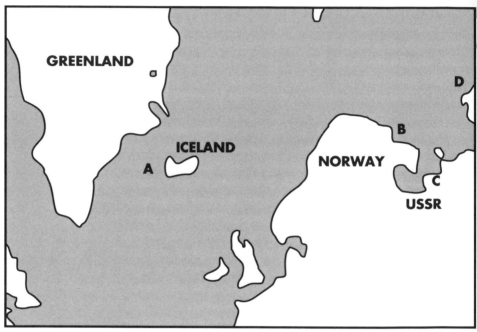

Map 1. Summer routes of Russian convoys: A. Reykjavik; B. Murmansk; C. Archangel; D. Novaya Zemlya.

supplying guns, tanks, planes, fuel, food, machinery, and hundreds of other essentials for its defense. Soviet steel mills and arms plants, some of which had been moved hundreds of miles into the interior, were working day and night, but they could not come close to producing all that was needed. The United States had to make up the difference.

Without the flour, wheat, milk, lard, eggs, and other foods sent from American ports, Russian resistance would have collapsed. Ships carried the millions of shoes, coats, boots, and gloves that enabled the Soviets to fight during their frigid winters. From America went planes, tanks, trucks, and other vehicles. Ships carried thousands of locomotives and railroad cars, plus enough rails to span the Soviet Union from border to border. They delivered steel, aluminum, chemicals, and vast amounts of barbed wire and telegraph wire. Even whole factories, including refineries, were freighted over the sea roads. The total value of

This photo, taken by a German reconnaissance plane, shows a convoy, probably PQ-17, in the early stage of its voyage after leaving Iceland. (U.S. Naval Historical Center, NH 71382)

this material exceeded ten billion dollars. A huge fleet of ships was used to deliver it.[1]

There were three primary supply routes to the Soviet Union. The first to be used, and one that has since become famous, was the route to the White Sea ports of Archangel and Murmansk. They were about 4,500 miles from American and Canadian East Coast ports by way of Iceland or Scotland, where convoys were made up for the final lap through the Arctic.

Little has been written about the second route, by which millions of tons of oil, food, and war equipment were shipped to the Soviet Union from the United States, across the North Pacific to the port of Vladivostok in Siberia. The American tankers *L. P. St. Clair* and *Associated* delivered oil there as early as September 1941.

This seaborne pipeline operated throughout the war without interference from the Japanese. The Soviets had enough to do against Germany without taking on the Japanese, and the latter were content to let sleeping dogs lie and not use their ships or submarines to interdict this important supply line to the Soviets.

The supply run to Vladivostok was almost entirely a Soviet operation, although much of the material was carried in the fifty-two Liberty ships "loaned" to the Soviet Union under Lend-Lease. Cargoes were shipped from Vladivostok to the fighting fronts over the Trans-Siberian Rail Road, but some were stockpiled at various places in Siberia. In 1944, a program called Operation Milepost was initiated. The United States supplied huge amounts of ammunition and other material to be stockpiled in Siberia for a Soviet offensive against Japan, which Premier Joseph Stalin had promised would take place after the defeat of Germany.[2]

As soon as adequate port facilities were built in Iran, the third primary route was opened up by way of the Persian Gulf. Ships bound for Iranian ports were routed in several ways to ensure minimum losses from submarines or surface raiders. Many sailed from American East Coast or Gulf ports across the South Atlantic, around the Cape of Good Hope, and up the East Coast of Africa to the Bay of Bengal and the Persian Gulf. Some were dispatched from the West Coast through the Panama Canal to use the same route, but a few West Coast cargoes went around Cape Horn and then across the South Atlantic. U-boats picked off many ships along the East Coast of Africa. The Mozambique Channel was a favorite lair for submarines.

Beginning in 1942, an additional route for ships from the East Coast or the Gulf was by way of the Panama Canal and then the long haul across the Pacific to Fremantle, Australia, via southern New Zealand. One ship, the *Jonathan Grout*, was almost two months in getting to Fremantle by this route and met only one ship—at a distance—during the entire crossing. No ships were sighted on the next leg of the trip from Fremantle to the Bay of Bengal. Crossing the Indian Ocean, the crew were on alert after a radio dispatch warned Captain Edward M. Foster that Japanese submarines were seen along his course. As the *Grout* steamed up the Persian Gulf toward the end of her long journey at the Shatt al-Arab River, the crew had a severe case of "channel fever"[3] after being so long at sea. They were excited by the prospects of going ashore for a drink and an assessment of the local women as soon as the hawsers were secured to a dock. Alas, the topmasts of many ships were spotted at the mouth of the Shatt al-Arab. After the *Grout* dropped her hook, visiting boats from other ships gave them the sad news of some ships riding at anchor for weeks as they waited to discharge. Fortunately for the crew, the *Grout* had a priority cargo and, within a few days, was sent to an anchorage near Ābādān, Iran, where barges discharged the most urgently needed material, including crated planes and high-explosive shells.

Any young man who joined the Merchant Marine for action and adventure was pretty sure to see more of both than he had ever wished for, especially if his ship was loaded with cargo for the Russians and sent off to England or Iceland to join a convoy heading toward Archangel or Murmansk. Freighters on the Russian run usually carried from several hundred to a thousand or more tons of ammunition and explosives. A torpedo hit or a well-

81

placed bomb could easily result in the obliteration of ship, crew, and cargo.

The first American ship on the Russian run, a member of convoy PQ-8, was the little *Larranga*. Switched from Panamanian to American registry in December 1941, she was equipped with six 30-caliber machine guns and a four-inch stern gun and carried a Naval Armed Guard of six men under Ens. H. A. Axtell. The merchant crew assisted at the guns and helped to beat off a submarine attack the day before Christmas. They claimed hits on a surfacing U-boat, but this could not be officially confirmed. German records show that three submarines took part in this attack on PQ-8 but do not indicate that any were sunk. After surviving several more U-boat attacks, the *Larranga* docked in Murmansk on 17 January 1942 and then returned safely to her home port.

The crews of most ships that made the northern run to the White Sea had thrilling stories to tell. The ships' logs were terse chronicles of high adventure.

The freighter *Michigan* shot down two planes, and the Liberty ship *John Randolph* recounted two near misses from torpedoes. The *Steel Worker* struck a mine and sank in Kola Strait. While fighting through to Archangel, the freighter *Ironclad* ran aground and was eventually given to the Soviets.

After stranding at Kildin Island, the *Ballot* became a total loss. The *J. L. Curry* was abandoned when her deck plates were crushed by heavy gales. Gunners on the *Expositor* blew off the conning tower of a submarine that tried to attack on the surface. The *Yaka* took a direct bomb hit in one of her boilers, then fought on to Murmansk and sweated out 156 German air attacks while unloading her cargo of guns and food.

In 1942, the armament of American freighters on the Russian run consisted principally of 30- and 50-caliber machine guns. Some ships also had three-inch surface and antiaircraft guns or four-inch guns mounted on the stern to repel surface attack, but others had nothing but machine guns.

The *West Hilus*, for instance, was defended with a four-inch stern gun, two 50-caliber Browning machine guns, and the captain's .45 Colt automatic pistol. By the time the ship reached the Russian coast in 1942, she had used up almost all of her ammunition. When eight Junkers bombers attacked, the guns could fire only a few rounds. "Sticks of bombs seemed to be coming right down the stack," said the vessel's log. Although surrounded by bomb bursts, the *West Hilus* wasn't hit.

In March 1942, the *Bateau*, an American-owned vessel under the Panamanian flag, became separated from her convoy in a heavy snowstorm. Suddenly coming out of the whirling snow, three German destroyers bore down on the ship. The two navy gunners, one American and one English, opened fire at once with the stern gun, but a destroyer hit the *Bateau* with two torpedoes before they could get more than three or four shells away.

The lifeboats were swung out, but they couldn't be launched because the launching gear was frozen. Within five minutes, the *Bateau* had disappeared. Forty-one men went with her.

In 1941 and early 1942, before the famous American Liberty ships began to roll down the launching ways in large numbers, the Allies scraped the bottom of the barrel for vessels to freight the mountain of Lend-Lease supplies piled up along the Atlantic coast. Many ships that should have been scrapped were loaded down to their Plimsoll marks and sent off on the dangerous sea roads to Russia.

One of these was the *Dunboyne*. She hit a horrendous gale off Newfoundland that pitched and tossed and battered her with terrible fury. The pounding of the seas loosed the midships deckhouse from its fastenings. The crew lashed the structure to the ship with cargo booms and cables to prevent the entire bridge section and officers' quarters from sliding over the side.

The old *Dunboyne* limped back into port, weak and tired. She was ready to leave the rigorous Russian run to younger ships, but there was no rest even for old-timers. After her deckhouse was fixed, she finally crossed the Atlantic and delivered her cargo to Murmansk.

Among the older ships in the early Russian convoys were some former Axis freighters that had been commandeered in American ports. They were placed under Panamanian registry and operated by the U.S. War Shipping Administration. The ships were renamed to commemorate famous champions of the American turf. They included the *Bold Venture, Blenheim, Pompoon, Reigh Count, Stone Street, Troubador,* and *Alan-A-Dale,* but they were unable to show German submarines the kind of speed attained by the fleet-footed fliers for whom they were named. Most of these ships went to the bottom before the end of the war.

Convoys PQ-9, -10, -11, and -12 delivered their cargoes mostly without loss, although the Germans made intense efforts to find and destroy PQ-12 with the battleship *Tirpitz,* based in Norway. In groping for the convoy through mists and fog, the *Tirpitz* at one point came close to finding it, but the ships slipped by undetected. Only the lack of good air reconnaissance by the *Tirpitz* saved PQ-12 from disaster.

A German flotilla of submarines, plus destroyers and a large number of bombers, was sent out to eliminate convoy PQ-13, whose nineteen merchant ships were heavily protected by a covering force of cruisers and destroyers. The *Effingham* was the only American freighter to be sunk, but classic sea duels took place between the escorting forces and attackers as the Germans tried to close with the convoy.

When convoy PQ-15 left Reykjavik, Iceland, on 26 April, it included the American freighters *Expositor, Deer Lodge,* and *Francis Scott Key,* one of the new Liberty ships. The *Expositor* was a floating powder keg, with five thousand tons of ammunition and TNT under hatches. Air attacks beginning on 2 May and continuing without letup for two days gave the American contingent a fiery baptism in battle.

The British ships *Bothaven* and *Jutland* were torpedoed and sunk. Either an aerial torpedo or a tin fish from a submarine hit the British freighter *Cape Corso,* which, according to an observer, "blew skyward in a mass of flame." There were no survivors.

This was a sobering spectacle for the crew of the *Expositor,* but they had little time to think about it. Moments later, lookouts reported the conning tower of a submarine just a few yards off the port quarter, so close that none of the guns could be depressed enough to open fire. But as the distance widened and the submarine did not seem intent on a crash dive, gunners on the *Expositor* got off several point-blank rounds. According to the official report of the Armed Guard officer, Ens. Robert E. Ricks, USNR:

> The second shot hit squarely on the conning tower. As the shell exploded, the top of the conning tower was blown off. The U-boat appeared to sink and the water boiled up in a froth of air and bubbles. An oil slick came to the surface. At this moment lookouts spotted a torpedo headed for the ship on the port beam. It missed by a few feet.[4]

Convoy PQ-16, with thirty-four merchant ships flying various flags, left Reykjavik on 20 May under heavy escort. Five days later, the Germans began concerted attacks with high- and low-level bombers, torpedo planes, and submarines. The American freighter *Syros* was hit by an aerial torpedo and sank with heavy loss of life. The British freighter *Empire Laurence*, packed to the hatch tops with ammunition, was bombed and set on fire. Crewmen lost no time in abandoning ship and for good reason. Before all hands could get away, the ship exploded. When the trawler *Lady Madeline* came up to rescue survivors, only an oil patch and floating bodies marked where the ship had been. A few badly wounded men were picked up, but they died soon after.

The American *City of Joliet* was attacked by eight torpedo planes and eighteen dive bombers during this battle but survived the onslaught, only to become a prime target again on 27 May. So many bombs were dropped close to the ship that rivets were blown out of the hull plating and water poured into the ship in such volume that the pumps could not handle it. She had to be abandoned, much to the chagrin of crewmen and gunners who had fought so bravely to get the cargo through. No lives were lost.

The battle report of the American freighter *Michigan* contained entries such as the following:

27 May 1025 hours: Attacked by a wave of six bombers from the starboard quarter. Five planes passed overhead. The sixth dove directly down on the *Michigan*. The guns opened fire as the plane began its dive. When within 1,000 feet of the ship, the plane released five bombs, then leveled off and strafed the ship with machine gun fire. Bombs landed within 100 feet of the ship.

27 May 1155 hours: Attacked by a formation of bombers from astern. One stick of bombs landed within 100 feet of the ship and the port gun platform. No casualties.[5]

Seven American ships in PQ-16 were sunk.

Allied sailors on the Russian run knew that they had only a fifty-fifty chance of survival if they had to take to lifeboats or rafts. Even in July, many crewman of the British freighter *Hartlebury* died of exposure after several days in a boat.

An unexplainable mystery to many of the sailors who made the trip to Murmansk was the roundabout routes their vessels took before they ever got there. For example, the American freighter *Beauregard* arrived in England in May 1942. After discharging her inbound cargo, she was sent to Hull, where she loaded tanks and other equipment for north Russia. By September, the *Beauregard* was in Loch Ewe, Scotland. Then to Glasgow for repairs. After that to Belfast, Ireland, and then back to Scotland—Kirkwall, the Firth o' Forth, and Edinburgh—where the tanks were taken out and replaced with newer models. The ship eventually arrived in Murmansk on Christmas day, 1942.

The freighter *Gateway City* rode at anchor for 107 days at Reykjavik before joining a convoy for Murmansk.

When the ships finally did reach Murmansk, they encountered frequent air attacks. Nor were there any shore-side attractions at Archangel or Murmansk to relieve the danger and boredom of a long voyage.

During one raid on Murmansk in April 1942, more than one hundred German and Russian planes were in the air. Gunners on the American freighter *Eldena* shot down three Nazi bombers and won a cash bonus from the Soviet government for their excellent marksmanship.

The *Eldena* and the freighter *Dunboyne* were berthed together. The following excerpt is from the voyage report of Ens. Fred S. Finke, Jr., of the *Eldena*:

> 3 April 1942—2100 air raid alarm. Shore batteries opened fire. *Dunboyne* and *Eldena* opened fire on plane 1000 feet overhead. Plane hit and crashed off starboard bow. Plane diving on the *Tobruk* on our port beam dropped bomb in a hatch. Ship sank. Bomb dropped in nearby building, killing several people. Plane dove on ship and machine gunned the decks but no one hurt!![6]

Until the *Eldena* sailed three weeks later, there were daily alarms and frequent raids. Two days after leaving Murmansk, her convoy was under heavy air attack and the escort beat off an attack by a German destroyer.

The trip home from the Barents Sea was hardly less dangerous than the run north. Many ships were sunk on the way back to Iceland or Scotland. Such was the fate of the freighter *Puerto Rican*. After delivering her war goods, she was homeward bound early in 1943 with 3,500 tons of ore under hatches.[7]

During a storm on the night of 6 March, the *Puerto Rican* lost the convoy but proceeded alone toward Iceland against rough seas and gales. The engine was forced to its limits in order to keep the heavily laden ship at six knots. By 9 March, the seas had not abated, nor had the cold, biting wind and a rainy mist that froze as it drove against the straining ship. The decks, rigging, superstructure, and lifeboats were heavily coated with ice. It was a miserable night to stand a deck watch, but there was no relenting by the lookouts as the lonely ship ploughed through the treacherous seas. They stared into the storm, but there was not much chance of seeing a submarine through the freezing spray and mist or against the black sky that joined with tumbling waves to form a bleak, forbidding cavern beyond the ship.

The end of the *Puerto Rican* came at about 2200. Fireman August Wallenhaupt was the only one who could tell about the vessel's last moments, for he alone survived.

Wallenhaupt was off watch and, like most of the crew, was sleeping "full rigged" in heavy underwear, socks, dungarees, and a woolen shirt. He heard no loud explosion when the torpedo hit, but he could not mistake the nature of the impact. Jumping out of his bunk, he grabbed an armful of clothes, hurriedly donning more trousers and socks and slipping into two sweaters over his woolen shirt. Preferring not to get off the ship at all than to be poorly clothed on that bitterly cold night, Wallenhaupt began to struggle into a heavy rubber suit that zipped tight around the neck and was fitted with heavy boots. Designed to protect men from freezing in such emergencies, the suit was watertight when properly put on.

Suddenly, the engine stopped and the lights dimmed. With no time left for dressing, Wallenhaupt ran for the open deck. The ship's lights went out as he groped through the passageway. The vessel was deathly quiet. Seas smashing against the hull sounded doubly loud and terrifying now that the usual noises of a moving ship were stilled.

Wallenhaupt made his way to a lifeboat on the port side aft, but the launching gear was so clogged with ice that the boat couldn't be lowered. Along with other crewmen, he sought the starboard boat.

"They're all frozen," someone shouted. "Not a damn one is any good."

Number three boat was lowered away, but when it hit the water the men couldn't release the frozen after-falls from the tripping gear. The ice had mated falls and block together into one solid cake.

"Here she comes . . . look out . . . God, she's going!"

There were screams of despair from the boat as the *Puerto Rican* suddenly heeled over the struggling men, canted at a sharp angle, and started her downward plunge, taking the boat with it.

Fireman Wallenhaupt jumped overside when the *Puerto Rican* sank. His heart seemed to stop for a few terrible moments as the icy water shocked the breath from his body and the suction of the sinking ship dragged him into the depths. Gasping for breath, he finally shot to the surface.

He heard shouts and cries from the men who had stood with him on the deck of the vessel only a few moments before. A small raft with several occupants drifted by, and he hung to the side of it until he could regain his breath and strength.

After fifteen minutes or so—no one could keep an accurate track of time during the long, terrible hours of the night—the men saw one of the large wooden life rafts floating some distance away.

"Let's go," Wallenhaupt shouted to the others, but they shook their heads in refusal. He dropped off the bobbing raft to fight his way alone to a more secure haven on the bigger float.

Spurred on by the desperate hope and determination to live through the ordeal, Wallenhaupt reached the raft. When he climbed into it, he found a dozen or more of the crew, all of them wet, shivering, and ill-attired for the frigid cold.

Later, they saw a capsized lifeboat with about ten of their shipmates clinging to the icy keel. It was too dark to tell who all the men were, but they recognized able seaman Robert Howard, George Reilly, and several gunners before the boat was lost to sight among the huge waves.

Two hours later, able seaman Robert Kaley, an Englishman, was wrested from the raft by a sudden, smashing comber. On the following day, two of the navy gunners were swept away when a wave broke over the huddled survivors and careened the raft precariously onto a precipice of foaming water. Half-conscious, Wallenhaupt also discovered that Joe Disange had died during the night and was frozen to the ice-covered float. Shortly afterward, the rest of the gunners, too weak to hold on any longer, relaxed their grips on the lifelines and were thrown into the sea when the raft bucked.

Two days went by—two raw, freezing days, during which it wouldn't seem possible for a human being to survive. Wallenhaupt was now alone on the raft.

When the *Puerto Rican* went down, the British destroyer *St. Elistin* had been searching the area for strays from the storm-battered convoy. She picked up the *Puerto Rican*'s SOS and was on the spot several hours after the freighter sank but her crew found only a capsized lifeboat and an oil slick on the deserted water.

Making a final sweep of the area, the *St. Elistin* then sighted the raft and its lone occupant. Although half-frozen, Wallenhaupt had won his fight against the sea.

A number of ships were dispatched from Iceland to Russia without convoy, the idea being that a lone ship might not attract the attention of German reconnaissance aircraft.

The *William Clark,* loaded with planes, tanks, tires, and ammunition, was en route from Iceland to Murmansk on 4 November 1942. A torpedo hit the engine room and killed the men below. Shortly after the ship was abandoned, she was hit by two more torpedoes that broke her in two. Survivors were rescued from lifeboats several days later. Of a crew of seventy-one, thirty were killed by the blast or later died of exposure.

The next day, the *John H. B. Latrobe,* steaming alone along the same route, was pounced on by five torpedo planes. Although each plane dropped a torpedo, none found its mark because of a heavy barrage from the ship's guns.

After the planes roared away, the officers of the *Latrobe* held a council of war. They assumed the planes would come back and decided to return to Iceland and await a convoy. This decision probably saved the ship and her valuable cargo.

German submarines and bombers continued to haunt the route to northern Russia almost until the end of the war. The

Horace Gray was torpedoed on 14 February 1945 at the entrance to the White Sea. Carrying 7,500 tons of potash, she was beached and declared a total loss. The Norwegian freighter *Norfjell* was sunk a short distance ahead of the *Gray.*

In the same area, the *Thomas Scott* was torpedoed on 17 February 1945 at the start of a return voyage from Murmansk to Scotland. All on board, including forty Norwegian refugees, were rescued by a British destroyer.

Not so fortunate was the *Horace Bushnell.* She was torpedoed on 20 March 1945 in convoy JW-65, almost at the end of a voyage to Murmansk from Scotland. The torpedo exploded in the engine room and killed the five men on watch. A Russian tug towed the shattered hulk to shore and beached her, so the cargo could be salvaged. The *Thomas Donaldson* was torpedoed the same day in the same area, with a load of locomotives and railroad cars.

Until Germany surrendered and the U-boats were gone from the seas, no ship could be sure of a safe passage to Archangel or Murmansk.

7
Convoy PQ-17

P Q-17 WAS PROBABLY the most celebrated convoy of the war.[1]
Shortly after the remnants of the convoy had battled their
way through to Archangel and Murmansk in 1942, *Life* magazine,
the mass-circulation picture journal of the time, featured in its 3
August issue a dramatic account of the convoy with photos of
ships being attacked and sunk by German bombers.

People who couldn't find Archangel or Murmansk on the
map were awed by this fleet of freighters that fought against
great odds to carry the material of war to the Soviets. Inevitably,
if someone knew a person had been in the Merchant Marine
during the war, the question would be asked, "Were you on the
Murmansk run?"

PQ-17 was arranged at the insistence of Roosevelt and Stalin, with the reluctant acquiescence of Churchill, who was still
suspicious of Stalin and bitter at his cooperation with Hitler.
Churchill considered it a dangerous and risky operation.

The convoy carried about everything that conceivably could
be needed by the Soviets—tanks, barbed wire, bullets, bombs,

black powder and nitroglycerin, Jeeps, chemicals, trucks, artillery shells, shoes, radios, dehydrated eggs, flour, and sugar. Most of the ships carried some granulated nitroglycerin, a cargo that could—and did—cause a ship and crew to vanish in a terrible detonation of fire, smoke, and flying metal.

The fleet of thirty-three freighters and tankers comprising PQ-17 made up in Reykjavik on 27 June. Twenty-one of the ships were American, including several new Liberty ships. Other ships flew the British, Russian, Dutch, or Panamanian flag.

Theoretically, the convoy had powerful protection to rebuff any German attack. Some miles to the north of the convoy's course were the British cruisers *Norfolk* and *London* and the American cruisers *Wichita* and *Tuscaloosa*, with a protective screen of destroyers.

Even more impressive was the distant covering force, intended to meet and destroy any German battleships that steamed out from their Norwegian lairs to attack the convoy. This force included the American battleship *Washington*, the British battleship *Duke of York*, and the aircraft carrier *Victorious*, in addition to the cruisers *Nigeria* and *Cumberland* and a fleet of destroyers. These ships were well removed from the convoy but positioned to come to its aid if it was attacked by capital ships.

Protecting the immediate area of the convoy against submarines and bombers were six destroyers, four corvettes, two submarines, and the antiaircraft ships *Palomares* and *Pozarica*, plus seven minesweepers and armed trawlers. Following in the rear of the convoy were three rescue ships, *Zafaran, Rathlin,* and *Zamalek,* an indication that the British Admiralty might have expected a dangerous voyage for PQ-17. Churchill and his naval advisers had reason to be concerned for its safety. The German battleship *Tirpitz,* the heavy cruiser *Hipper,* and a number of destroyers were known to be in Trondheim, Norway, and the battleships *Admiral Scheer* and *Lutzow* were reported to be in Narvik, all within easy striking distance of the convoy. The Admiralty's uncertainty about these ships was to trigger the disaster of PQ-17.

At noon on 1 July, German reconnaissance planes discovered the convoy and leisurely circled the ships at a safe altitude.

The navigators plotted the convoy's course, and the radio operators sent the information back to their bases in Norway.

The next day, several U-boats were detected near the convoy. Although the escorts attacked them, none of the U-boats was sunk. A flight of eight torpedo planes attacked but made no hits. One of the bombers was shot down. As the U-boats also tried to get into position for torpedo attacks, the destroyers dropped depth charges and drove them away. The ships steamed on unscathed. At 1500 on 3 July, twenty-six bombers attempted a mass assault, but they were unable to score any hits, thanks to heavy fire from the merchant ships and their escorts. So far, the crews of PQ-17 had reason to feel good about their chances.

A lone bomber drew first blood on the afternoon of 4 July. Streaking in low over the water and dodging a stream of anti-aircraft fire, it torpedoed the American Liberty ship *Christopher Newport*. The *Newport* did not sink, but it was impossible to tow her to port or to salvage any of the cargo. She was sunk by gunfire from one of the escorts. Meanwhile, the fate of PQ-17 was being decided at the Admiralty, far away in London. As the ships plodded on, with guns manned and waiting for another attack, naval headquarters was nearing a tragic decision. Believing that a German battle fleet had left its base in Norway and was probably heading for the convoy, the Admiralty decided that the fleet should break up and every ship proceed on her own.[2]

The cruisers of the covering force were to withdraw immediately with their escorting destroyers.

The convoy commodore received an ominous order to "scatter and proceed independently to your destinations" at 1900 on 4 July. The order seemed so inconceivable that he radioed twice for confirmation before he passed it on by flag signal to the other ships. The order was received with consternation and with not a little cursing about the "idiots" and "dunderheads" who were running the convoy from offices in London.

"I couldn't believe it," Captain John Thevik of the Panamanian *El Capitan* said. "I thought some signalman had blundered and sent the wrong order. But there was no recall. I rang the engine room for full speed, went into the chart room and plotted

94

a course for Nova Zembla [Novaya Zemlya, an island just north of the Soviet mainland]."[3]

Throughout the fleet, captains and crews shared the same thoughts, as they saw the destroyer escorts pull away and race off toward the west: "They're deserting us . . . they're giving us away to the Germans."

This, of course, was not what the cruiser commanders or the destroyer skippers wanted. They were only reluctantly obeying orders.

Thirty merchant ships loaded with war supplies for the Russians took off at their best speed, which, for some, was no better than eight knots. Most of them headed for Nova Zembla, which was the nearest land. For many of them, the ensuing hours to safe haven or to destruction evolved into a wartime saga.

A freighter carrying a barrage balloon in convoy PQ-17 goes down after being torpedoed by a U-boat, July 1942. This photo was taken from the submarine that torpedoed the ship. (U.S. Naval Historical Center, NH 71303)

As the destroyers dashed away, Captain Mortensen of the freighter *Bellingham* told Chief Engineer Saltsman to "give us everything you've got." The pistons of the old ship pounded with a fury unknown before, and the boilers produced more steam than any inspector would have allowed. The needles on the steam gauge danced dangerously beyond the red lines indicating the safety limits. Thanks to the black gang, the *Bellingham* logged fourteen knots in her hours of crisis and eventually docked in Archangel.

The Germans soon took advantage of this gift from the Admiralty.

At about supper time, a signal from the convoy commodore on the British freighter *River Afton* warned the ships that an air attack was imminent. Within minutes, there was a roar of airplane engines. Twenty-four German torpedo planes, breaking through patches of fog, bore in low over the water.

Lt. (jg) Willard Brown, Armed Guard commander on the *Bellingham,* said a plane came so close that he could see the pilot in the cockpit and the torpedoes slung under the fuselage. "They had bright green bellies and yellow heads," he said. "I watched the torpedoes drop and I waited for the explosion. By some miracle they just missed us but they hit the British ship *Navarino* in the next column."[4]

Also hit was the Liberty ship *William Hooper.* The crews of both ships were picked up by a rescue ship.

Three planes were shot down, one by the freighter *Washington.* Bullets sliced it in two as it banked over the ship's bow.

The Russian tanker *Azerbaijan* was also hit and dropped back, with a gaping hole in her side. But her captain did not give up his ship, and the tanker later limped on.

Armed Guard Ens. Rudolph Kravetz said that bullets from the American freighter *John Witherspoon* hit the bombers "and bounced off," but the fire was so heavy that the attackers "veered off and climbed out of range."

Convoy PQ-17 had now lost three ships and some 20,000 tons of war supplies. As the convoy was scattering, the armed trawler *Ayrshire* led the freighters *Silver Sword, Troubador,* and *Ironclad* some thirty miles northward to the edge of the ice pack, where submarines could not attack so easily. At the suggestion of Captain George Salveson of the *Troubador*, the crews gathered all the white paint they could find and smeared it on masts and deckhouses to make the ships blend in with the ice pack. The *Ayrshire* then led its flock to Matochkin Strait at the barren, forbidding island of Nova Zembla.

On 5 July, the American freighter *Carlton* was steaming at nine knots with all guns manned and ready and not another ship to be seen. At 1710, a plane broke through the fog bank and dropped a torpedo that exploded in the fireroom and killed all the men below.

Forty-five merchant seamen and Armed Guard gunners abandoned ship. Some were picked up by a German seaplane, others by a submarine, and all were landed in Norway. Their adventure was not yet over—they were later sent to Germany on a troopship that was torpedoed with great loss of life. The *Carlton*'s men survived.

The next victim from convoy PQ-17 was the American ship *Honomu*, also sunk on the afternoon of 5 July. Nineteen men were killed. The survivors drifted on a raft for thirteen days before they were picked up.

The same day, the *John Witherspoon* was only twenty miles from a refuge at Nova Zembla when she was hit by two torpedoes. When a third torpedo struck, the ship broke in two. A submarine surfaced and gave the survivors bread and water and a course to the nearest land. Ensign Kroetz, two of his Armed Guard, and sixteen of the merchant crew were in the boat for fifty-three hours before being picked up by the *El Capitan*. Captain Thevik took considerable risk in rescuing the *Witherspoon* survivors. Lookouts had heard the faint piping of a whistle from among the heavy mists. It sounded like the whistles carried by torpedoed crewmen on their lifejackets, but it could have been from a wily submarine luring a rescue ship to within torpedo range. Should the captain probe the mists to investigate? Or should he go on, ignoring the possibility that some survivors were calling for help? He was faced with a weighty decision.

"I couldn't ignore the whistle," he said later, "It could be men in a boat. Time between life and death could be a matter of hours in those waters. I couldn't have been at peace with myself again if I hadn't slowed down to investigate. All hands were at the guns, just in case."[5]

This terse notation in the ship's log tells what happened:

> Heard a whistle which, after investigation, proved to be a lifeboat with nineteen men from the S. S. *John Witherspoon,* American. Approximately 70 degrees, 28 minutes North, 50 degrees, 00 minutes East. We took the men on board and proceeded in dense fog.

The convoy commodore's ship, the *River Afton,* was sunk soon after. The ship went down so fast that the crew had to jump into the icy waters and swim to rafts.

Commodore J. C. Dowding, who previously had been torpedoed three times, swam to a raft and helped to rescue a wounded officer and two young cooks. The survivors would have surely frozen to death if the rafts had not been provided with flares. The red smoke from these flares was seen by the corvette *Lotus,* which came to their rescue. *Lotus* had already rescued forty men from the American freighter *Pan Kraft.*

By the time 5 July, "the day of massacre," was over, the toll of lost ships also included the British ships *Bolton Castle, Empire Byron,* and *Zafaran;* the Dutch *Paulus Potter;* and the American freighters *Peter Kerr, Washington, Fairfield City, Pan Kraft, Honomu,* and *Carlton.* Lifeboats from the *Fairfield City,* and *Washington* reached Nova Zembla after six days. A motor lifeboat towing another lifeboat from the British *Empire Morn* traveled 250 miles before being rescued. Seven men died during the trip. After the *Empire Byron* went down, the submarine surfaced and provided the survivors with sausages, wine, and biscuits.

The *Peter Kerr* tried to beat off an attack by four torpedo planes with 30- and 50-caliber machine guns. All of the torpedoes missed, but when the torpedo planes left, dive-bombers with bright yellow-tipped wings took over. The first bombs were direct hits and started fires in the deckhouse. The Armed Guard gunners, remaining at their posts, peppered the next bomber with bullets as it roared down on them until all their ammunition was expended. More than thirty bombs were aimed at the ship, which zigzagged, twisted, and turned. Many bombs were near misses that exploded close aboard. Steam lines burst from the concussions, and the ship slowed to a stop.

After the order was given to abandon ship, the crew lost no time in getting away in the boats. Now that the ship could not move, the dive-bombers quickly finished the job. She went down with 6,000 tons of trucks, bombs, and other war supplies.

As the *Peter Kerr* sank, the *Washington* was heading for Nova Zembla with the ice pack on her port side. Nearby were the *Bolton Castle* and *Paulus Potter*.

At about 0300, dive-bombers hit the *Bolton Castle* and sent her down in a pillar of smoke. There were so many close misses around the *Washington* and so many hull plates sprung by their concussions that, as the chief engineer reported to the captain, "She's leaking like a sieve." The ship was abandoned, and all hands got away in the boats. While they watched the *Paulus Potter* being blasted several miles away, the *Olopana* came alongside and offered to take them on board. They declined the invitation because they believed that the *Olopana* would be the next victim. And so she was. She was sunk later that day, with many fatalities.

The British freighter *Earlston*, armed with a four-inch gun and several 20-millimeter Oerlikons, beat off dive-bombers in a bitter battle that lasted half an hour. While the crew was resting from this assault, torpedo planes attacked. For over an hour, they beat them off, too, but concussions from near misses broke the steam lines. Repairs were under way when two submarines surfaced nearby—at a point where the four-inch gun could not bear on them. The gallant ship had to be abandoned, after which she was torpedoed. The Germans did not interfere with the crew as they left the ship. One lifeboat reached the Russian mainland; the other landed on the coast of Norway.

After the convoy had scattered on 4 July, the crews of every ship in convoy PQ-17—the ships that were sunk and those that survived—went through thrilling and dramatic adventures that would make books in themselves.

The Liberty ships *Daniel Morgan* and *Samuel Chase* headed for Nova Zembla. On the 5 July, they were joined by several other ships, but they all became separated in the fog. That afternoon, as the fog began to dissipate, the *Morgan* found herself near the *Fairfield City*. Junkers bombers roared through drifting fog banks and quickly sank the *Fairfield City*. They then turned their attention to the *Morgan* in a battle that lasted, off and on, for three hours. About thirty bombs exploded on or close aboard this fighting Liberty, but she did not give up easily. The enemy aircraft paid for their success. One plane was last seen flying just above the waves, with fire coming from an engine. A second plane, riddled with shells, splashed into the sea.

So many near misses had opened up plates in the hull. After three holds flooded, the *Morgan* was abandoned. The ship was then torpedoed by a submarine that surfaced and gave the crew in the lifeboats a course to steer to Nova Zembla. One lifeboat capsized, and the survivors were picked up by the Russian tanker *Donbass*.[6] They volunteered to help her gunners defend the ship until she arrived in the White Sea on 8 July.

The *Samuel Chase* made it to Matochkin Strait and joined five other merchant ships and several of the smaller escorts from the convoy. From there, they made a dash for the White Sea, during which the *Chase*'s gunners were credited with shooting down two bombers. Near misses from bombs broke steam lines, but the black gang made repairs and the *Chase*, aided by protective fire from two British sloops and an armed trawler, made it to Molotovsk on the White Sea.

Not so fortunate were the *Hoosier* and *El Capitan*, as they neared their destination of Archangel.

Ens. W. L. Blackwell, Jr., Armed Guard commander on the *Hoosier*, described the fatal attack in his voyage report:

7 July—At 2230 hours, when approximately 200 miles from the entrance to the White Sea, a flight of Junkers came over on our port quarter at about 1500 feet and circled for an attack. All our guns were ready for them. As soon as the planes started their dive, we opened fire [50-caliber machine guns were the *Hoosier*'s principal armament]. Three bombs hit 50 yards off the port bow. No damage. The second attack of bombs hit close beside us amidships on the starboard side. Several gunners were thrown flat on the deck.

The third stick of bombs hit on the port side just abaft the beam and about 20 yards away, with great impact on us from the concussion. The Chief Engineer went below to see how much damage had been done and if we could continue. The ship was fast losing way because of broken steam lines. Planes were circling us again, getting ready for another attack when a submarine surfaced about a mile off. The captain then gave the order to abandon ship. The ship settled slowly as all hands left her in the lifeboats. We were picked up by a HMS *Poppy*, a corvette.

The Armed Guard gunners and the merchant crew who were helping us never faltered at the guns, even with the bombs coming right down at them.[7]

After polishing off the *Hoosier*, planes dove on *El Capitan* one after another while Captain Thevik maneuvered his ship to escape a rain of bombs. When the gunners ran out of ammunition, they broached the cargo, found boxes of bullets, and reloaded their guns. So many near misses from exploding bombs opened hull plates, and leaks soon exceeded the ability of the pumps to handle them. When the air attack was resumed an hour or so later and more bombs exploded alongside the ship, the inrush of water spelled the *El Capitan*'s doom. When the steam lines had been ruptured and the engine room and holds flooded, Thevik gave the order to abandon ship.

"Another few hours and we would have had protection from Russian planes," he said.[8]

The old freighter *Bellingham* was fighting for her life on the 7 July, too. At 0605, she was hit amidships on the starboard side by a torpedo but, the tin fish did not explode, although it drilled a sizable hole in the side of the ship. The vessel continued on, as she changed course frequently to avoid ice packs.

At 2230, several dive-bombers circled the *Bellingham* and then attacked her from the port quarter. The ship's meager armament of 50- and 30-caliber guns opened fire, point-blank when the planes were about one hundred yards away. One of the bombers burst into flames but continued on to drop three bombs that missed the stern by less than fifty feet. The plane then strafed the decks with cannon fire before splashing in flames off the bow.

The *Bellingham* had seven machine guns but only seven gunners, so the merchant crew were an essential help in passing ammunition. In this battle, the *Bellingham*'s gunners expended 1,500 rounds of 50-caliber bullets and 500 rounds of 30-caliber bullets.

The Russians had reason to bemoan the loss of the *Alcoa Ranger*, also torpedoed during the morning of 7 July; she was carrying much-needed steel and armor plate, plus nineteen tanks.

One saga of PQ-17 involved lifeboats from the *Washington* and *Paulus Potter*. Survivors from the *Washington* rowed for six days through floating ice and snowstorms to reach the coast of Nova Zembla, where they captured birds, found some driftwood, and made a soup. Continuing along the island's coast, they met the boats from the *Paulus Potter*, and the crews teamed up to kill helldiver ducks for another dinner of soup. By then, many of the men could not walk because of frostbite.

On 15 July, as the little fleet of lifeboats continued rowing, they came across the freighter *Winston-Salem*, which had run aground in the fog. Already straining the provisions of this ship were survivors of the *Olopana* and several men from the British freighter *Hartlebury*, who had drifted ashore on a raft. The *Winston-Salem* was discovered by a Russian whaling ship, which rescued all on board and delivered them to the British freighter *Empire Tide*, another refugee that made it to Nova Zembla. *Empire Tide* was now overloaded with two hundred survivors of PQ-17.

Several days later, the *Empire Tide*, along with four other freighters, two Russian destroyers, and several small escorts from PQ-17, left Nova Zembla and made it safely to Archangel.

The *Winston-Salem* was eventually pulled free by a Russian trawler, after some of her cargo had been off-loaded into a Russian freighter, and she arrived at Molotovsk on 28 July.

When the escort trawler *Ayrshire* arrived at Archangel, the firemen were shoveling the last bit of coal onto the fires. Another hour or so and they would have been burning the tables and lifeboats.

The group of ships that had followed the example of the *Troubador* and others in painting hulls and deckhouses white also found refuge at Nova Zembla. They were joined by several other refugees from PQ-17. After hiding out there for two weeks, they all made a dash for Archangel and arrived there on 25 July.

In describing the loss of the *El Capitan,* Captain Thevik said, "We almost made it. *El Capitan* and her crew did all that they could to get the cargo through."[9]

Such could have been a tribute to all of the ships and men in convoy PQ-17: "They did all they could."

Of the thirty-three ships that left Iceland, twenty-three were sunk by bombs and torpedoes. Lost in the cold waters of the Arctic were 100,000 tons of war supplies, including 430 tanks, 210 crated airplanes, and some 3,300 vehicles.

8
Convoy PQ-18

WHEN THE UNITED STATES AND GREAT BRITAIN decided to send another large convoy to northern Russia, no chances were taken for a repeat of the PQ-17 disaster, with the tragic loss of ships, men, and vital war cargoes. Designated PQ-18, this convoy left Loch Ewe, Scotland, on 2 September 1942 and took a circuitous route north of Iceland.[1]

Interestingly, a difference exists between the British and American official histories of the war as to how many merchant ships were in the convoy. The American version says thirty-three, the British thirty-nine. As the convoy was under British organization and control, its count of ships and escorts is accepted here. In addition to the merchant ships, there were three oilers to refuel the escorts and a rescue ship to pick up survivors. One of the freighters, the British *Empire Morn,* was equipped with a platform for launching a Hurricane fighter plane.

Immediate protection against attack by planes or submarines was provided by destroyers, corvettes, minesweepers, armed trawlers, and two "ack-ack" ships—vessels bristling with antiaircraft guns. Two submarines accompanied the fleet. Also, many of the merchant ships had been given more and heavier guns before leaving Scotland.

In addition, a submarine patrol line had been set up between the convoy and German bases in Norway to detect any sortie by capital ships and intercept them. A number of long-range Catalina flying boats were to provide reconnaissance part of the way.

Valuable support was also provided by the escort carrier *Avenger*, which carried twelve Hurricane fighter planes. Ironically, these planes were older and slower than the crated Hurricanes being carried by the merchant ships for the Russians. This was the first time that a small escort-type carrier was used for convoy protection. It proved to be an effective weapon for PQ-18 and a great morale builder as well.

A friend of the author, fireman Al Bernstein of the freighter *Scoharie*, put it this way:

> When we saw planes taking off from that carrier we knew that German bombers would be getting a hot reception. It was a big boost knowing there was a hornet's nest riding along with us. We weren't going to be sitting ducks for bombers.[2]

For defense against any sortie by the *Tirpitz* or other German capital ships from Norwegian fjords, there were the cruiser *Scylla* and a fleet of sixteen destroyers armed with torpedoes.

Added insurance for the convoy's safe transit was a distant covering force, beyond bomber range, that included the battleships *Anson* and *Duke of York* and destroyers. They would, presumably, dash to the convoy's aid if the *Tirpitz* or other German ships tried to intercept it. Also, planes and submarines were on the lookout for the Germans.

The British felt that they had done everything they could to get the vital cargoes of PQ-18 to the Soviet Union. The Germans were equally determined to destroy the convoy.

105

Long-range German reconnaissance planes discovered the convoy north of Iceland on 8 September. All hands on board the ships knew this was the prelude of unpleasant things to come.

The Germans directed twelve submarines to intercept the convoy. It was learned after the war that the enemy, at that time, had 92 JU-88s equipped with torpedoes and 133 JU-88s carrying bombs at airfields in northern Norway.

The first U-boats arrived on 12 September. U-88 was spotted ahead of the convoy and was sunk by depth charges, but, on the 13th, two ships on the starboard wing of the fleet were torpedoed by U-408 and U-589.

Crewmen James Harrington and Scotty Turner of the *John Penn* were on deck together when the Russian freighter *Stalingrad* was hit. Harrington relates:

> A great column of water cascaded over the ship. She was about 600 yards abeam of us. Clouds of steam poured out amidships as she went down. A corvette came up and picked up survivors. Other escorts were rushing around hunting for the sub and dropping depth charges. Subs! . . . Maybe we would be next.[3]

Hardly had the *Stalingrad* gone down before there were two more explosions. The Liberty ship *Oliver Ellsworth*, just astern of the *Penn*, swung out of line and listed heavily to starboard. When it became evident that she wasn't going to sink, two corvettes sank her with gunfire.

Later that day, the crew of the *John Penn* saw the sudden end of the British freighter *Empire Stevenson*, which blew up in "a terrifying sheet of flame," with parts of the ship flying in all directions. A torpedo had found its cargo of TNT.

The *John Penn* was also torpedoed that day. The torpedo hit in the engine room and killed all of the men below.

The convoy was now 150 miles northwest of Bear Island. The first air attack was made that afternoon by six JU-88 high-level torpedo bombers, with no hits. But at 0330, some thirty JU-88s attacked in a line abreast. An observer called it "an awe-inspiring sight . . . like an old-time cavalry charge, with the pilots disregarding the rain of shells pouring into them."

The attackers maintained a perfect formation, with about three hundred feet between planes. They roared in at their targets, each plane launching two torpedoes. The sea was alive with tin fish. Eight ships were hit and sunk, six on the starboard wing of the convoy and two in the middle.

Eight bombers were shot down, but the convoy had lost fifty thousand tons of cargo.

Lt. (jg) Wesley Miller, Armed Guard commander on the *St. Olaf,* told how all merchant ships and escorts were firing with every gun they had:

> The noise was deafening . . . on and on came the torpedo planes in an unending line. They darted up, then down, to confuse the aim of our gunners. Some of the planes were painted solid black with the tips of their wings painted orange or green. They were weird and awful to behold.[4]

The Armed Guard commander on the *Scoharie,* Lt. (jg) Albert Maynard, watched his gunners pour shells into a formation of torpedo bombers. He said:

> They weren't more than 30 feet above the water. . . . They let their torpedoes go at point-blank range. It didn't seem possible that any could have missed. After they dropped their torpedoes they zoomed up and away and strafed our gun crews from their belly turrets.[5]

Two torpedoes launched at the *Scoharie* missed by less than twenty feet off the stern.

The four-inch guns of the *Scylla* shot down several bombers. The Germans lost eight planes.

During an attack by fifteen torpedo planes, there occurred one of the most dramatic sea disasters of the war, all the more impressive because the incident was photographed from the deck of a ship two columns away. This was the death of the American freighter *Mary Luckenbach* and all on board. The event was vividly remembered by men on the *Nathanael Greene, Lafayette,* and *Scoharie.* Al Bernstein described it:

> I saw two planes going at the *Luckenbach.* One was headed for her broadside. The other one seemed to be making a strafing run, or banking over the ship after it had launched a torpedo. And then it all happened so fast—whether a torpedo hit the ship or whether a plane crashed on her deck. The *Luckenbach* erupted like a volcano in a huge cloud of billowing gray smoke. In a flash the *Luckenbach* had disappeared.[6]

Most of the ships in PQ-18 carried a thousand tons or more of dynamite.

Lt. (jg) R. M. Billings, Armed Guard commander on the Liberty ship *Nathanael Greene,* had equally vivid memories of the battle. The *Luckenbach* had been less than three hundred yards off the *Greene*'s starboard quarter when she blew up. Billings reported:

> Planes were so close, you couldn't miss with a machine gun . . . suddenly our ship experienced a terrific explosion. My helmet and phone were blown off and much debris was dropping all over the ship. I thought we had been torpedoed.
>
> All the cargo boxes on deck were smashed by the concussions. Doors and bulkheads were blown down and smashed. Cast-iron ventilators were buckled. Shrapnel and scraps of metal covered the decks. Glass ports were smashed. The ship's hospital room aft was almost demolished. Bullets were picked up all over the deck. How everyone topside escaped from being killed I don't know. It is impossible to put into words the force of that explosion and the amount of debris that hit our ship.[7]

The freighter Mary Luckenbach *blows up and completely disintegrates after being hit by an aerial torpedo in convoy PQ-18, September 1942. A classic from World War II, this photo was taken by crewman Al Bernstein from the deck of the freighter* Scoharie. *(Author's Collection)*

Several men on the *Nathanael Greene* were wounded by flying metal and were transferred to the *Scylla*.

Captain William Shearer was second mate on the freighter *Wacosta* during the attack. "The *Mary Luckenbach* was directly head of us in the next lane," he said. "One minute she was there. The next minute there was nothing but a cloud of smoke. She blew a big hole in the ocean."[8]

Captain Richard Hocken of the *William Moultrie*, steaming in the same column behind the *Mary Luckenbach*, said that when his ship passed over the spot "there was nothing left of her at all . . . not even a box or a board. It was like the ship had never even been there . . . only ripples on the sea."[9]

This disaster, among many others that occurred during the war, reminded the men of PQ-18 what could happen when ships had lethal cargoes on board, as did most of them on the Russian run.

A few minutes after the *Luckenbach* explosion, the *Wacosta* took a torpedo in the starboard side. Bullets from ships firing at the attackers zinged around the crew as they launched the lifeboats. All hands were picked up by a minesweeper.

There were more attacks on 15 September. Escorts sank U-457.

Torpedo planes attacked again three days later, when the convoy had almost reached its destination. The American freighter *Kentucky* was a victim in this attack.

Ens. W. H. Farrar, commanding the *Kentucky*'s fourteen-man gun crew, reported:

> Friday, 18 September: 0605 Land sighted off the port bow. Identified as Cape Kanin.
>
> 1025: Ten enemy aircraft sighted astern.
>
> 1030: Torpedo sighted coming in at 15 degrees to our course on the starboard side. Despite maneuvering, the torpedo hit at our number two hold. The hatch covers were blown up into the rigging. The port side of the bridge was carried away. The captain ordered the ship abandoned.[10]

After making sure that all his men had left the ship, Ensign Farrar jumped into the sea and swam to a life raft. Fortunately, all hands were soon picked up by minesweepers.

Shortly after the *Kentucky* was sunk, the Hurricane fighter on the *Empire Morn* took off and shot down an attacker. The convoy finally reached Archangel on 19 September.

Of the thirty-nine ships that had left Scotland, thirteen were sunk. The Germans lost thirty-four planes and three submarines.

Despite the heavy loss in ships and cargoes, PQ-18 was considered a success. The convoy had fought its way through the seas despite the all-out attempts of the Germans to stop it.

9
Battle of the North Atlantic: Phase II

T HE CRUCIAL PERIOD in the Battle of the Atlantic occurred during the latter part of 1942 and the first half of 1943. It was touch and go as to who would win—the convoys or the submarines.

Before the war, the U.S. Merchant Marine had included passenger ships operating along the coast and to Cuba and the Caribbean. The ships were pressed into service as U.S. Army transports. A great tragedy of the war was the torpedoing of one of these liners, the *Dorchester*. She was hit at night on 3 February 1943 while bound in convoy toward Greenland with more than 800 soldiers and civilian construction workers, plus 130 crewmen and U.S. Army gunners (in place of the usual Naval Armed Guard). The cargo included one thousand tons of lumber. The convoy was escorted by three slow Coast Guard cutters, all poorly equipped for detecting and harrying submarines. U-456 had no difficulty in slipping past the escorts at a point ninety miles southwest of Julianehåb, Greenland, and putting a torpedo into the *Dorchester*'s engine room.

The passenger ship Dorchester *in happier days. In festive dress, with pennants flying, she comes into port to board passengers for a holiday cruise. The* Dorchester *was one of many coastal liners popular with vacationers before the war. (The Peabody Essex Museum, Salem, Massachusetts, 20,410)*

The ship carried fourteen lifeboats, eight large life rafts, and forty small rafts, but so great was the confusion and near panic among passengers and crew that few of the boats and rafts were lowered in an orderly fashion. Fifteen minutes after being hit, the *Dorchester* took a heavy list to starboard and went down by the head.

Second Mate Samuel Dix ran along the deck among the throng of troops milling around in the dark and loosened the toggles of the life rafts so they could slide overboard. "As the ship went down," he said, "I stepped off the deck into the water and struck out for a raft. We tried to pick up some men floating in life preservers, but they were already dead."[1] The water was about

30°F. Dix and several companions were picked up by the cutter *Commanche.*

The sinking of the *Dorchester* showed the danger of sending out ships packed with troops and with crews not properly trained to handle lifeboats and react in emergency situations.

Radio operators William McGill, Frank Pataleve, and Walter Linstrom stayed in the radio shack to use the emergency equipment. They went down with the ship, as did Captain Hans Danielsen.

Another hero of this tragic night was Bos'n Knute Knutsen, who unfastened many of the small doughnut rafts and threw them overboard as the ship went down. More than 600 people were lost, including some 400 soldiers.

Only a few days after the loss of the *Dorchester,* the *Henry R. Mallory* was part of a slow convoy of sixty-five ships steaming toward Iceland. The night was dark and overcast, with a brisk wind. There were 493 on board; a merchant crew of 77, a 34-man Naval Armed Guard; 137 army officers and men, 173 navy personnel, and 72 marines.

The ships were spread out in fourteen columns, four ships to a column, the *Mallory* being the third ship in the third column. U-boats were known to be in the area, and an alert for the gun crew had been sounded at 0100. The convoy was about 540 miles south of Iceland.

At 0352, a torpedo hit at number three hold, just aft of the engine room bulkhead. The ship took a sharp list immediately as water poured into the hold.

The *Mallory* carried ten lifeboats, four large rafts, and ten small rafts, a bare minimum for the large complement on board. It always had to be assumed that, as a result of weather conditions, it would be possible to launch boats only on the leeward side.

Only three lifeboats cleared the ship, probably because of the lack of seamen trained in boat handling. Three lifeboats capsized, one full of injured men. Another boat was launched, but inexpert handling caused it to fill with water. Number seven boat and the men in it were swamped. Another boat was destroyed by the torpedo blast. Number ten boat could not be launched because the launching gear did not work. Apparently, only a few of the rafts were launched.

The sinking of this troop transport again emphasized the importance of training in lifeboat launching and handling. Inexperienced men often panic when a ship is sinking in the dark of night.

Third Mate Herbert Trenowith, asleep when the torpedo hit, relates the events that followed:

> As I jumped out of my bunk and grabbed some cold weather clothes, the ship was already starting to list. I ran on deck to my station at number six boat. It took several minutes to work the launching gear and lower it into the water. There was a fairly rough sea and the boat was so packed with men that we could barely ship the oars and pull away. Pretty soon, a snow squall came up. The last we saw of the *Mallory*, her stern was awash. When dawn came, the ship had disappeared.[2]

The survivors in this boat were picked up by the Coast Guard cutter *Bibb*. Water temperature was 28°F, so those floundering in the sea after the ship sank did not have long to live.

Cadet Joseph Best, Jr., one of four young maritime training school cadets on the *Mallory*, was among the eighty survivors in number eight boat, intended to hold fifty.

"It was a miracle we didn't swamp," Best said. "Water was lapping over the gunwales. We bailed with buckets and with our caps and our hands."[3] This boat was also picked up by the *Bibb*.

Survivors reported many incidents of heroism. Crewmen, searching the shattered troop quarters for the injured, rescued two marines with broken legs, carried them on deck, and placed them in a lifeboat. Seamen Walter Carson and Enos Chandler found a sailor with a broken back, carried him on deck, and

Exhausted, half-frozen survivors of the torpedoed transport Henry R. Mallory *are hoisted on board the Coast Guard cutter* Bibb *in the wintry North Atlantic. The cutter* Ingham *also rescued survivors. (U.S. Coast Guard)*

placed him in a lifeboat. Radio operators John Leahan and Arnold Tanger stayed at their posts to send out calls for help, as the rest of the convoy moved on, and went down with the *Mallory*. Captain Horace R. Weaver also went down with his ship.

A typical Armed Guard voyage report during the harrowing days of early 1943 is the following by Ens. Lewis Coleman on the tanker *Pan Maine*:

> Enemy action commenced the afternoon of 21 February, with depth charges by the escorts. Immediately, there were flag hoists by the convoy commodore indicating that submarines were in the area. Many

depth charges throughout the afternoon. Watches increased at dark and all hands on the alert.

The first sinkings came the night of 21–22 February. At 2030 ship 21 was hit and dropped out of the convoy.

The night of 22–23 February was the worst. Four ships were torpedoed. Occasional gunfire during the night. Another ship hit near us. It went down in about three minutes.[4]

Pan Maine was part of convoy ON-166, a fleet of sixty-six ships westbound from England. The U.S. Coast Guard cutters *Campbell* and *Spencer* had detected U-boats following the convoy on 21 February and the *Spencer* had attacked with depth charges. It was determined later from German records that the attack was successful; the victim was U-225. Waiting for opportunities to attack, the U-boats persisted and tagged along with the convoy. Their first hit was on the British freighter *Empire Trader*.

U-606 torpedoed three ships. Shortly after sunset, she was depth-charged by the Polish destroyer *Burza*. In trying to escape the explosive charges by diving too deep, the submarine's pressure hull cracked. To keep from coming apart in the depths, she blew all tanks and rose to the surface. The *Campbell* was nearby and rammed the submarine, which resulted in considerable damage to the *Campbell*. She had to leave the convoy and head to port for repairs. As many of the submarine's crew as were able scrambled to the deck and jumped overside before she plunged to the bottom. Twelve of the forty-eight man crew were rescued.

The next night, the *Chattanooga City* was hit. The voyage report stated:

At 2120 there was a tremendous explosion at number four hold on the starboard side. It seemed to lift the ship out of the water; blew off all the hatch covers of number three and number four holds. The shaft was broken. The ship was stopped. There was nothing to do but abandon ship.

116

The entire crew of thirty-seven merchant seamen and twenty-one Armed Guards got away safely and were picked up by the Canadian corvette *Trillium*.

ON-166 had a multinational escort. In addition to the *Spencer*, *Campbell*, and *Burza*, it included the British corvette *Dianthus* and the Canadian corvettes *Chilliwick, Rosthern, Trillium,* and *Dauphin*.

One of the great convoy battles of the war involved convoys HX-229 and SC-122, both of which were bound from New York to the United Kingdom in March 1943. Alerted to the movement of these ships, Admiral Dönitz directed a fleet of forty U-boats against them. Before a week of frantic action was over, a total of twenty-six ships went to the bottom, with 160,000 tons of cargo.

The Coast Guard cutter Spencer *attacking U-175 with depth charges, 17 April 1943. The explosions forced the submarine to surface, and she was then sunk by gunfire. Convoy HX-233, bound for England, is seen in the distance. (U.S. Coast Guard)*

Some 372 seamen, gunners, and passengers lost their lives.

When the battle began, convoy SC-122 was about sixty miles ahead of the HX-229, but the large mass of ships was so close together and the number of attackers so numerous that, for all intents and purposes, it was a single, wide-ranging engagement. The first American ship in HX-229 to be hit was the *James Oglethorpe*, a new Liberty ship carrying steel, cotton, and food, plus a deckload of planes, tractors, and trucks, on 17 March. Some of the crew were in such a hurry to leave the *Oglethorpe* before the order was given to abandon that they piled into a lifeboat without taking care to have it properly lowered. The boat was upended, and thirteen men were spilled into the sea.

Convinced that the vessel was not about to go down right away, Captain A. W. Long refused to abandon her and told the escorts he would try to get to Newfoundland. Some thirty men, who were made of sterner stuff than the "panic party" that left the ship, volunteered to stay on board with him. The *Oglethorpe* was never seen again. Perhaps she encountered heavy weather and foundered on the way to Newfoundland.

St. Patrick's Day was a sad occasion for HX-229. U-boats bagged six more ships, four of them American. The brand-new Liberty ship *William Eustis* was carrying more than 9,000 tons of sugar, enough to sweeten a cup of tea for every Briton. She was torpedoed shortly before midnight, but all hands were saved.

The next victim was the *Harry Luckenbach*. Most of the crew got away safely in lifeboats and were probably expecting to be picked up soon by the escorts, for at least three escorts saw the boats. Whether because of a misunderstanding among the escorts or perhaps an overly intent desire to sink U-boats instead of rescuing survivors, the escorts let the boats drift away and the convoy moved on. This type of unnecessary tragedy occurred more than once during the war. Seamen who saw these derelict boats, sometimes with bodies sprawled across the thwarts, might have wondered what untold stories of the sea they represented.

No rescue ships had been assigned to HX-229.

The U-boats added one more American victim that night, the *Irenee du Pont*, which was hit by two torpedoes. On board were forty-nine in the merchant crew, twenty-six in the Armed Guard, and nine U.S. Navy officers bound for England as passengers. When last seen, she was slowly sinking with a general cargo and a deckload of eleven medium bombers. Twenty of the ship's crew were lost, some because they had jumped over the side before the life rafts were launched, in addition to ten of the Armed Guard and two passengers.

The submarines were not yet finished. The *Walter Q. Gresham* was torpedoed on 18 March, with a loss of twenty-seven seamen and Armed Guard from her complement of sixty-nine.

In exchange for the loss of only one U-boat, the Germans had sunk eleven ships in HX-229 and nine in SC-122.

The battle of the Atlantic did not end for the U.S. Merchant Marine until 5 May 1945, when the collier *Black Point* was blasted by a torpedo just six miles northeast of Point Judith, Rhode Island, only a short distance from the Cape Cod Canal, Massachusetts. Throughout the war, Captain C. H. Prior and the *Black Point* had been hauling coal from Hampton Roads, Virginia, to Boston.

For armament, there was a six-pounder on the stern and two 30-caliber machine guns on the bridge. Bos'n Mate Second Class Lonnie Lloyd, who commanded the six-man gun crew, was standing on the poop deck by the gun crew's quarters when the torpedo hit, and he was blown overboard.

One boat was launched with seven men. Another boat was swamped. Some jumped overboard and climbed onto a raft. After twenty minutes or so, the collier capsized. Eleven men were lost.

The commander of the submarine, U-853, that sank the *Black Point* had acted very foolishly in bagging a relatively unimportant victim when it was evident to all submariners that the sea war was over. An armada of ships and planes were soon on the scene. U-853 paid for her folly in a watery grave off Block Island, Rhode Island.

From the beginning of the war, British escort vessels were equipped with ASDIC, similar to the U.S. Navy's sonar.

ASDIC is a term derived from the Allied Submarine Detector Investigation Committee, a group of British naval officers and scientists who developed antisubmarine measures during World War I.

In both ASDIC and sonar, sound impulses were sent out from a retractable dome on the bottom of the ship. When the sound waves made contact with a submerged object, such as a submarine, an echo was sent back to the source and picked up by an operator using microphones and a display panel. From the time lapse between transmission and reception, a trained operator could fix the distance of the target. He could also determine the bearing of the target by knowing the angle of the ship to the target.

All escort ships were also eventually equipped with radar, which gives the range and bearing of any object on or above the surface (ships and airplanes). Radar was invaluable in detecting surfaced submarines and on a calm day could even pick up a drifting lifeboat.

Throughout the war, ASDIC and sonar were the chief means of detecting submarines and following their movements while they were submerged. Escorts had guns and depth charges, but they were of little use if a U-boat's position could not be discovered and plotted in order to use depth charges effectively or to flush the submarine to the surface.

During World War II, the most effective weapon against the submarine was the depth charge, a large canister of dynamite that was projected or dropped from racks at the stern of the escort vessel and timed to explode at a certain depth or on contact with the submarine. Also used in World War I as a main weapon against U-boats, the depth charge contained 300 to 600 pounds of TNT.

Submarines, of course, submerged to the greatest possible depth to evade depth charges and took evasive action to throw off their pursuers. Although they often underwent hours of nerve-racking depth charge attacks and still survived, well-placed, well-timed patterns of depth charges destroyed many undersea raiders. The most successful depth charge attacks against the U-boats were made by escorts working in pairs, when vessels could be spared for this type of operation.

At the end of the war, the British government paid this tribute to the men who sailed the ships and kept open the lifelines of liberty:

> A debt we can never repay is due to the men of the Merchant Marine who, true to their fine tradition, and with steadfast courage, devotion and endurance, refused to be intimidated by the heavy toll of sinkings and to threat of their ships being blown to pieces in one of the stormiest oceans of the world. An extra need of praise is due to those who manned the ships carrying ammunition and explosives and the tankers which carried the highly inflammable fuel and aviation spirits.[5]

The Battle of the Atlantic lasted sixty-eight months.

Hundreds of hulks—shattered by torpedoes, gutted by fire, blown to pieces by terrible explosions—line the ocean floor between the United States and Canada and Great Britain. Many more ships lie on the bottom in other areas of the Atlantic Ocean. Their cargoes of tanks, planes, machinery, guns, bombs, steel, and food strewn about the wrecks give testimony to the senseless waste of war.

Thousands of seamen lie with their ships—the tragedy of the human sacrifice in the Battle of the Atlantic.

The crews of more than one hundred German U-boats also went to their deaths in the dark depths of the embattled sea. They were no less determined and brave than the men who manned the ships destroyed by their submarines.

10
Fighting Fleets

WORLD WAR II WAS A CONTINUING battle of Allied convoys—merchant ships and their naval escorts—against German U-boats. Half a hundred ships spread out over many square miles of ocean, each of them following a prescribed position in a well-planned, precise pattern. On any one day, up to seven hundred ships might be crossing the Atlantic in convoys.

High adventure often lay ahead. The far horizon might be a curtain about to rise on a drama of life and death, or it could just hide so many more miles of trackless routine. Like a regiment on parade, the fleet plowed on, ship by ship, toward the battle-fronts.

All manner of ships traveled in a convoy. A typical convoy might include a one-time fruit ship, her coat of yachtlike tropic white exchanged for wartime gray, and a blunt-nosed tramp slushing along at the tail end of the fleet, her firemen sweating at the boilers as they try to maintain enough steam to keep up. The old tramp is down to her marks with a load of bombs and ammunition, but what is that to her? She has freighted all manner of cargoes in her time and survived many a winter gale laden "full and down."

Over in the next column might be a three-island freighter with ponderous Oregon pine on her foredeck and crates on her after hatches. "Tell me where they're building a dock, sailor, and you'll know where she's bound." And those crates! What's in them? Bulldozers for an airstrip or tanks for Suez? Seamen aren't told where they're going. "Take the stuff where it will help to win the war. That's your job, sailor!"

A bulky Norwegian whaler now carries tanks instead of oil. In place of whaling guns, they've mounted a four-inch rifle on her bow. Next to her is one of those new American Liberty ships. She looks long and rangy, and rugged, too, with a clean sweep of hull and a pleasing sheer.

They sure pile the freight on these Libertys! Tanks and planes and crates filled with aircraft engines. The deck is so full of cargo that they built a catwalk on top of it so the crew and gunners can move fore and aft.

Hardly two ships are alike in the entire fleet. There is a ship with two funnels and a Norwegian motorship with no funnels at all—a converted windjammer with the after mast serving as a stack. Another ship once carried pilgrims from the Dutch East Indies to the holy shrines of Mecca. Over there are a lumber carrier, a former collier, and an old liner that plied the China seas before the war.

No names are painted on the bows or the sterns of these ships. Temporary name boards are carried on bridge decks to help the escorts identify them when the convoy makes up and each ship is assigned her position. If a submarine sinks the ship right beside another one, the crew of the second ship might never learn her name or what flag she flew.

Ships of all the Allied nations are in the convoy. Their names read like a recital from Lloyds Register of Shipping: *Trojan Star, Oriental, William B. Giles, West Ivis, Cumberland, Calaban,*

Borgestad, Flomar, Nicolas Stolpoulas, Russosoviet, Anna Maersk, Day Rose, and *Barrington Court.*

Two destroyers, sailing in the van of the convoy, look like cowhands leading a herd of cattle. They are on the lookout for coyotes of the deep, those undersea wolves that hope to slip in among this plodding herd and bag two or three before the escort knows they are anywhere around. The destroyers steam ahead of the ships and stop occasionally to listen for the "ping" of a U-boat's hull on their sound-detecting gear.

A quartet of corvettes and frigates patrol the flanks, and two more corvettes comprise a rear guard a mile or two astern. Manned by tough Britons and Canadians, the corvettes roll and plunge their way across the ocean day after day, voyage after voyage, with not much time in port. They call them the "buckin' broncos" of the North Atlantic. Little ships, with white spume showering over their bows. Rugged, trusty watchdogs of the war's most vital lifeline.

The merchantmen cannot rely entirely on their escorts. They stand constant lookout, their own Merchant Marine gunners and the Naval Armed Guard scanning the sea for the lacy track of a speeding torpedo or the telltale wash from a U-boat periscope. If the convoy is on the Russian run, in the Mediterranean, or on the western approaches to Europe, the lookouts must watch for aircraft, too. Many ships that outrun the U-boat gauntlet are sunk by bombs when they near the British Isles.

When the meals are done, the galley boys haul the refuse to garbage barrels on the stern, where it will be dumped into the sea after dark. There's no better way for a submarine to track a convoy than by a trail of table leavings and floating vegetable crates.

Smoke, too, can give an accurate fix on the convoy's position and progress, so the convoy commodore keeps a weather eye on the funnels of the fleet.

"Cut down on that smoke," he signals to an old tanker in the third column. "They can see you coming all the way to Berlin."

At nightfall, in the queer half-light between day and night, extra precautions are taken. This is a time favored by U-boats for attacking convoys.

From about an hour before dusk until the sun has set, it is "general quarters" for the Armed Guard gunners, who stand by the guns ready to fire at any suspicious object. Myriad lights appear to flicker on the horizon, as though a fleet of U-boats is riding atop the distant sea.

All portholes on board ship are tightly closed, and the watch makes the rounds to see that all cabins have blackout screens fitted over their ports. Against the backdrop of a dark night on the ocean, even a pinpoint of light can be seen for miles.

Doors are kept open from cabins to passageways. That's important, because a torpedo blast can cause a closed door to jam and imprison the men inside, leaving them to die like rats in a trap. It has happened many times.

The sleeping men have turned in "full rigged," as sailors say, wearing trousers, shirts, and socks. They don't always have time to dress when a tin fish comes knocking at the door.

Where are you bound, sailor? To Cardiff or Glasgow, perhaps? Or they might be sending you to the Bristol Channel for orders and, after that, who knows—maybe to Murmansk or Suez? If you're lucky, you could be back in the States within six months . . . or a year. But everybody has a job in this war, sailor, and delivering the cargo is yours. Steady as she goes and "keep 'em sailing."

The convoy system was not new to World War II. The British eventually used it during World War I after suffering tremendous shipping losses, but its origins go back many centuries.

The ancient Greeks convoyed their grain ships in the Mediterranean. Roman triremes convoyed their freighters to protect them against the Carthaginians and other marauders. At times during the frequent wars of the eighteenth and nineteenth centuries, fleets of merchantmen in convoy from the West Indies and the Spanish Main contained 150 sail. Such convoys covered a huge expanse of ocean, for sailing ships needed room in which to maneuver. Many a Yankee privateer dogged the fringes of a convoy and darted in to capture a fat prize before the escort could protect the ship. During the Napoleonic wars, there were convoys of 500 sail.

If a World War II convoy was too well protected to permit a successful attack, submarines often tagged the fleet for days in the hope of snaring some straggler forced to drop behind because of engine or steering failure. They bagged many "lame ducks." A number of ships that disappeared during the war probably fell victim to U-boats lurking in the convoy's wake.

The *Colin* experienced the typical fate of a convoy straggler. She had left Halifax for England on 17 April 1944 in a convoy of sixty ships escorted by six corvettes and two "jeep" carriers. On the sixth day out, the *Colin*'s steering gear broke and she fell behind for repairs. By the time the repairs were made, the convoy was long gone and the *Colin* could not catch up. She was ideal U-boat bait.

On the evening of 26 April, a submarine on the lookout for lame ducks hit the *Colin* with three torpedoes, one forward, one midships and one aft. The explosion broke the ship in two.

"The ship was sinking before the debris had stopped falling," Lt. S. R. Navickas, the Armed Guard officer, reported.[1] Fortunately, only one man was lost and survivors were picked up by the CNS *Bentley*.

At least one convoy suffered severe losses when the whistle signals for an emergency turn were misunderstood. Half of the convoy turned to the left and half to the right. Before the ships could reorganize, a U-boat wolf pack slipped between the columns and sank several ships.

Costly accidents also dogged convoys, especially when steering mechanisms failed. Ships laden with gasoline or explosives came together in a holocaust of fire and smoke. Such a collision caused heavy loss of life when the Panamanian freighter

El Coston and the tanker *Murfreesboro* collided in the mid-Atlantic on the night of 25 February 1944. The ammunition-laden *El Coston* had trouble with her steering gear and crashed, bow on, into the *Murfreesboro*, which was carrying 125,000 barrels of 87-octane gasoline for air bases in England.[2]

In a matter of seconds, the tanker was a mass of fire. The fiery fuel spilled out of the broken tanks and covered the sea with a terrible blanket of flame. Some men chose to jump into the sea rather than remain on the tanker's decks. One boat was launched, but it was badly overcrowded and spilled its occupants into the flames dancing across the water.

The *El Coston* was also a roaring furnace. Added to the shouts of the crew as they tried to launch the boats and the screams of men trapped in the flaming water was the wail of the freighter's whistle. The whistle cord had become stuck when the call was given to abandon ship, and the dying vessel sounded her own requiem within the fire that lit up the sky.

There was an extraordinary instance of heroism on the *El Coston* that night.

The forward hold contained a cargo of fuses and bombs—a potent package of sudden death and destruction. Lt. Sanford Bale of the Naval Armed Guard led some of his men along the blazing deck. They kept the flames away from this powder keg by lowering a hose into the hold through a ventilator and dousing the bomb-laden crates with water.

The *El Coston* foundered early the next morning. The Navy tug *Choctaw* picked up the *Murfreesboro* after her fires had burned out and, against stormy winds and seas, towed her into New York in a remarkable effort of salvage. Sixty men were lost in this convoy collision, including Captain Olson of the *El Coston* and three of his officers.

Some of the heaviest ship losses of the war occurred in convoys. For example, convoy LC-107, crossing the North Atlantic to the United Kingdom in November 1942, lost sixteen ships out of forty-four to a U-boat wolf pack. The freighter *Nahira* made

The Coast Guard cutter Bibb *rescued many men in North Atlantic convoys after their ships were torpedoed. She also conducted numerous attacks against marauding U-boats. (U.S. Coast Guard)*

a hard right turn to miss a torpedo and then was sunk by another one coming from the opposite direction. The tanker *L.V. Sanford* dodged two torpedoes, and her gunners claimed a hit on a U-boat. The tanker *Tidewater* fired at three torpedoes coming toward her. One of them missed her stern by a few feet and sank a British ship in the next column. The freighter *Olney* hit a submerged object that shook the ship as though it had run on a reef. The crew believed they accounted for one U-boat that never went back to Germany.

During 1943, about forty American merchant ships in convoy were sunk in the North Atlantic.

A large number of escorts were needed to protect the merchant ships, and both England and the United States built hundreds of vessels especially designed and equipped for convoy escort work. The British and Canadians provided most of the escorts and their crews in 1942 and 1943, with small but highly efficient sloops, frigates, and corvettes. There were variations of each type, but sloops generally were 260-foot vessels with a speed of sixteen knots. Corvettes were much more numerous and measured about 205 feet overall, with a speed of sixteen knots. Frigates were 300 feet long and had a speed of twenty knots. Duty on these ships was the most rigorous of any during the war. Besides the exhausting nature of convoy protection, the escorts were in such demand that they had little time in port. Except when they required extensive overhaul, their crews enjoyed little shore leave.

Destroyers also escorted convoys when possible, but there were never enough of these ships to go around.

Starting in 1943, convoys occasionally included escort carriers. These were small aircraft carriers, built on merchant ship hulls, with such short flight decks that they became known as "jeep carriers" or "baby flattops." Also coming into production that year in American shipyards was a class of small destroyers called destroyer escorts (DEs) in two types, one measuring 289 feet overall and the other 306 feet. They each had a complement of about two hundred men and did twenty knots.

The destruction of U-boats accelerated and convoys enjoyed much greater protection as more escort carriers went into operation during 1944. Planes operating from escort carriers could detect surfaced submarines many miles from a convoy, thanks to an advanced type of long-range radar. In some cases, it enabled planes to pounce on submarines and bomb them before they had a chance to submerge.

There were several classes of escort carriers, but a typical "jeep" of the *Bogue* class of 1944 was 492 feet long, made seventeen knots and carried twenty-eight planes. With a cruising range of 26,000 miles, she could stay at sea for extended periods.

Some 400 DEs were commissioned, but most of them were completed too late to take part in the Battle of the Atlantic during its crucial months.

129

Details of convoy operations, U-boat attacks, and escort tactics are found in official American and British histories of the war at sea and in a number of books written by commanders of escort vessels and escort groups. There are several personal memoirs by U-boat skippers that give their side of the convoy war.

A typical convoy in 1943 consisted of fifty merchant ships, with no more than five escorts: a destroyer and four frigates and / or corvettes. The size of the convoy depended on the availability of escorts. The destroyer patrolled about 1,500 yards ahead, and escorts were on each flank. At night, the favorite time of submarines to attack, the five columns closed up somewhat, and the escorts moved in closer to the ships.[3]

If available, a rescue ship was assigned to tag along in the rear of the convoy to pick up survivors from torpedoed ships. These small and very maneuverable vessels, outfitted from a variety of prewar commercial craft, were commanded by men from the British merchant service, with merchant crewmen. They carried one or more doctors and a small hospital for treating frostbite and more serious injuries. The ships' courageous crews rescued hundreds of men in often remarkable displays of seamanship and ship handling. There were never enough rescue ships to assign one to every convoy.

In a fifty-ship convoy, the spacing of ships was usually about 1,000 yards between columns and 600 yards between ships. According to U.S. naval historian Samuel Eliot Morison, a convoy with nine columns could be spread 9 miles in width and 1½ miles in depth. Obviously, five escorts had their hands full trying to ride herd on such a far-flung fleet.

Looking at a diagram of such a convoy, it would appear to be a nice, neat arrangement, but a storm could play havoc with the positioning of ships. After a gale had blown out, there was often little semblance of order, and it might be hours or days before all ships were back within the fold and in their right places. After a storm, a few ships sometimes did not find the convoy and proceeded on their own.

No exterior lights were allowed in convoys, although some convoy commodores might permit a vessel to show a very–low-power, well-shielded blue light at the stern to prevent a collision with the ship behind it. Even a crewman lighting a cigarette on deck at night could position his ship to a lurking submarine, and such instances actually occurred.

Some hours before a convoy was ready to sail, the captains attended a convoy conference in naval headquarters to be briefed on details of the voyage, including the known disposition of submarines at the time and the type of escorts that would accompany the convoy. Each captain was told the number and position of his ship in the fleet, and each received a sealed envelope with other information that was to be opened after a few hours at sea.

A ship captain described a convoy conference, in which he participated in 1942:

> All hands were pretty somber. We knew we weren't going on a picnic. We didn't have to be told to cut down on the smoke or don't show any lights or don't dump garbage in the day time. Most of us had been through the mill. Some had been torpedoed or attacked by aircraft. There wasn't a uniform among the whole lot of us . . . only the naval officers on the platform had uniforms.
>
> When all the talk was over we tucked our envelopes in our pockets or our briefcases and filed out to go back to our ships. The waiting was over. For good or bad it was time to "roll and go."[4]

After the ticklish job of steaming out of harbor and "forming up"—taking assigned positions—the convoy commodore gave the signal to proceed, and the ships moved on at the designated speed.

To keep her assigned position, each vessel was required to maintain a fairly constant number of engine revolutions. An officer on watch, day or night, had to keep a steady eye on the ship ahead, as well as on ships to port and starboard. A watch could be a harrowing experience for an officer on foggy days, and many harassed captains lived on the bridge while their ships steamed through heavy fogs. There were disastrous collisions in such weather. It was very unnerving to know that the ship ahead or just astern was a tanker loaded with aviation gasoline or a freighter carrying high explosives.

The tanker *Boston* rammed the tanker *Altair* during a fog in convoy in November 1943.

"In a minute or so," said Cadet Midshipman Laurence Ransom of the *Altair*, "the entire ship was in flames. Pretty soon it was an inferno."[5]

So enveloping were the flames that there was only time to launch one lifeboat with thirty men, who were picked up by the *Boston*. Twenty-one men were lost.

Danger and death could lie ahead, but these possibilities never kept the men from sailing the ships. They never kept a ship in port for lack of a crew. Nor did the uncertain prospects ahead keep the black gang from tending the boilers and the machinery, although these men knew that U-boats aimed for the engine room. So often in the official reports of a sinking were the words, "The men on watch in the engine room and the fireroom were killed in the explosion."

When they saw ships burning and sinking around them, some captains signaled the engine room for full speed, posted extra lookouts, manned all guns, said goodbye to the convoy, and took off on their own. One of these was W. A. Hutchins, master of the freighter *Liberty Glo,* a product of the World War I emergency shipbuilding program. The *Liberty Glo* was westbound in convoy ON-127, with thirty-one other ships, in September 1942 when a wolfpack attacked. Over a period of several days, the U-boats sank several merchant ships, damaged four more, and sank the Canadian destroyer *Ottawa.*

Several times on the 19 September, the *Liberty Glo* narrowly missed torpedoes by taking evasive action. A U-boat surfaced so close to the ship that the guns couldn't be depressed enough to hit her.[6]

"It was so close we could have bombarded it with eggs," Captain Hutchins said. *Liberty Glo* tried to ram but missed as the submarine, whose commander was probably more amazed than Hutchins at their cozy proximity, made an evasive turn and dived.

At that point, Hutchins and First Mate William Lesite decided that the *Liberty Glo* would be safer well beyond the wolf-pack. It was time to go it alone. Slipping away from the convoy that night, the *Liberty Glo* made a beeline for Halifax. All seemed well until the sun came up and lookouts reported a U-boat in their path about two miles ahead. Captain Hutchins took immediate evasive action by zigzagging.

"We made so many zigs and zags it almost made us dizzy," the Captain said. "The sub tried to keep up with us for a while but it eventually took off on the surface. It probably had other business—like scouting for an eastbound convoy from Halifax."

The *Liberty Glo* made port ahead of the convoy. Although officials were not too happy with her "free-lance" tactics, she had survived to sail another day.

11
Battles of the Central and South Atlantic

T HE BATTLE OF THE ATLANTIC is usually thought of as the long contest between convoys and U-boats in the ocean's northern latitudes. That was the area of high drama, as well as the major line of supply to Britain—a lifeline that had to be preserved or the entire war would be lost.

Other battles extended over the vast reaches of the Central and South Atlantic. In the south, particularly, there were few convoys except near the African and South American coasts; for the most part, the ships ran alone and unescorted. In these wide reaches of lonely sea, a ship's only protection was her guns and the ability to outrun a submarine or a surface raider.

The *American Leader* could do neither. This new freighter, a type C-1, left Cape Town on 7 September 1942. She was bound for New York with a cargo of rubber, copra, spices, coconut oil, hides, and twenty tons of opium.[1]

On the night of 10 September, a dark shape loomed out of the blackness ahead. Before the ghostly vessel could be identified, she began pouring shells, interlaced with red tracers, into the unsuspecting freighter. Captain Haakon Pedersen told radio operator Joseph Cohen to send out an SOS, but before Cohen could get his set activated, shells were turning the radio room into a shambles. Obviously, the attacker was a German raider. Moving slowly around the *American Leader,* she blasted the wheelhouse and shelled the lifeboats. Some of the crew took refuge in the passageways; others congregated in the galley, where there was hot coffee while they waited out the shelling.

"Coffee never tasted better," said one of the survivors. "It helped to stop the jitters."

When there was a sudden lull in the firing, some of the crew ran to the open deck and jumped overboard. Others released life rafts and helped Captain Pedersen lower the only lifeboat that hadn't been shot to pieces.

It soon became evident why the firing had stopped. Two torpedoes hit the deserted ship. Ten minutes later, the raider came up to the lifeboat and the rafts and played a spotlight over the survivors. For a few moments, the men thought they might be machine-gunned, but this was not the raider's intention.

"Stay where you are," someone shouted to them. "We will pick you up."

A ladder was lowered over the side. One by one, the men were helped on board by strong-armed sailors. They were quickly ushered below decks, and the raider got under way.

The crew learned that they were on the *Michel.* They shared the crowded space below decks with almost five hundred other survivors from ships that the *Michel* had sunk. The *American Leader* was the raider's sixteenth victim.

The *Michel* was unable to care for so many "guests." On 7 October, the men of the *American Leader,* along with some others, were transferred to the *Uckermark,* a tanker supply ship, in the Indian Ocean. The *Uckermark* took the men to Batavia Dutch East Asia, and turned thirty-eight of them over to the Japanese. From that day until the end of the war or until they died, life was a continuing hell for the prisoners. They were regularly beaten and forced to grovel before sadistic guards.

Most of them never returned home. They were drafted to labor details at various Japanese bases, and some were drowned, ironically, when a transport carrying POWs to Japan was torpedoed by an American submarine. Crewman Walter Portia survived this disaster because, just before the torpedo hit, he was one of a group brought up on deck for air and exercise.

Captain Pedersen and his officers were sent in labor details to Singapore and Formosa, then to Japan and Korea, where they were liberated at the end of the war.

Many ships during the war carried four cadets or "cadet-midshipmen," as they were called, from the U.S. Merchant Marine Academy at Kings Point, New York, who served on board to obtain practical experience at sea. There were usually two deck cadets and two engine cadets. These young men stood watches, had stations at the guns, and acquitted themselves quite admirably throughout the war. More than one hundred were lost. Others could recount narrow escapes from death.

Cadet William J. DeRemer, for instance, was sleeping on a hatch top to enjoy the cooling breeze on a hot night when the *Cape Sable* was torpedoed on 13 April 1942.[2]

"The explosion," DeRemer said, "threw me from the hatch cover where I was sleeping over to the railing. It knocked me unconscious. Fortunately, a wave broke over the deck and doused me and I regained consciousness just in time. The force of the wave stripped me of my life jacket and most of my clothes but I was able to get to my lifeboat station just before the boat was lowered away."

The survivors of the *Cape Sable* were picked up by the British armed trawler *St. Wiston* and were taken to Freetown, Sierra Leone.

"Although the British had little to give us," DeRemer said, "they offered us anything we needed and we feasted for several days on tea and stew."

A U-boat was waiting for the Liberty ship *John Carter Rose* as she headed for Freetown, Sierra Leone, in 1942 with a high-priority cargo of trucks, machine tools, iron pipe, and 26,000 drums of aviation gasoline.[3]

On 6 October, lookouts reported a surfaced submarine running parallel to the ship's course several miles away. The *Rose* changed course to present her stern to the U-boat, and her five-inch gun opened fire. The gunners jumped and cheered when their fifth shot appeared to have hit the conning tower and the submarine submerged. With ten lookouts and all guns manned and ready to fire, the *Rose* zigzagged and, for a while, seemed to have eluded the enemy. But her good fortune did not last long. Shortly after midnight on 8 October, two torpedoes exploded in quick succession on the starboard side at number two hold and set fire to the gasoline drums.

When a third torpedo hit and the forward part of the vessel was ablaze, the order was given to abandon ship. Three lifeboats got away. The submarine came up and gave the men cigarettes and loaves of brown bread. An officer passed a paper to men in the lifeboat. On it was written the name of *John Carter Rose* and the names of two other ships.

"Which ship is yours?" he asked. Evidently, the Germans knew of three ships that would be transiting this area of the Atlantic.

On 13 October, one lifeboat was picked up by the American freighter *West Humhaw* and taken to Freetown. The tanker *Santa Cruz* rescued the survivors in the other two boats and took them to Recife, Brazil. Five crewmen and three men in the Armed Guard had been killed.

The freighter *East Indian*, steaming without convoy, was bound for New York with a valuable cargo of tea and manganese when she was torpedoed on the evening of 3 November 1942 at approximately 317 miles southwest of the Cape of Good Hope. On board were twelve passengers and a crew of sixty-two merchant seamen and Armed Guard. Her heavy load of manganese took the ship under in less than three minutes. Forty-nine people survived the sinking in a lifeboat and several rafts.[4]

After the ship went down, the submarine came up to the survivors and the commander asked for the captain. He was told that the third mate was the only surviving officer.

137

"What was your ship?" the commander asked the third mate.

"What was your cargo?"

"Where were you bound?"

"Why were you so far to the southwest?"

The third mate tried to be evasive, but it was evident from other questions that the U-boat commander knew a lot about the ship and her point of embarkation.

Finally, he laughed and said: "If you had not wasted so much time zigzagging I would have sunk you by 0900 this morning and you would have saved yourselves one hundred miles at the oars."

The survivors in the lifeboat reached Cape Town after a week of rowing and sailing. There is no indication in the records as to what happened to those on the rafts or why some of them were not taken into the lifeboat. Official records have many gaps of information about the fate of survivors from torpedoed ships.

Also in the broad reaches of the South Atlantic, the tall-masted *Star of Scotland,* one of the few big sailing ships to see service in World War II, met her fate from a German submarine.

The *Star,* built in 1887 as the four-masted British bark *Kennilworth,* had sailed in the commercial ocean trades for half a century. When World War II broke out, she was a gambling ship, anchored beyond the three-mile limit off Long Beach, California. Because there was a demand for any vessel that could float and the *Star's* iron hull was still stout and seaworthy, she was put into drydock, sandblasted, repaired, painted, and rerigged as a six-masted schooner.

She sailed for Cape Town from Aberdeen, Washington, with two million feet of lumber under command of a veteran "square rigger," Captain Constantin Flink. The outward voyage was made without incident, and the big ship, seemingly proud to be under sail again, showed a good turn of speed. After unloading at Cape Town, Captain Flink set a course for Rio de Janeiro, Brazil, where a cargo had been arranged.[5]

On 13 November 1942, ten days after leaving the Cape, the *Star* was running with a quartering breeze, all sails set. By Flink's morning sight, she was at 26°30' south latitude and making twelve knots.

While the crew were busy at ship's work and enjoying the warm sun and brisk breeze of an idyllic day afloat, a U-boat skipper was gauging the schooner's course and speed and planning the best way to attack. He decided to save a torpedo and sink her with gunfire.

At 0815, the first shell whistled overhead, just above the masts. More shots followed quickly. Several missed, but others smashed into the vessel amidships. One blasted a deckhouse containing drums of gasoline. Fire soon spread fore and aft.

Captain Flink told the crew to abandon ship, but she was moving too fast for launching the lifeboats. They had to take the way off her by lowering the sails, but there was no time to take in the canvas.

"Let the halyards go on the run," the captain shouted.

Shells continued to smash into the ship as the Germans used this opportunity to practice their gunnery. When speed was reduced to a few knots, the crew launched a boat. The mate tried to slide down the falls into the boat but fell against the hull and was drowned.

Captain Flink had gone below for his sextant, a chart, and the ship's papers. When he came on deck, the lifeboat was gone. After a few hearty curses for the crew, he launched the remaining lifeboat himself and safely got away.

The submarine maneuvered up to Flink's boat. Her youthful commander, speaking good English, apologized for sinking the *Star*, "Such a beautiful ship. "I am sorry, but this is war."

For a few minutes, Flink was sure he was to be an unwilling passenger on a submarine when the U-boat skipper said, "Perhaps we should give you a ride to Germany."

He was ordered on board the U-boat, where the commander questioned him about the ship's cargo, port of origin, and destination. Flink explained that the first mate had been lost overboard and that he was the only one who knew navigation. The submarine cruised around the area for an hour or so to look for the missing mate. When there was no sign of him, Flink was allowed to leave the U-boat and join the men in the life-boat.

The submarine then approached the *Star,* which was ablaze forward, and launched two rubber boats. Suntanned young Germans, laughing and shouting as though they were embarking on a picnic, paddled to the ship and climbed on board. In a way, they were on a picnic. They were soon raiding the galley and store-rooms and filling their rubber boats with potatoes, meat, fruit, and canned goods, which they took back to the U-boat.

When the *Star* was almost completely enveloped in flames, the U-boat fired about thirty shells into her hull. She finally sank slowly by the head around 1600. The submarine then moved leisurely away. Standing on deck, the U-boat's crew waved to the castaways and shouted, "Good luck."

"It was time then to be on our way," Flink said. "We set our sail to a good breeze and I laid a course for the coast of Africa."

The lifeboat had been well stocked with cans of milk and fruit, cheese, and biscuits. The captain set a strict schedule of food and water rationing. The crew caught flying fish, and there was rain.

Flink told the men that, if the winds held fair and there were no storms, they would reach the coast in nineteen days. They made it in eighteen and landed on a sandy beach in Angola, near a place called Lucidra, after traveling more than one thousand miles!

Not a man was lost, and all hands were in good health when a nearby lighthouse keeper saw them and summoned help.

"It was sad to lose the old ship," Flink said, "but at least she didn't end her days as a barge—or a gambling ship. She met her fate as an old windjammer should—out at sea, with all sail set."

The *Deer Lodge,* a product of America's World War I "bridge of ships," was taking the long route around Cape Horn, bound for Durban, South Africa. Twenty miles off the coast, lookouts spotted a surfaced submarine in the early hours of 17 February 1943.[6]

Guns were manned, but visibility was poor and the submarine had evidently submerged before sending a torpedo into the ship at number two hold. At this crucial moment, the steering gear broke and there was no way to avoid the second torpedo. The order was given to abandon ship, but several gunners remained on board. They were hoping the submarine would surface to inspect her handiwork. When the ship started to go down, these reluctant gunners threw over a doughnut raft and jumped into the water. A lifeboat picked them up. After thirty-two hours, forty-five survivors, all but two of the ship's crew, were rescued and taken to Port Elizabeth, South Africa.

Violent storms were not confined to the turbulent North Atlantic. When the *William B. Giles* was returning in convoy from the Mediterranean to New York in January 1944, the ships experienced huge seas and winds of terrific force. Several of the lightly ballasted ships were blown out of their positions and across the convoy, narrowly missing collisions.

The voyage report of the *Giles* stated:

> For hours during the morning we watched a ship being blown toward us from two columns on our starboard hand. There was nothing either one of us could do but wait and watch. It finally passed us a hundred yards or so astern, still at the mercy of the wind.[7]

Lack of sufficient ballasting was a problem for many ships returning home after discharging their cargoes.

On her way from New York to the Mediterranean in March 1944, the Liberty ship *William M. Meredith* encountered such heavy weather that Captain L. J. Greene was forced to heave to. He described the storm to the vessel's operators, the Weyerhaeuser Steamship Company:

> On the 29th, mountainous seas broke over the upper bridge, pouring water down the ventilators into the master's cabin, the cadet's quarters and the radio room, and filled numbers four and six boats with wa-

ter. The strain caused by this broke wire grips on both boats and the worm gear on the davits. Called out the crew to secure the boats. On the 30th, mountainous quartering seas boarded the vessel and carried away the after falls of number four boat, so it hung down by the forward fall, banging against the side of the ship. Had to cut the boat adrift, ship laboring heavily in whole gale and rolling violently. Weather finally moderated and we passed through the Straits of Gibralter on April 9.[8]

As in the North Atlantic, the Central and South Atlantic saw many dramatic and tragic events. Especially sad was the sinking of the Dutch *Zaandam*. She was repatriating 200 men who had survived the torpedoing of other ships and had been waiting at Durban and Cape Town for a ship going to the States. Among them were survivors from the *Swiftsure, Examelia, Coloradan,* and *Chickasaw City,* all U.S. ships.

A submarine found the *Zaandam* several hundred miles off the coast of Brazil on 2 November 1942; two torpedoes had broken the ship in two. She sank so fast there was only time to launch two boats. One leaked so badly that it could hold only 27 men. The other boat was dangerously overcrowded with 78. There was no room on the thwarts for all of them, and most had to stand. Fortunately, the weather was mild or the boat would have soon capsized. Some of the men had left the ship on rafts. The survivors were picked up after drifting for six days. Of the 300 men on board the *Zaandam,* 115 were saved. One of those rescued was Jan Hoogerwerf, already a survivor of four previous torpedoings at the age of twenty-four.

Also in the South Atlantic, two heroic ship-to-ship battles of the war took place. The tanker *Stanvac Calcutta* and the Liberty ship *Stephen Hopkins* each refused orders from German raiders to surrender. Their crews manned the guns, hoisted the battle flags, and fought until their ships sank.

142

12

"We Won't Surrender without a Fight"

STEAMING NORTHWARD IN THE SOUTH ATLANTIC on 6 June 1942, the tanker *Stanvac Calcutta* was eight days out of Montevideo, Uruguay, bound for Caripito, Venezuela, to pick up a cargo of oil. She was in dangerous waters. Nazi U-boats were staging a carnival of death and destruction in the Caribbean and its approaches. They were so bold that much of the time, they approached their victims on the surface because they knew there would be no planes or warships to attack them.

Captain Gustaf O. Karlsson had posted extra lookouts. All hands were on alert and guns were readied for instant action. There had been intermittent rain squalls, with occasional banks of scudding rain momentarily hiding parts of the sea and horizon. Otherwise, visibility was good. The sea was almost calm, with a slight swell.

At about 1000, Karlsson and First Mate Aage Knudsen were drinking coffee in the mess room and talking about what the mate was having the men do in routine ship's work that day. At the same time, a lookout on the bow had focused his binoculars on a spot where a thinning rain squall was blowing away. No doubt about it. The indistinct shape he had been watching was visible now as a ship. He shouted the information to the bridge, "Ship ahead—off the starboard bow."

Studying the vessel through his glasses, the third mate, who was the officer on watch, could see that it had the outline of a merchant ship. While he was trying to identify her further, there was a puff of white smoke from the vessel's foredeck and, seconds later, a muffled sound of gunfire. A shell plummeted into the sea a hundred yards or so off the tanker's bow.

There was no need to call the captain. He and Knudsen had heard the shot. Taking the steps two at a time, they ran for the bridge. Karlsson was quick to act. After one look at the stranger, he sounded the general alarm, calling all hands to battle stations.[1]

The *Stanvac Calcutta* was owned by the Socony-Vacuum Oil Company of New York but, like many American-owned tankers, she flew the Panamanian flag and carried a small contingent of Naval Armed Guard gunners. There were not enough of them to man all the guns, so the merchant crew also served as gunners, loaders, and shell handlers. Navy Ens. Edward Anderson was in charge of the gun crew.

As the captain and first mate watched, the stranger came closer.

A shell was rammed into the breech of the three-inch gun on the tanker's bow, and the gun pointer trained his piece on the oncoming ship. The gun captain adjusted the telephone headset firmly over his ears and reported to Ensign Anderson on the bridge, "Bow gun ready, sir."

Again, there was a puff of smoke on the stranger's bow followed in seconds by a plume of water a hundred yards or so away as another warning shell fell into the sea. At the same time, a signal in international code was run up on the vessel's halyards. "Stop your engines." A Nazi flag whipped out at the gaff on her mainmast.

"She's a German raider, all right," the captain said. "But if he thinks we're going to lay down and give up he's mistaken. We're not surrendering this ship without a fight."

He ordered a sharp turn to starboard so that the four-inch stern gun, the largest gun with the longest range, could bear on the enemy. Hoping his ship was faster than the raider, he rang the engine room and asked for every possible revolution they could produce. "Give us everything you can," he said. "This is for life or death."

At the forward gun were able seamen Champagne, Larsen, and Reed; Sarrazin, the pumpman; and fireman DeLong. All were part of the ship's regular crew—no professional gunners these. As the *Calcutta* began her turn, they received the order to fire and answered the raider's shot with two of their own. No hits, but the shells were close.

Every man, with a steel helmet and life jacket, was now at his battle station and waiting orders from the bridge.

Able seaman Saedie Ben Hassan was standing on the bridge when the captain turned to him and said, "Run up the ensign. Break out a hoist with our code number."

It was probably the first time that the flag of Panama ever went into battle on the high seas, and it couldn't have flown over more undaunted men.

After hoisting the flag to the truck of the mainmast, Ben Hassan ran back to the top of the pilot house to help run up the ship's identification in code on the signal halyards. As soon as the flag and pennants whipped into the breeze, the raider was spurred to action. There was a flash of fire from one of the guns on her foredeck, and a shell soon hit the tanker along the waterline.

Down in the engine room, the fireman and third assistant engineer on watch hurried from fire door to fire door at the boilers. They took out the burners and inserted small-sized tips that would shoot a fine, hard stream of oil into the furnaces for a hotter fire and more speed. The needle on the steam gauge passed the thin, red danger line, but they paid no heed to this warning. The oil pressure pump was speeded up, and the third assistant engineer wired down the safety valve on top of the boilers. Every pound of steam would count. Every knot of speed was vital. The ship was only a year old, and Karlsson hoped to outrun the raider.

During the next ten minutes, the raider's guns hulled the *Stanvac Calcutta* in a dozen places. Men had to shout to be heard above the bark of the 20-millimeters, the roar of the big guns, and the crash and grind of the shattered steel. A shell smashed the after crew's quarters and wounded two men.

Karlsson maneuvered his ship calmly and deliberately, swinging to left or right so that the bow and stern guns, the only effective pieces in such an action, could take shots at the raider. Ensign Anderson, directing his gun crews as though they were at target practice, gave the gunners the range and reporting results of their fire over the intercom.

"Bow gun . . . bow gun . . . more elevation . . . doing fine . . . doing fine."

"Stern gun . . . that was a close one . . . smash 'em with the next one."

Many of the *Calcutta*'s shells misfired, and the gunners lost precious opportunities to score hits because of the faulty ammunition. The fifth shot from the stern gun was well aimed, knocking out one of the raider's guns and, they later found out, killing the gun crew.

The German raider now concentrated her fire on the stern gun. Shrapnel shattered the pointer's telescope and bent the sighting bar. Miraculously, the gun pointer was not killed, nor did the courageous sailors leave their posts when more shrapnel burst around them. Although the sighting mechanism was now useless, they kept ramming shells into the breech, laying the gun on the target, and firing without mechanical aids. Seventeen rounds were fired in this way before a shell from the raider pierced the magazine beneath the gun platform. Anderson now ordered his men to leave their dangerous position. The magazine was afire and could explode at any moment.

"Just give us three more rounds," the gun captain replied. "We've got three more shells to throw at 'em."

Several of the gun crew tried to clear a path through a shattered hatch down to the flaming magazine to obtain more ammunition. The magazine blew up beneath them.

The forward gun kept firing.

Determined to end this unwanted battle as quickly as possible, the raider poured shell after shell into the battered tanker with such precision and accuracy that it was evident that the men of the *Stanvac Calcutta* were dueling with well-trained naval gunners.

After taking more than a dozen hits below the waterline, the tanker developed a heavy list. When water poured into the shell-pierced tanks, Karlsson ordered Knudsen to shift ballast so the vessel could be brought back on an even keel. The mate responded instantly, although he had been badly wounded by a shell fragment and was bleeding profusely. As he was working valves along the main deck, a shell smashed into the bridge and turned the entire steering and navigating section into a smoking, battered shambles. Running back to the bridge, Knudsen found the captain dead from multiple wounds. Able Seaman Neldon Okander was slumped over the wheel, his hands still clutching the spokes as though he was determined, even in death, to keep the valiant ship on her course. He, too, had been killed by flying steel.

At the foot of the broken stairs leading to the bridge, Knudsen found radio operator Philip Heath dead at his instrument panel. He had been killed while sending out the SOS. The radio room had been all but blown to pieces.

With the vessel now out of control and sinking from holes in the hull, as well as from water pouring in through the shattered stern, Knudsen pulled the whistle cord and sounded the call to abandon ship.

At the forward gun, the crew waited to get off one last shot, but their gallant gesture proved fatal. As they left the gun platform and ran down the deck toward lifeboats near the stern, an exploding shell killed Larsen and Champagne and wounded Sarrazin, Reed, and DeLong.

The *Stanvac Calcutta* went down soon after the survivors got away in the lifeboats. But the raider had to launch a small torpedo boat and send two tin fish into her torn, shell-gashed side before the waves engulfed her; the signals still whipping from the halyards and the flag of Panama still flying at the gaff. Eleven men had been killed.

Survivors were taken aboard the German ship, which turned out to be Raider 23, otherwise known as the *Stier*. Converted from a fast freighter, she was a large ship armed with six large five-inch guns, plus smaller guns, and carrying two aircraft for reconnaissance. The Germans said they had fired a total of 123 shells at the fighting *Stanvac Calcutta*. They admired the tanker's spirit and regretted that such a brave captain had to go down with his ship.

After taking the survivors on board, Raider 23 hurried away from the scene of battle; the Germans knew that the tanker's SOS might have been heard and that any warships in the area soon would be on their trail. Several days later, they rendezvoused with a supply ship and transferred the survivors, including eleven wounded. Ben Hassan, who was too badly hurt to be moved, was kept on board the *Stier*. All of the wounded men had been given good care by the ship's doctor.

From then until 21 October, the men of *Stanvac Calcutta* were crowded together with 171 survivors from other sunken vessels in the forward hold of the supply ship, which had been the Australian steamer *Nanking* until she was captured. On 6 November, the *Stanvac Calcutta*'s crew were turned over to the Japanese and spent thirty-four months in various POW camps in Japan.

Ben Hassan was still on board the *Stier* as a bed patient when the raider challenged the *Stephen Hopkins*, another lone ship in the South Atlantic and gave her orders to stop. This time, the *Stier* met her match. Instead of stopping, the intended victim opened fire. The ensuing battle became one of the most gallant sea fights of the war, an all-time epic battle of the sea.[2]

13

The Stark Courage of a Valiant Crew

THE *STEPHEN HOPKINS* was a typical Liberty ship, but she was an extraordinary fighter. The battle that she waged against great odds was one of the most gallant events in the history of World War II. The *Hopkins* and her crew won a place in the annals of the sea among the other bold ships and brave men who manned their guns, ran up their battle ensigns, and fought to the end in the face of almost certain death.

The *Stephen Hopkins* left Cape Town in a ballast on 19 September 1942 and proceeded on a course for Dutch Guinea to load bauxite for the States.[1]

The sea was calm and the trip uneventful until 0930 on 27 September, when two strange ships, bearing from the north, suddenly broke out of a bank of haze about three points off the starboard bow.

As soon as the unknown craft were sighted, Third Mate Walter Nyberg called Captain Paul Buck, who hurried from his cabin to the flying bridge and took a quick look through his glasses at the oncoming ships. He told Nyberg to sound the general alarm. In a moment, the wild clanging of bells woke the sleeping men who were off watch and sent naval and merchant crewmen scrambling for steel helmets and life jackets.

"Battle stations . . . battle stations . . . man your guns."

"What is it? What's up? Another practice?"

"No gun drill this time . . . action . . . action."

"I don't like the looks of them," the captain said to Nyberg. "That big ship has too many guns to be a freighter. The small one looks like she's got guns in turrets—warship of some kind." He took another searching look at the menacing strangers, then turned to First Mate Richard Woyhoski with a solemn command, "Break out the ensign and check all boats."

From the flag locker on the bridge, Woyhoski selected a new flag that had never yet been run to the masthead. It was a battle flag, larger than the usual ensign, bright and proud. The cloth was soft in his hands—a fitting flag for men to fight under.

A sudden rainsquall made it difficult to make out details of the approaching ships, but Captain Buck could see through the glasses that they appeared to be heavily armed converted merchant vessels traveling in close consort. One was a large ship, 7,000-tonner at least. Her companion was smaller, but further inspection through the glasses satisfied Buck that she, too, was bristling with guns.

Even as the general alarm ended its ominous call to battle stations, Captain Buck saw each ship run up the German flag and simultaneously open fire. A black puff of smoke hung for a few seconds above the foredeck of the smaller vessel, then drifted into the overcast; the shell splashed into the sea not a hundred yards off the bow of the *Stephen Hopkins*. Naval gunners and merchant crewmen assigned to help them at the gun stations hunched against the steel shields of the gun tubs. Gunners strapped themselves to the 20-millimeters, with merchant crewmen standing by to pass the shells and take over the weapons if the gunners were killed.

The *Stephen Hopkins* was armed with a four-inch gun aft for use against such an enemy. Her antiaircraft armament included two 37-millimeter guns, also effective against the superstructure of surface craft, and four 50-caliber and two 30-caliber machine guns, which were useless in this kind of a duel except at very short range.

Ford Stilson, the chief steward, had been in his cabin when he heard the alarm bells and the crack of the first shell. Stepping into the passageway, he met several men running for battle stations. One of the youngsters was laughing with excited anticipation. "This is it, steward," he yelled. "This is it. Here's our chance to see some real action." Real action! How little they knew what was ahead.

The steward went to his battle station in the officers mess room and laid out bandages and other first aid equipment on one of the tables. The mess room would become a hospital. The cooks and messboy would help him to carry the wounded, it was his duty to bandage wounds. He tried to remember what he had read about applying tourniquets.

"Get lots of sheets and towels," he yelled. "A bucket of water. Rig up the stretcher."

Before these preparations could be made, a second shell hit amidships and killed oiler Gus Taiforos and First Assistant Charles Fitzgerald as they stepped out onto the open deck with their helmets and life jackets. Two more shells fired in salvo struck the *Hopkins* seconds later. Captain Buck ordered a turn to port, and able seaman George Papas, on watch at the wheel, threw the helm hard over so that the ship could turn and give the four-inch stern gun a chance to bear on the enemy.

Shrapnel from one of the first shells to hit the *Hopkins* struck Ens. Kenneth Willett, the Armed Guard commander, as he ran across the boat deck toward his men on the stern gun platform. Hitting him in the stomach, the jagged steel staggered the young officer, but he reeled along the deck to take charge of the big gun roaring out the freighter's first answer to the German attack.

Navy gunners and merchant seamen who were feeding shells into the gun cheered as the first shot from the *Hopkins* threw a sheet of spray over the foredeck of the smaller ship, which was pressing toward the Liberty slightly in advance of her companion.

"That was close," the gun pointer shouted. "Next time we'll have him for sure."

He wheeled up the barrel ever so slightly. The big brass shell was thrown in the breech.

The men held their hands over their ears as the rifle roared again and the gun tub shivered from the recoil. There were yells and cheers when they saw the shell hit squarely on the pursuing ship. Smoke and a plume of fire proved that it had smashed into wood and steel and done damage. "We got him. We got him!"

Ensign Willett directed the fire. Leaning against one of the ready boxes with the intercom phone on his ears, he exhorted the gun captain to "aim low and make every shot count." His crew urged him to leave the gun station and go forward for attention to his wound, but he insisted on staying at his post. "I'm all right," he kept saying, "I'm all right."

He shouted encouragement through the ammunition hoist to merchant seamen and the Armed Guard who were passing up shells and powder from the magazine under the steering engine room at the far end of the ship. The men down there knew they didn't have much chance of getting out, but no one faltered or shirked.

When the Germans had closed the range to a thousand yards or so, their small guns opened up, cutting a swathe of blood and death along the freighter's decks and showering the gun emplacements with hot, jagged steel that pinged in a murderous chatter against the gun tubs, steel deckhouses, and hull.

In the first exhilaration of battle, there had been excited talking around the big gun on the stern, with everyone trying to say something all at once, but the deadly spatter of bullets sobered the first binge of excitement. When one of the gunners reeled against the splinter shield of the gun tub with blood streaming from his chest, the conversation was stilled. Moments later, the gunner fell onto the shivering deck plates and died without saying a word.

Down below in the engine room, the boiler fires sputtered with each boom of the stern gun and more lights went out in the engine spaces. One by one, the electric bulbs broke from the concussion, and the emergency lamps had to be switched on. The lonely vitals of the ship seemed to be fenced by the eerie shadows of steam pipes, ladders, and gratings.

Fireman Mike Fitzpatrick was on watch. He was probably standing between the boilers with a rag in his hand and trying to see the water as it jumped in the gauge glasses with the burst of each shell. When a shot from the raiders hit amidships, every floor plate in the engine room jumped and clattered. Heavy concussions broke the gauge glasses, and the hot water dripped onto the deck in front of the fire doors. The vibration from the guns knocked packing off the steam lines and covered the floor plates with a snowlike shower of asbestos.

With Fitzpatrick in the engine room were Third Assistant Kenneth Vaughan, the watch engineer, and Andy Tsigonis, the oiler. They must have listened to the chatter of the machine guns coming down the funnel over the log desk and the 20-millimeters sounding like the noise from a battery of riveting machines. What they said no one will ever know, but they surely wondered what was going on topside and wished they could have been on deck. Being scared is not as bad when one can see the fighting and take some part in the battle.

It was hard to stay calm down there so far below the open air and the stimulating sights of battle. Isolated at their vital posts by the engine and the boilers, hemmed in by a maze of pipes and steel bulkheads, knowing only what the men on the bridge would tell them over the phone, the black gang could only steady their nerves and wait, listen, and pray. A shell hitting the boilers could bathe the engine spaces in scalding steam.

The three men probably never knew what happened when the salvo smashed through the thin, steel shell that separated the boilers from the sea. There was a crash of steel against steel, followed by the roar of live steam. The men on the bridge rang the watch in the engine room, but there was no answer. The engine spaces were filled with steam and water and choking cordite.

Speed dropped quickly after the boilers were hit. Although the engine still turned for a while, it soon slowed to little more than a few revolutions.

But the guns of the fighting freighter did not slow down. When the raiders swung around to try for a broadside salvo, the 37-millimeters on the Liberty's bow barked some telling bites. Navy gunners and merchant crewmen fired shell after shell until the gun tub was filled with scorched shell cases.

Although it was evident that the engagement would soon be over, no one suggested that the flag be struck. The Stars and Stripes whipped from the gaff—a bright battle flag under which some sixty men were putting up a fight worthy of a warship.

The battered ship fought on.

Second Mate Joseph Layman directed the fire of the two forward guns, the 37-millimeters, which scored hit after hit on the raiders. The guns kept firing till their crews were all killed or wounded and the gun platform was a mass of twisted metal. Every gun crew on the *Hopkins* did its share. During the last few minutes of action, the raiders were close enough for the *Hopkins* to use machine guns. Her gunners kept up a steady fire that swept the decks of both enemy ships until they, too, were silenced and their gunners killed or wounded.

When all the shell handlers and gunners lay dead or wounded around the after gun, Ensign Willett, barely able to stand, tried valiantly to lift another shell into the breach but his strength was too far gone. One of the ship's cadets, Edwin O'Hara, ran up and fired the last five shells left in the ready boxes.

Hardly had he rammed the last one home—the fortieth shell fired from the hard-fought gun that morning—when the ammunition magazine blew up below him. The blast rocked the ship and filled the air with bitter fumes. Flames shot up the ammunition hoist. The war had no braver men than those sailors and merchant crewmen who stayed at their posts in that unar-

Cadet Edwin O'Hara fires the last shell from the stern gun of the Stephen Hopkins. *The gun tub has been shattered by enemy shells. Dead and wounded members of the gun crew lie sprawled around him. O'Hara died soon after. From a painting by W. M. Wilson. (National Merchant Marine Academy, Kings Point, New York)*

mored ammunition locker below the water line, although they knew that they probably could not get out.

Hit by incendiaries, as well as high-explosive shells, the *Stephen Hopkins* was burning in a dozen places fore and aft. Her decks were littered with death and destruction. Deckhouses were pocked with holes. Steel plating was ripped and torn like jagged saw teeth.

The shot that hit the magazine was followed by two more that wrecked what remained of the midships house, demolished the radio room, and killed radio officer Hudson Hewey while he tapped out the SOS—calls for help that were never heard.

Twenty minutes after the fight began, with his ship already sinking by the stern, the captain blew the whistle to abandon ship. Seconds later, a shell hit the bridge where he stood with the weighted box containing the ship's confidential papers. Captain Buck was not seen again.

The first mate was seriously wounded by the same shell burst. When Chief Steward Stilson and seaman James Burke tried to carry him to one of the boats, he refused to go and waved them off. "Get into the boats yourselves," he said. "Get off before it's too late. I'm done for. Don't bother with me."

There were no emotional heroics as those left alive prepared to abandon the embattled ship.

Carpenter Hugh Kuhle and Ensign Willett slipped the pin from one of the life rafts so that it could slide off the cradle into the water overside. As they ducked across the bullet-swept deck to release a second raft, both of them, according to survivors, were cut down by machine-gun slugs that rained on the Liberty like hail. Engine Cadet O'Hara had been running along the deck to help Kuhle and Willett with the rafts, but he, too, was felled by bullets.

George D. Cronk, the second engineer, helped to tend the falls as the lifeboat left the ship. He then jumped overside and, after being pulled into the boat, assumed command.

As the boat was being lowered away, a shell hit just above it, the shrapnel killing Andy Yanz and Bill Adrian and wounding four others. The small boat was badly holed and took to the water in poor shape for a long ocean voyage. Worse still, the wounded men were hundreds of miles from the nearest medical aid.

With more than the usual foreboding of castaways, the survivors of the *Stephen Hopkins* put out their oars, stuffed the holes in the boat with pieces of blanket, and pulled away from the sinking ship.

At 1130, the gallant *Stephen Hopkins,* ablaze fore and aft and her decks a mass of shattered, shell-torn steel, sank by the stern with the American flag still flying at the gaff. Waves were making up under the force of a freshening wind as the lifeboat moved among the wreckage to pick up several of the crew who had jumped overboard and were clinging to pieces of planking or rafts; however, there were few to be found.

While the survivors were engaged in this work, they drifted to within five hundred yards of the two raiders, the smaller of which was down by the stern, with huge rolls of smoke billowing high into the sky. The gunners of the *Hopkins* had done well. The German was soon a flaming derelict, and her companion ship hurried up to take off the crew. Even the wounded who lay in the bottom of the bullet-pocked lifeboat felt a thrill of elation to know that their brave defense of the ship had not been all in vain.

The crew of the *Hopkins* didn't know it, but they had engaged the German commerce raider *Stier* and the blockade runner *Tannenfels*. The enemy's rate of fire was estimated at three rounds a minute from the heavier guns, plus a steady stream of machine-gun fire that swept the Liberty's decks. Both raiders used incendiaries, shrapnel, and contact fuses. The *Stier* carried six 5.9-inch guns, plus two torpedo tubes. The *Tannenfels* had a considerably lighter armament.

The Germans made no effort to detain the drifting boat or question the survivors. The *Tannenfels* was overly burdened with captured crews and anxious to be rid of the scene as quickly as possible. Unlike the Japanese on similar occasions, the Germans did not try to obliterate all traces of the ship and kill the survivors in order to throw trackers off the scent. Perhaps the attackers admired the spirited battle put up by the freighter's men in defense of their ship, for it was not a naval vessel. Being outnumbered and outgunned, the ship, in all honor, could have surrendered without firing a shot, but her men chose to do battle. And fight they did, until the seas poured in through her shell-pocked sides and, with red tongues of flame licking her ravaged decks, she settled beneath the waves—the American flag still whipping at the gaff.

157

As the men in the lifeboat sailed away from the scene that afternoon, they heard a dull explosion far astern. The distant raider was obscured by mist and rain, but the thunderous blast indicated that the vessel had blown up and probably settled quickly to the bottom.

In the lifeboat, tossing among the waves, were nineteen men, five of them painfully wounded by shrapnel. Trying to keep the boat on a course with the aid of a sail, they recounted the battle, as each one of them had seen it, and reported on the fate of their shipmates.

Second Mate Layman, they said, had been killed at the forward gun, along with Herbert Love, a messboy. When they last saw Bos'n Allyn Phelps, he was clearing away the wires of the shattered aerial so that Sparks could send an SOS.

"The chief engineer?" They remembered that he had picked up Pedro Valez, a wiper who had been hit by a shell, and had laid him on the mess room table for emergency aid. Just about then, a salvo had smashed into the midships and turned it into a twisted wreck.

"Henry Engle was crawling up to my room for first aid," the steward reported. "I found him in the passageway when I ran up for bandages. I couldn't do anything for him . . . nothing at all."

And so it went—a grim recital of death, yet a story of great courage, for none of them had complained or asked to quit. When they were wounded, it was in the line of duty. Theirs had been courage fit for the best man-of-war.

Later that afternoon, the men in the lifeboat sighted six of their shipmates on a small doughnut raft. Although they couldn't see their faces because of the distance, they thought they recognized raft second cook Jean Zimsel and at least one of the navy gunners. They shouted and waved, but the wind was blowing hard and carried the drifting raft far out of sight in a bank of mist as they tried unsuccessfully to overtake it.

Sometime after this, they also saw Third Mate Nyberg in a shell-shattered lifeboat that he had kept afloat by stuffing pieces of a life jacket into the holes. He, too, disappeared in the drifting banks of mist before they could reach him in a cross-wind pull.

From then on, the log of the lifeboat reveals a terse story of tragedy and perseverance. On 28 September, the crew sighted two abandoned rafts—the sign of another ship gone down. They saw no evidence of survivors, and they took food and water from supplies on board the rafts. That night, they had to heave to in heavy seas.

The log continues:

29 September: "Rationed food and water. Wounded men in bad shape."

30 September: "Becalmed. Tried to make wounded more comfortable by bathing their bandages in salt water."

1 October: "Cut rations to six ounces per man per day so to have more for the wounded."

6 October: "Eugene McDaniels, second cook and baker, died at 6:30. Stopped ship and buried him at 10:30."

8 October: "Leonardo Romero, steward's utility, died at 2:30. Buried him at sunset. His only possession was a ring."

9 October: "Operated on gunner Wallace Breck. Bad wound. No anaesthesia. Got piece of shell out of his shoulder."

11 October: "Green flares from unseen craft ahead at 3:15 A.M. Think it was a submarine. Answered with a Very pistol."

Two more men, firemen Demetrades and Gelagates, died before the lifeboat finally reached the shore of Brazil, twenty-two miles north of Rio, on the 27 October. On board the little boat pulled from the surf were fifteen survivors from the gallant Liberty ship, whose lone battle against a brace of heavily armed raiders is one of the truly heroic epics of the sea.

Royal Navy Capt. S. W. Roskill said:

They fought an action of which all the Allied Navies and merchant marines should be proud, and had rid the oceans of one of the heavily armed and dangerous German raiders.[2]

The U.S. Maritime Commission later honored this Liberty by naming her one of the "Gallant Ships" of World War II and commending "the stark courage of her valiant crew in their heroic stand."

14

Boats Away

AMONG THE MANY SAGAS of the sea during World War II, none were more dramatic or better demonstrated human courage than the stories of seamen who left their sinking ships in lifeboats to brave the hazards of the deep with the most elementary of equipment and frequently with the most meager of supplies. The sinking of a ship by storms or enemy action brought seamen to a shocking confrontation with the hardest school of seafaring—small boat navigation and seamanship—that tested their ingenuity, skill, strength, and fortitude.

Many men did not survive this cruel test by sea, wind, and weather, but the often incredible voyages of those who did are the epics of the war at sea. Winter in the Atlantic, especially, was not conducive to survival in open lifeboats. Floating lifeboats were frequently spotted, but most of them—tiny, wave-tossed mysteries of the sea—were the mute, and only, evidence of U-boat victims.

Most lifeboats were from twenty-six to twenty-eight feet long and about eight feet wide. They were constructed of either metal or wood; all ships built during World War II had metal boats. Most ships carried four lifeboats, two on each side, and, on war-built American ships, one of the four was equipped with a gasoline engine.

Lifeboats were fitted with a mast that could be stepped after the boat was away from the ship and with a sail. There were usually about four oars for each side.

Boats were required to have water in beakers or sealed cans and food, such as biscuits and pemmican, which was a concentrated mixture of dried beef, flour, and molasses. Some boats were stocked with dried milk and chocolate. When there was time before a ship sank, smart crewmen augmented the food supply with bread and canned fruit from the galley.

Also, boat equipment included such useful items as flares, mirrors for signaling, fishing kit, compass, matches, knife, bucket for bailing, and sea anchor (a drag put over the stern in stormy weather to prevent broaching or capsizing). A bucket with a lanyard attached was often used as a sea anchor.

A ship was required to have enough boats to accommodate all on board, but torpedoed freighter or tanker crews seldom had the luxury of using four lifeboats. Usually, there was no time to launch four boats, and one or more boats were often destroyed by a torpedo blast. In heavy weather, it was impossible to launch boats on the weather side because waves smashed them against the side of the ship or capsized them.

The rafts, which probably saved as many men as lifeboats, were wooden platforms, about ten feet square, attached to empty drums. They offered no protection from wind and waves. Rafts were carried on skids and could be launched instantly by tripping a releasing gear. They were stocked with most types of equipment carried by lifeboats.

Even one who has never had to abandon ship can imagine the desolate feeling of being adrift in a boat or a raft with the water just inches below the gunwales, being drenched with cold spindrift or baked by a burning tropic sun. Often, more mental than physical stamina was required to survive. Physically strong men frequently gave up after a few days and died, or they became victims of delusions and hallucinations. Electrician Michael Wajda of the tanker *T. C. McCobb*, sunk off French Guinea on 31 March 1942, drifted for forty-six days on a raft. Wajda said he survived because he never gave up hope.

"Every day when the sun came up," he said, "I thought this would be the day a ship would find me. Somehow, I knew it would happen."[1]

Ingenuity, plus excellent boatmanship and navigation, wrote a happy ending to the voyage of the *Prusa*'s boats after that ship was sunk by a Japanese submarine on 19 December 1941. Two boats left the *Prusa*, one with twelve men and the other with thirteen. Nine of the crew had been killed in the attack. The ship disappeared beneath the waves in less than ten minutes after the torpedo hit.[2]

At first, the situation did not seem bad at all, and the two boats managed to stay together. They were only 500 miles southeast of Honolulu and close to well-traveled steamer tracks. The nearest land was about 250 miles away.

But winds were adverse, and no ships were sighted. Trying to beat against the wind proved fruitless in such clumsy craft. All the men could do was to turn and run before it, with every mile taking them farther out into the wide reaches of the vast Pacific.

When it became evident that Hawaii was beyond reach, they took stock of their supplies. Each boat had about eighty pounds of biscuits, twenty-eight gallons of water, forty-eight cans of milk, and a case of cherries. Captain G. H. Boy set up a ration schedule, allowing each man one biscuit and about half a cup of water morning and evening, plus a can of milk among several men for each meal.

The boats parted on 20 December. The chief mate's boat was picked up eight days later.

Captain Boy, holding to a southerly course at first, planned to run just south of the trades where there was more likelihood of rain to replenish the water supply.

By the 23d, the weather had worsened so much that the boat began to leak badly. Chief Engineer Knee plugged the holes with pieces of bandage, but two men had to bail continuously. Those not bailing steered or took turns pulling on the heavy oars to keep the boat from being swamped.

After twenty-four hours of continuous rowing and bailing, the storm passed. Completely exhausted and with their hands worn almost raw with blisters, the men curled up in the limited space and slept.

Sail was set, and Captain Boy plotted a course for the Gilbert Islands, hundreds of miles away. There was no paper or pencil, so a sliver of wood was used to work out navigation problems, with figures scratched on the thwarts and the captain's boots. Boy had his sextant, Bowditch, and the nautical almanac.

One of the men had to be forcibly restrained from drinking sea water, a common event on lifeboat voyages.

On 23 December, a heavy sea broke the tiller. Using his pocket knife, Third Mate Baker carved a new tiller from a broken oar.

Heavy weather persisted. On the day before Christmas, the leaks got worse. Chief Knee, remarkably versatile in the tradition of "old-time" ship engineers, plugged them again, this time using a spare life preserver. Two men were now kept bailing at all times on two-hour shifts.

When the mast broke during a squall, Baker repaired it with rope lashings and splints fashioned with his handy jackknife.

Christmas was celebrated with an extra ration of cherries.

In midafternoon of 31 December, the boat sailed into a school of gamboling whales. For several hours, it was touch and go—the huge mammals slapping their flukes so close to the boat that the flailing blubber showered the men with water.

On 4 January, a heavy rain drenched the boat and provided welcome refill for the water beakers.

Leaks worsened, but the chief came through again. He took an air tank from under one of the thwarts and lashed it to the side above the worst of the leaks, so that the boat rode a little higher there.

Second Mate Ed Banvard died on 16 January. The boat was headed into the wind, and his body was reverently lowered over the side. Captain Boy recited all he could remember of the Ninety-first Psalm:

> I will say of the Lord, he is my refuge and my fortress; my God; in him will I trust . . .

Two days later, Boy was afraid that he had missed the Gilberts by sailing through or to the north of them. He checked and rechecked his position the best he could on such an unstable platform and with a limited horizon.

After trying for a star sighting that evening and working his computations again, he told the crew, "It looks like we missed the islands. My figures show we should be in the middle of the Gilberts right now. But this isn't the best way to do navigation. We might have missed 'em by a hundred miles. There's only one thing to do. No use backing and filling here. We'll have to try for the Solomons."

The Solomons—hundreds of miles more in a leaky boat.

The wind started to blow again that night. While a crewman kept a flashlight on the compass, Boy tried to keep the bucking boat on a WSW heading, but the boat would not hold the course. It seemed determined to go due west. Others tried the tiller, with similar results. They finally gave the boat its head and coursed west, intending to change direction when the gale died down.

It was lucky for the *Prusa*'s men that their boat was determined to follow its own course. On the afternoon of the next day—their thirty-first day adrift—a low-lying atoll broke over the horizon ahead. They didn't believe it at first—it must be a mirage—but the shoreline persisted and became more firmly delineated. The joyous crew broke out the oars and pulled with all their might. Forgotten were empty stomachs, sore hands, and cramped muscles. The boat seemed to fly through a windless, sparkling sea.

Waving to them from the shore, the island's natives watched them head the boat into the breakers, ship the oars, and shoot onto the beach like harpooners on a Nantucket sleigh ride.[3] The natives helped them out of the boat and into the shade of coconut palms.

The *Prusa*'s men had landed on the island of Nukunau, one of the southernmost atolls of the Gilbert group. They spent several weeks on Nukunau before being picked up by a copra trader and taken to Australia.

Within a few weeks, most of them were again sailing merchant ships to the fighting fronts.

Their voyage could have ended in disaster several times, but good boat handling, ingenuity, and discipline carried them through. The *Prusa*'s crew added their own chapter to the epic of the merchant seamen of World War II.

The survivors of the *Prusa* sailed through dangerous, but warm, waters of the mid-Pacific, but the men of the Standard Oil Company tanker, *W. L. Steed* had to battle for survival in the worst kind of winter weather in the North Atlantic. Northbound with a full cargo of Colombia crude oil on 2 February 1942, she was bucking heavy seas and a strong southwesterly wind when a torpedo hit on the starboard side just forward of the bridge. The blast set the cargo of fuel on fire, and it was soon evident to Captain Harold McAvenia that his ship was doomed. Almost as soon as the torpedo hit, radio operator Francis Siltz sent out distress calls giving the vessel's position at about ninety miles off the Delaware capes and asking for assistance: "Torpedoed . . . torpedoed . . . ship on fire . . . request help." As learned later, the message was picked up by a British tanker that was torpedoed before she could help.

Captain McAvenia decided that probably there would be no chance to launch lifeboats if a second torpedo hit, so he ordered the boats away and sounded the mournful whistle signal to abandon ship. Despite heavy seas that made launching difficult and dangerous, four boats managed to leave the ship in an exceptionally fine display of boat handling and seamanship. Last to leave was number two boat containing fifteen men, including the captain, Chief Mate Einar Nilsson, and Second Mate Sydney Weyland. Weyland later reported that he saw all lifeboats get safely away from the burning hulk. The boats were soon separated in a driving snowstorm that blanketed the sea. Winds were increasing, and seas were rising.

While one U-boat surfaced and circled the tanker, a second one shelled the hulk. Some thirty minutes after being abandoned, the *Steed* exploded and the men in number two boat saw it sink by the head. Unintentionally because of the snow squall, number three boat came close to the submarine doing the shelling and almost rammed it, but the Germans made no attempt to interfere.

McAvenia, Nilsson, Weyland, and their companions in number two boat suffered intensely from the cold, snow, and driven spray. None was adequately dressed for such weather. By the end of the third day adrift, the captain and twelve of the boat's crew had died from the cold. Only Weyland and Nilsson, both half-conscious, were left when the British steamer *Hartlepool*, which would be sunk later on the Russian run, picked them up. Nilsson died soon after being landed at Halifax and rushed to a hospital.

The experiences of the men in number three boat were dramatically recounted in the Standard Oil Company's history of Ships of World War II. Able seaman Ralph Mazzucco gives this account:

> Finding it impossible to catch up with the other boats, we started to put out our sea anchor. The canvas carried away and we hauled in the frame. At this time we noticed that our water keg was empty. When the boat was suspended slantwise (going down the falls) the water keg had got loose and rolled to the bow, breaking the spigot and letting out the water.
>
> We made a sea anchor out of the water keg, first chopping a hole in the top and a hole on each side near the top. We had about six feet of two-inch manila line which we passed through the two holes on the sides of

167

the keg and secured with a square knot. We then made the line for the sea anchor fast to the bight of the two-inch line.

After finishing this makeshift sea anchor, we transferred all the heavy weights to the forward end of the boat to get the head down and lighten the stern. This worked very nicely and we started to bail the water out of the boat, hoping to be picked up by some naval vessel.

The sea was running heavier and the weather was getting intensely cold. We stretched our lifeboat cover over the center thwarts to protect us from the wind.

After it grew dark, we lighted some of our distress flares in the hope of being rescued.[4]

When they saw a pistol flare from one of the other boats, they headed toward it, only to have a big sea smash into the boat and carry away rudder, tiller, sails, and all but three of the oars. The boat was half full of water and the men were soaked to the skin.

Mazzucco continues:

After struggling for a couple of hours, we had the boat bailed out and crawled under the canvas hood for protection from the heavy spray and strong wind. We kept talking and joking through the night in an effort to keep up our morale.

[Arthur] Chandler lay down on a life preserver and fell asleep. The next morning I tried to wake him and realized he was dead and we carried him to the forward end of the boat. The same morning Burkholder became delirious. Shortly before noon he died.

It was so bitterly cold that we decided to start a fire. The lamp in the boat being broken, we poured oil on some wood we had chopped up and placed it in the water bucket. The fire burned steadily and helped to dry out our wet clothes and thaw us out to some extent. By cutting up the thwarts, stern sheets, forward sheets and the bottom board we managed to keep the fire going for the rest of the day and during the night until we were picked up by the Canadian cruiser *Alcantara*.

The morning we were picked up I came from under the boat cover and when I stood up I saw the ship. I grabbed a flare and lighted it. The cruiser turned around and came slowly toward us, cautious for fear of a possible submarine attack. They stopped about 200 feet away. The bluejackets on the cruiser were lined up all along the deck with heaving lines, ready to throw them to us. I secured a line around the bosun [Joaquin Brea], and he made it up the scramble net. I fastend a line to [Louis] Hartz, who was then hauled on board. I climbed up the net myself.

We were taken to the ship's hospital, undressed and put to bed.

We arrived at Halifax 7 February. We arrived in New York 11 February.[5]

Another boat from the *Steed* was sighted on 12 February by the British freighter *Raby Castle*. There were four men in it, but the only one still alive, Second Assistant Engineer Elmer Maihiot, Jr., died soon after being rescued. The fourth boat was never found.[6]

Ingenuity—an improvised sea anchor and a fire in a bucket—spelled the difference between life and death for three of these torpedoed tankermen. Physical toughness and a will to live helped, too.

Physical toughness, more than anything else, enabled some crewmen of the Panamanian freighter *Raceland* to survive. The ship, with a U.S. Naval Armed Guard crew and other Americans in the ship's crew, was sunk on 28 March 1942 in a bombing attack on a convoy heading toward North Russia.

Two of the four boats launched were lost amid heavy seas and never seen again. The others finally reached the coast of Norway, with twenty-two of the men dead from the bitter cold. Constant rowing, the survivors said, kept them alive.

Another story of men against the sea followed the torpedo-ing of the Liberty ship *Roger B. Taney* in the South Atlantic on 9 February 1943.[7]

The *Taney,* under command of Captain Tom Potter, was homeward bound from Cape Town by way of Brazil when look-outs reported a white streak about twenty feet beyond the bow. Torpedo!

The alarm bells called all hands to general quarters. Donald Zubrod, the purser, relates:

> That was a feeling of excitement no words can express. Running alone . . . a black, windy night. An unseen sub out there trying to sink us. It was so dark you could hardly see anything more than six feet in front of you. After a while we could hear the distinct "whoop . . . whoop . . . whoop" of the U-boat's die-sels. It was following us.[8]

The chase continued for an hour, but the *Taney's* ten knots were not enough to outrun the raider. At exactly 2200, a torpedo exploded in the engine room and killed the fireman, oiler, and engineer on watch.

Zubrod continues:

> I was standing on a wing of the bridge. All our guns were firing at imaginary targets but it was im-possible to see anything. Two lifeboats were smashed by the explosion.
>
> The ship was dead in the water so Captain Potter gave the order to lower the boats. It was my job to collect the code book and other confidential papers and throw them overside in a weighted box. By the

time I did all this the boats had got away. I could hear voices and the clatter of oars in the oarlocks, but I couldn't see anyone. I yelled as loud as I could. I was alone on a sinking ship. Every time the ship rolled the blocks from the lifeboat falls banged against the hull. It was like a requiem. Only one thing to do—jump. The boats couldn't be too far away. I jumped into the blackness.[9]

Fortunately, someone heard Zubrod shouting. A lifeboat came back to find him, and he was hauled on board.

A second torpedo then hit the *Taney*. The men watched the big, indistinct bulk disappear beneath the waves.

The U-boat came within a few yards of the boats, and an officer asked the name of the ship. When no one answered, he laughed and said, "Never mind we know all about your ship." His offer to tow the boats for several hours was declined, and the submarine slipped away into the night.

After a conference between the two boats, the officers decided to strike out for the southeast trades and the coast of Brazil, but the boats soon became separated by rough weather. The first mate's boat was picked up twenty-one days later. The captain's boat, in which Zubrod was riding, continued on for another twenty-one days, during which the weather varied from flat calm to half gales to a violent tropic storm, in which winds were close to hurricane force for a brief period.

With twenty-three men crowded into the boat, there was no room for stretching out or even a minimal amount of exercise. The days were long, and the nights were cold. The wind whipped the spray over the crowded crew as they hunched their backs and bent their heads trying to escape the salty blast.

Worst of all was the confinement. "Try sitting in a chair for a full day without getting up," Zubrod suggests. "Sometimes you get so nervous you want to jump overboard."[10]

Potter navigated by dead reckoning, using the stars at night and a small sextant that was in the boat's equipment.

The biggest worry was water. There was no rain for thirty days. Just as they used the last drops of water in the beakers, a rain squall appeared.

On the thirty-fifth day, Sam Lo Presti, the cox'n of the gun crew who had been a famous hockey player, attached a knife on the end of a boat hook and speared a dolphin. Cutting up an extra oar for fuel, the men cooked the meat in a bucket.

A distant glow of lights was seen on the fortieth night. They were brighter the next night so, on the forty-second day, the men shipped their oars and started to pull. For the first time since the torpedoing, they saw the distant silhouette of a ship. They spotted several more ships over a period of several hours, but none of them took notice of the tiny boat or the shirts waving at the end of oars. Finally, a Brazilian passenger ship spotted them and changed course to pick them up.

Despite the ordeal and their cramped condition, all hands were able to climb up the Jacob's ladder unaided and reach the vessel's deck. They had logged more than 2,600 miles in one of the longest lifeboat sagas of the war.

In April 1943, the brand-new Liberty ship *James W. Denver*, east-bound on the Atlantic, became lost from her convoy after a heavy fog. Despite this, all might have been well if the *Denver* hadn't developed engine trouble. The reciprocating engines of Liberty ships were simple mechanisms that performed wonderfully during the war, considering their harsh treatment and frequently inexpert handling. Even new machinery can be temperamental until it is broken in, however, and that was the case on the *Denver*.

The heavily laden Liberty squatted on the sea like a tin duck in a shooting gallery while the black gang hurried with sledges, calipers, and scrapers to get the pistons moving again. The ship steamed on after a few hours' delay, but the engine trouble persisted. On 11 April, the long, gray bulk of the *Denver* was once again sitting lonely and helpless in the mid-Atlantic when a German submarine found her.

A stationary Liberty ship presented more than four hundred feet of perfect target in good weather and, with only a slight sea running, a U-boat commander would have been particularly inept to miss the *Denver*, even at long range. No destroyer was fussing about the ship, and no telltale smoke from the stacks of other freighters on the horizon was visible. The commander took his time inspecting her, figuring the wind and drift, and calibrating the distance. He then pressed the button to release compressed air into the torpedo chamber and send the lethal missile racing through the waves.

Not a shot was fired in retaliation. The undersea raider couldn't be seen from the ship as she hit and ducked. The commander wisely waited for the ship to sink before exposing the U-boat. Besides her crew of forty-two merchant seamen, the *Denver*, like other ships of her size at this period of the war, also carried an Armed Guard ensign and a force of twenty gunners manning antisubmarine and ack-ack guns. But the *Denver*'s armament might as well have been resting back in a shoreside armory.

The Liberty sank as smoothly and effortlessly as though she had been scuttled by her crew. She took with her to the bottom thousands of tons of machinery, food, guns, and the myriad tools of war consigned to the holds of most ships bound for the European fronts.

In the excitement of leaving the ship, one of the boat crews spilled into the sea when they overturned the boat in their haste to get down the ship's side. The well-doused men were quickly rescued and distributed among the other three boats without injury, but the incident resulted in crowded conditions in the other boats and fewer rations per man.

Apparently, the deck officers all crowded into one boat. Dolar Stone, the *Denver*'s deck engineer and a friend of the author, says that the craft in which he was riding had only two men who knew anything about seamanship. Almost all of the eighteen men on board were engine and steward department personnel and Armed Guard gunners. Able seamanship is needed to handle a boat in the open sea and navigate it hundreds of miles to a safe haven.[11]

The men in the boats looked around to see if the submarine was going to surface and spray them with machine-gun fire. The U-boat commander must have decided to stay down and bag any other ships that might be attracted to the scene because the survivors didn't see any signs of the raider.

Stone talked about the crew's odyssey that lasted thirty-four days, "There was a little half-hearted joking at first, but all-in-all it was a pretty solemn affair. We hated to lose our ship and especially to see her go down without ever having fired a shot from all those brand-new guns."

The skipper gave the three boats a course to steer toward the nearest land and then told the officers in charge of each boat to hoist sail and "get going."

"Good luck," he told them. "It's going to be a long trip and there's no use hanging around here."

Stone's boat stepped its mast, hoisted the little red sail with which most Liberty ship lifeboats were equipped, and set out for the east. Seas were making up fast under a sharpening wind. The crew soon had to rig a sea anchor so they could heave to and ride the waves. By this time, the other boats were out of sight and Stone's boat rode the sea alone—a tiny flotsam, it seemed, on that huge expanse of darkening sea and breaking whitecaps.

Even in placid waters, a lifeboat is anything but comfortable. The keel-less craft pitched, rolled, and wallowed all that first night and into the day and night that followed. All hands were wet and miserably seasick.

A Liberty ship lifeboat was a twenty-four–foot metal affair, with a watertight compartment built into the bow and stern and under the seats that ran around the gunwales on both sides. It had no provision for comfort, especially with a full complement. There was hardly room for lying down, even with a moderate crew of eighteen, and the miseries of mal de mer must be "sat out" and endured. Seasickness, cold, cramps, and the exercise of bodily functions were but a few of the unpleasant aspects of being adrift in the small boat.

Just at dusk on the third night, the lookout stationed in the bow sighted a vague shape looming up ahead. In the excitement of his discovery, he yelled, "Destroyer." Dusk at sea can cause confusion as shadows mix with the wave tops and form illusive patterns, especially in the minds of harried men, but Stone lit the boat's lantern and, standing erect on the thwart with one hand on the mast, waved it back and forth on the chance that there was a ship ahead. To attract more attention, each man in the boat also switched on the tiny emergency light fastened by a safety pin and lanyard to his life jacket.

And then—almost before the men realized what was happening—a shape did loom up ahead, directly in their path, the black, bulging hull of a submarine. "It was a hell of a big sub," Stone said, "and we were sailing right down on top of it."

Only a few minutes later, as the men watched the raider in amazement, the lifeboat grated against the submersible's hull. It sheered off just in time to keep from riding right up onto the cigar-shaped side and turning over. One of the U-boat's officers shouted at them from the conning tower as the surprised survivors of the *Denver* bumped across his afterdeck grating.

"Where are you from?" he yelled.

"Brooklyn," they shouted back and fended their boat away from the submarine's hull.

"Brooklyn. That's where baseball and ships come from."

This appeared to be a good joke, and they could hear the U-boat officer having a hearty laugh on the conning tower. He spoke very good English.

"What ship are you from?" was his next question.

They knew that the German could find out readily enough if he was much interested, so they yelled back, "*James Denver.*"

Again, the officer and a companion had a long laugh. The men guessed, with good reason, that this was probably the U-boat that had sunk them, and she could have surfaced later and identified the vessel from the overturned lifeboat or other debris.

"Well, well. You lads are from one of those Liberty ships." The remark sounded sarcastic, but before the submarine moved off in the darkness, a sailor came down the deck and handed them a carton of cigarettes. From the bridge, the officer shouted the course for them to steer in order to reach the nearest land. Although they heard the hum of the U-boat's diesels as she moved off, they saw within the hour what was apparently a different submarine. Obviously, they had bumped into a rendezvous point for a wolf pack. They were relieved that the Germans didn't sink or capture them to prevent their revealing the presence of the undersea flotilla.

The heavy weather persisted. All hands continued to be miserably seasick during the next few days, and the lifeboat made more mileage up and down than it did toward land. Stone and several others took turns at the tiller as they tried, with aching arms and blistered hands, to keep the cranky boat on a course. They talked about girls in Baltimore, Puerto Rico, Rio, and Le Havre. They talked about hot dogs, ice cream cones, and juicy steaks.

At dusk on 19 April, they sighted a small steamer, but it turned tail and ran when they set off flares. From a distance, the lifeboat probably looked like a submarine.

During their last fourteen days at sea, the rations got low. Water was rationed to three ounces per man per day, and all they had to eat were malted milk tablets. Flying fish that landed in the boat were devoured raw. On the night of 11 May, they saw blue signal lights, but when they waved a lantern and shot flares, the lights disappeared. Once again, they surmised they had met a Nazi wolf pack.

Rescue came on 14 May when Spanish fishermen found them and took them to La Aguerra in the Canary Islands. They were given quarters across from a swastika-draped German consulate and, after a few days, obtained passage to Cádiz, Spain. Then, packed into two trucks loaded with Polish and Czech refugees, they were hauled to Gibraltar. When the truck suddenly swerved to avoid a tree, Virgil Hurd, one of the crew, was thrown against the side of the truck and badly injured. He later died at Gibraltar—an ironic end to a voyage in a lifeboat amid the hazards of the sea.

The survivors were repatriated to the United States on the *Seatrain Texas,* but not until the *Texas* had idled for thirty days at Gibraltar while waiting for a convoy.

"I'm not superstitious," Stone told the author, "but from now on I am going to spend every Friday the 13th bellying up to some bar watching the suds go down."

15

The Man Who Refused to Die

AMONG THE INSPIRING INCIDENTS of almost superhuman determination and courage on the high seas during World War II, none surpasses the dramatic story of Able Seaman Rexford Dickey of the Liberty ship *Wade Hampton* and his battle against seemingly impossible weather conditions.

Two days out of New York on 28 February 1943, the *Wade Hampton* was bound for Loch Ewe, Scotland. The deeply laden ship had dropped back from the convoy so that crewmen could check the fastenings on a deckload of motor torpedo boats.[1]

When the job was finally done and Captain John Reynolds rang for "full ahead" on the engine room telegraph, the *Wade Hampton* was five to six miles behind the rest of the convoy. There were no escorts to spare for a straggler; the lone ship was free prey for a lurking U-boat. The night was pitch black, and the vessel bucked heavy seas as she tried to catch up with the convoy.

The *Wade Hampton* appeared to be steaming on a sea of black ink. A thick overcast hid the stars. The lookouts could see no farther than the whitecaps breaking ghostlike just beyond the vessel's side. They did not see the submarine or the torpedo that smashed into the port side of number five hold. The muffled explosion shook the 10,000-ton ship as though it had run onto a reef. Cordite fumes filled the air.

Alarm bells on the passageways sounded the call for general quarters. Crewmen pulled on coats and life jackets and ran to battle stations.

The torpedo had knocked off the propeller and damaged the shaft. The ship was dead in the water.

The second torpedo hit almost in the same place as the first. The stern was shattered by the blast, and part of it fell into the sea. Several crewmen were carried along with it.

Two torpedoes could not sink a Liberty ship, however, and the *Wade Hampton* remained afloat, badly hurt but seemingly in no danger of sinking immediately.

Captain Reynolds did not know when a third or a fourth torpedo might come streaking into the helpless ship and send it plunging to the bottom. Thinking that the crew would be safer in the lifeboats, he gave the order to abandon ship. The radio operator was sending an SOS with the ship's position, and the captain felt that it would not take long for one of the convoy escorts to come to their aid.

"Man the lifeboats," he yelled from the bridge into the coal-tar blackness fore and aft, where the Armed Guard gunners were standing by at useless battle stations. "Man the boats and lower away!" Moments later, he pulled the whistle cord to signal the three long blasts of abandon ship.

Despite heavy seas, the lifeboats were safely lowered. Each boat pushed away from the side of the ship and quickly became lost from sight of one another in the darkness.

But four men remained on board.

Bos'n John Sandova and able seaman Rexford Dickey had stayed on board to tend the falls as the lifeboats, one by one, went over the side. On Liberty ships and other vessels with similar lifeboat equipment, at least two crewmen had to remain on the ship and help to lower away so that the boats went down the falls evenly and safely, without being upended and capsized.

When the last boat was lowered, the crew pushed away in the dark. In the confusion, they did not wait for Dickey and Sandova to slide down the falls and join them. The two men were soon marooned on what they thought was a deserted ship.

They were unaware that Captain Reynolds and Chief Engineer Worsham Chandler had stayed on the ship, too, and were attempting to determine how much damage had been done by the torpedoes. They still hoped some way could be found of towing the *Wade Hampton* to port and saving her multimillion dollar cargo.

"It was a strange feeling," Dickey said. "We heard the waves breaking against the side. As we stood there on that empty deck, they sounded like the combers beating on some deserted beach."

When the ship rolled, the steel blocks at the end of the falls thumped against the steel hull like a death knoll: bong, bong, bong, bong.

"For all we knew," Dickey said, "another torpedo might smash into the ship at any moment. We decided to leave her while there was still a chance."

The *Wade Hampton*, like other Liberty ships, was equipped with big rafts lashed to special launching racks on each side, fore and aft.

Dickey and Sandova pulled the pin from a raft on the lee side, and the heavy wooden float plummeted into the sea. Wind and sea soon carried it to the end of a long painter, and they couldn't pull it back to where they could jump into it. There was only one way to get on board the bobbing raft—jump over the side into the frigid, black, wind-whipped water.

Sandova jumped first. Sitting on the rail for a moment, Dickey stared at the breaking sea, then closed his eyes and pushed off.

The shock of the cold water swept his breath away. He bobbed to the surface and gasped for air. Grabbing the painter, he pulled himself to the raft, about twenty feet away. Sandova was climbing on board as he reached it. As Dickey heaved himself

On a spray-swept raft such as this, Able Seaman Rexford Dickey survived in the cold and wintry North Atlantic. This photo shows three exhausted British seamen awaiting rescue by a U.S. Coast Guard cutter. (U.S. Coast Guard)

onto the wave-washed float, he felt like someone was pouring ice water down his back. The wind cut like a knife.

"God, it's cold," Sandova muttered. "Let's find those lifeboats. We can't take much of this."

For a few minutes, they listened for voices from the lifeboats, but they couldn't hear a thing. The dense blanket of darkness seemed to stifle all sound: the grating of oarlocks, the shrill peep of lifeboat whistles, the commands of officers guiding their crews through the wind and sea.

They shouted, "Hall-oo, hall-oo. Lifeboats! Lifeboats!"

There was no answer.

"They couldn't hear us in this wind," Sandova said. "It's no use. We'll blow our lungs out, and they'll never hear us."

They broke out the oars and started to row—not to make any progress in the heavy seas, but as an effort to keep warm.

Rafts weren't made for rowing, but the men took turns pulling at the oars. They hoped they might be making some progress in the right direction. The exertion at least warmed them and took their minds off the cruel bite of the wind.

"I don't know how much time went by," Dickey related. "It might have been a couple of hours. Sometime that night we saw the black hulk of a ship. It probably was a corvette sent by the convoy escort when they picked up our SOS. Our life jackets had little red lights on them, and we flashed the lights so they could see us. We shouted, and we pounded on the boards till our fists were sore and we couldn't shout any longer. They never saw us."

The corvette was busy picking up men from the lifeboats. The raft was hidden in the wave troughs, and the life jacket lights were probably never seen by the men on the rescue ship.

The wind carried Dickey and Sandova slowly away from the corvette. The raft was rolling and pitching so wildly now that it was all they could do to hang on as it teetered on the crest of one big wave and then plunged into the trough of another. Sheets of spray swept the miserable survivors and made talk and movement almost impossible. They gave up trying to row.

Later that night, a warship ran so close by that she almost overturned the raft in its wake, but the ship swept on into the night. No one heard their frantic calls for help.

Meanwhile, Captain Reynolds and Chandler remained on the ship throughout the night. The next morning, a convoy escort rescued them. They were still hoping that a tug could be summoned and the *Hampton* towed into port. The navy considered this impossible, however, and sunk the ship by gunfire.

By early morning, Dickey and Sandova knew they were freezing. Their legs and feet became painful, and their ears and cheeks burned as though with fever. They exercised as best they could, bending their knees, swinging their arms, and rubbing their bodies, but it took almost all of their strength and energy just to hold onto the plunging raft. (Convoy records indicate that a force seven—a moderate gale—was blowing that night.)

White foam from breaking waves streaked across the sky. Dickey and Sandova were constantly drenched with cold spray. Added to this misery was violent seasickness caused by the constant motion of the raft.

After swallowing so much salt water and spray, they were terribly thirsty, but there was no water on the raft. The water beakers had been either broken by heavy seas or cracked by the concussion of the torpedo blast. When it rained on the following day, they held up the oars and licked the moisture from the blades.

The gale was abating somewhat now. They saw occasional streaks of blue across the slate-gray overcast.

In the midafternoon of the second day, a ship broke over their limited horizon on a course straight for the raft and not more than a mile or two away.

They waved a shirt fastened to the end of an oar, but the vessel ignored them completely. When she passed by a half mile or so distant, they could see no one on deck, no watch on the bridge, and no lookouts in the gun tubs.

Was this a ghost ship? A trick of the mind? Just an illusion? Dickey believes that he saw a real ship.

After the ship passed without any sign of recognition, Sandova gave up. He refused to fight the cold any longer.

"There isn't a chance," he insisted. "We haven't got a chance. I don't want to freeze on this raft and be chopped up by the surgeons if we do get rescued. I'd rather have it over with right now."

Dickey gave his companion a jacket, but it made no difference. Sandova went out of his mind. He soon became oblivious to the sea, the cold spray, and the chilling wind.

But Dickey refused to die.

"I won't, he kept muttering, "I won't die. I'll stick it out. I'll stick it out."

Still believing that rescue was possible, that a ship would somehow spot them on that wild expanse of lonely, tumbling sea, Dickey kept moving and exercising.

The seas had calmed somewhat, and the motions of the raft were not as violent as they had been. He lay on his back and did bicycle movements with his legs. With every ounce of his energy, he tried to keep up the vital circulation through his limbs. When the pain began to ease in his legs and a cold numbness took its place, he knew that it was more important than ever to move and exercise. If he did get picked up, he wanted hands and feet. A seaman wouldn't be any good without them.

Dickey didn't allow himself to fall asleep. To fall asleep would mean freezing to death. When he did doze off for a few minutes, it was always with the dream of a convoy steaming by. He would wake with a start only to see the empty, heaving ocean.

On the evening of the third day, he awoke from one of these momentary slumbers and saw ships. It took him a few seconds to realize that this convoy was no dream. The ships were real, with masts and hulls and wisps of smoke rising from their stacks.

Waving an oar to attract attention, Dickey mustered every last bit of strength. He shouted and yelled and then cried in desperation as the ships kept moving on. One by one, they passed him until their hulls disappeared beyond the rolling wave tops and only the tips of their masts could be seen above the combers.

Exhausted, Dickey dropped his oar and collapsed on the raft. He was sobbing in utter frustration, crying, and beating his fists against the sodden planking of the raft, when he heard a shout nearby.

He turned to see a destroyer so close aboard that he could almost have reached out and touched her sharp, knifelike bow. She was one of the old four-stackers that the United States had turned over to Great Britain under Lend-Lease.

The destroyer stopped, and two men jumped down onto the raft to pass lines around Dickey and Sandova.

Dickey waved to the men on deck. He tried to stand but couldn't. When the sailors helped him to his feet, it felt like a million needles were pricking him. They heaved him gently onto the ship's low-lying afterdeck, then rushed him below for warm clothes, hot coffee, and medical attention. They told him he was on board His Majesty's Ship *Beverly.*

"You're lucky," they told him. "It was only by accident that we found you at all. The skipper had a report of a submarine conning tower, and we were running down full speed to let you have some canned dynamite when we saw that piece of shirt you were waving on the end of an oar. Our three-inch gun was already to open up when someone shouted, 'Delay that, it's a bloody raft.'"

"Sandova?" Dickey asked.

The destroyer's doctor shook his head. "He's been gone for hours. Funny thing. He's a much bigger man than you are. Younger, too."

As the *Beverly's* screws bit the water again and she ran back to her patrol station on the convoy's quarter, the empty raft bobbed away on the cold, windswept sea, one of many to be sighted by freighters on the North Atlantic shipping lanes till long after the war. No shipmaster who saw it and reported its position to the Navy Hydrographic Office would know that this floating bit of wood and canvas was a mute testimonial to the courage of a merchant seaman who refused to die.

Later that day, the *Beverly's* crew buried John Sandova in the traditional service of the sea. An American flag draped the body as it slid from the destroyer's deck toward the sailor's last haven.

16

The Tankermen

Plodding, rust-streaked, squatty tankers
Decks awash on lonely way;
Filled deep with hell-brewed lightning,
Lifeblood of the battle fray.
Reeling decks, man-made volcanoes;
Heroes where true seamen meet
Are men of daring, men of courage,
Sailors of the tanker fleet.

"... TOP 'N LIFT"
SEAFARERS LOG, 1944

TANKERS FILLED WITH OIL and gasoline were indeed "man-made volcanoes." The men who rode them knew that a torpedo, a stick of bombs, or a collision in convoy might set off that cargo of "lightning" in a holocaust that would take not only the ship but many, or perhaps all, of the crew as well.

Despite this hazard, there was no scarcity of men to ride the volcano fleet on dangerous voyages around the world. The United States furnished 80 percent of the oil and gasoline that powered the bombers, tanks, Jeeps, and ships of World War II. The tankermen—the merchant sailors of the tanker fleet and their U.S. Naval Armed Guard comrades at the guns—delivered this lifeblood of battle.

To Salerno and Murmansk and Liverpool, across the lonely Pacific to Freemantle with fuel for our Australian-based submarines, through the buzz-bomb barrage to fill the oil tanks at Antwerp, on all the oceans of the world—the vital petroleum carriers steamed toward potential disaster. The war would have been lost without them. They were hunted ships, easily identified by the

*"Decks Awash on Lonely Way." Waves roll across the deck of a
tanker in the Atlantic, December 1941. This photo was taken from
the USS Aquila. (National Archives, 80-G-405291)*

special trademarks of their profession—navigating bridge and
deckhouse forward and engines aft.

From 7 December 1941 until VJ-day in 1945, nearly 65 million tons of oil and gasoline were carried from the United States
and the Caribbean to our Allies, the beachheads, and the fighting
fronts. This vast movement of precious fuel entailed hundreds
of voyages, many over waters infested by submarines, planted
with mines, and haunted by bombers. According to the U.S. Maritime Commission, American tankers made 6,500 voyages during
the war.

This was only part of the job. The tankers also supplied oil
and gasoline to the home front for the nation's vastly increased
wartime need for fuel. Throughout the war, our tankermen kept
the "black gold" flowing from Texas and the Caribbean to ports
throughout the United States and Canada.

187

Many seamen preferred tankers. The seagoing profession called these men "tanker stiffs." Their preference stemmed from the fact that tankers have little in the way of cargo gear to worry about. There are no booms and tackle to rig or hatch covers to remove before the vessel gets to port or when she leaves. On a tanker, the hose is connected, the pumps are started, and the cargo flows ashore effortlessly and quickly. The process is so speedy, in fact, that tanker life is disagreeable to men who like time ashore at the end of a trip. When a tanker gets into port, she ties up at an oil dock, which is, almost invariably, an inconvenient distance from the nearest sailor haunts. Within twenty-four hours—perhaps forty-eight at the most—the tanks are empty, and the skipper takes his vessel out to anchor. If the crew is lucky, they get ashore for a few hours. Then it's "make up convoy" again and back to sea. Tankers are too vital to stay long in port. It's always "hello" and "farewell" for the tankerman, scarcely seeing a new place before it fades fast astern.

Crews manning tankers on the Ābādān run and freighting oil from refineries in the Persian Gulf to Australia, and later to Gen. Douglas MacArthur's forces in the South Pacific, felt as though they were orphans of the sea.

The War Shipping Administration assigned between sixty and seventy of the T-2 war-built tankers to a shuttle service between the Persian Gulf and the Pacific. Many of the T-2s were on this shuttle for a year or more, with the crews remaining on board for the duration of a vessel's assignment. Staying in Ābādān about forty-eight hours to load, then outboard bound for her solitary passage down the Persian Gulf and the Arabian Sea and across the Indian Ocean to the South Pacific, a tanker offered her crew little time for recreation or amusement ashore. Entertainment in Ābādān was almost nonexistent, and the discharge points were often only island bases, bleak atolls, or advanced fleet operation points where the crew had little shore even to look at, much less to enjoy.

Added to the monotony and boredom of tanker service was the problem of food. Ships that ran out of galley and slop chest supplies found it difficult to replenish them. Nor were tankermen stuck on the Persian Gulf shuttle always sure of being homeward bound at the end of a year. When the ship's articles, which bound the men to twelve months' service, expired, new articles were drawn up and the crews generally signed on again for another year. Their only alternative was packing their bags and swimming home.

A typical tanker of World War II vintage might carry 140,000 barrels of oil or gasoline. A torpedo or a collision in convoy could turn this cargo into a flaming inferno. The *C. J. Barkdull*, with a crew of fifty-eight merchant seamen and Armed Guard gunners, was lost with all hands when U-632 torpedoed her in the North Atlantic on 1 January 1943.

On 30 August 1944 off the coast of Ireland, Frank Hodges, a fireman-watertender on the new tanker *Jacksonville*, was having a cup of coffee in the mess room before going on watch when a torpedo struck the ship. He relates:

> I ran on deck and found the ship enveloped in flames and smoke. I tried to reach the boat deck but a wall of fire roared up in front of me. The only clear place was at the stern. In a few seconds the flames were coming at me there and the smoke was so thick I could hardly breathe. I jumped over the side and when I came to the surface there was fire around me on the water. I took a deep breath and swam underwater to a clear spot.
>
> Flames on the ship were shooting higher than the masts. I heard men screaming. There were some bodies floating around but they were all badly burned. I found a path of clear water and paddled to the windward side of the ship where it was clear. There were ten or twelve men in the mess room when we got hit. They all died.[1]

Hodges and a gunner, Marcellus R. Wegs, were picked up an hour or so later by a destroyer. They were the only survivors of a crew of fifty merchant seamen and Armed Guard gunners. The *Jacksonville* had been commanded by Captain Edgar Winter.[2]

Many more tankers met equally fiery destruction from torpedoes.

Collisions were another dreaded hazard for men of the tanker fleet. In March 1945, tanker *St. Mihiel* was making her maiden voyage with 140,000 barrels of gasoline for the Allied forces in Europe when she collided with the tanker *Nashbulk* in the North Atlantic. The *St. Mihiel* was soon enveloped by flames that trapped and killed twenty-seven of the crew and made it impossible to launch lifeboats or rafts. Fourteen men jumped overboard and were picked up by the USS *Edsal,* a destroyer escort. They all volunteered to reboard the ship after the flames had been extinguished and help to take her into port. The *Nashbulk* also made port.

Oil was also a lethal cargo, such as when the tanker *Virginia* was hit in May 1942 in the Gulf of Mexico. Flaming oil spilled out of the tanks onto the sea. Crewmen jumped overboard, only to be trapped in the flames. Ordinary seaman Mike Kuzma, although badly burned himself, towed two injured shipmates away from the flames and helped support them until they were picked up. Kuzma was awarded the Distinguished Service Medal of the Merchant Marine for his actions.

Men of the tanker fleet performed many deeds of heroism. Only a few are mentioned here.

The tanker *Dixie Arrow,* loaded deep with crude oil, was steaming from Texas City, Texas, toward Bayonne, New Jersey on the morning of 26 March 1942. She was hit amidships by three torpedoes fired in quick succession from an unseen submarine. The heroic self-sacrifice of one crewman helped to save many of his shipmates.[3]

Within seconds, the vessel was on fire and much of the sea around her was covered with flaming oil. Flames quickly destroyed all but one lifeboat and one raft. Eight men managed to get into the boat and seven onto the raft, which drifted into the fiery oil. Other men leaped off the tanker's bow. The heroism of helmsman Oscar Chappell made it possible for these men to clear the flames and survive.

Able seaman Paul Myers saw what happened:

> Chappell was at the wheel. Fire was shooting up all around the wheelhouse. He saw that the men on the bow would be caught by the flames because the wind was blowing the fire that way. He turned the ship hard right, which took the flames away from the bow, but onto the wheelhouse. He lasted only a few minutes. He died at the helm, saving his shipmates. Radio operator James Flynn stayed at his post in the forward deckhouse while the radio room was engulfed by fire.[4]

A Liberty ship was named *Oscar Chappell* to honor this hero of the tanker fleet.

Captain A. M. Johansen, First Mate William Scott, Second Mate George MacNamee, and Third Mate H. E. Dailey were also trapped in the deckhouse of the *Dixie Arrow* and killed in the flames.

The *Pan New York* was carrying high-octane aviation fuel when she was torpedoed about 650 miles west of Ireland on October 29, 1942. Only eighteen men out of a crew of sixty survived. Armed Guard Lt. William Herzog lost his life as he tried to free several of his men trapped in their quarters by the torpedo blast.

The Distinguished Service Medal of the Merchant Marine was awarded to galleyman Russell Wirtz of the tanker *Esso Baton Rouge* for heroism of a different kind.

When this ship was torpedoed on 23 February 1943 in the Eastern Atlantic, several crewman were severely burned. Two men, an Armed Guard gunner who had been blinded and burned over a third of his body and a merchant seaman who also had been blinded, were pushed overboard by Wirtz. He then sup-

The tanker Dixie Arrow *in flames off Cape Hatteras, North Carolina, March 1942. The wheelhouse, with helmsman Oscar Chappell, is engulfed in fire. (National Archives, 80-G-2183)*

ported them in the water until they were picked up by a British corvette.

The corvette already had on board more than two hundred survivors from other torpedoed ships, and her doctor was unable to care for all the wounded. Wirtz volunteered to help. He was assigned the care of nine patients. For nine days and nights, he administered sedatives and helped the doctor in delicate operations.

"By his unselfish devotion and untiring efforts," read a citation from the U.S. Maritime Commission, "he helped to save the lives of seven men. He is an inspiration to the men of the Merchant Marine."[5]

When a man escaped from a flaming tanker, he needed determination and stamina to survive. The tanker *W. D. Anderson* was steaming north fourteen miles off Stuart, Florida, on 22 February 1942. Frank Terry, a wiper and former lifeguard, was drinking coffee at the fantail and listening to shipmates tell about their favorite ports of call. He recalls:

> Suddenly, there was an explosion. I knew it must be a torpedo. There were flames almost instantly. They blocked the way to my boat station, so I ran to the side and jumped over. When I came to the surface and looked back the ship was a mass of flames and burning oil was pouring out of the tanks onto the sea. I swam away from the oil as hard as I could. I bumped into a man who was badly burned and I tried to swim with him, then I realized he was dead. The heat from the burning oil was intense. I took off my shirt and shoes and struck out again to the windward side of the ship. After an hour or so I got way clear of the flames and was able to tread water. Several times I almost gave up because I was so exhausted. After a while a fishing boat came by and picked me up.
>
> I didn't see any of my shipmates alive in the water. I think they were trapped aboard ship.[6]

Of the thirty-six men in the crew, Terry was the only survivor.

As the war years went by and ships became more adequately armed, the submarine attacking a tanker frequently got much more than she bargained for. The battle put up by the tanker *Yamhill* against a Japanese submarine is one such instance.[7]

During the *Yamhill*'s voyage to the South Pacific in 1944, a lookout on the early morning watch was amazed to see a torpedo streaking toward the ship on the port side. As soon as he yelled the alarm, the man at the wheel swung the helm hard over and the tin fish missed the stern by a few feet. The alarm was ringing by this time, as merchant seamen and navy gunners ran to battle stations.

While the guns were being manned, a second torpedo sped at the *Yamhill* but missed when the vessel was deftly maneuvered out of the way by a hard turn of the helm. Three more torpedoes were fired by the unseen submarine, and they all missed. Determined that her fat prize should not get away after this lavish waste of costly torpedoes, the submarine broke the surface close by on the starboard side. Her crew poured out of the conning tower and a deck hatch to man the gun on the raider's forward deck.

Even as the *Yamhill* turned sharply about to present her stern to the enemy, two shells from the submarine were near misses. The tanker's gunners answered the fire and saw their shell skip over the water just beyond the raider's deck, so close that it seemed to have cleared the submarine by little more than inches. The Japanese must have shivered from the breeze. The next shot was just short of the submarine. The gunners had her bracketed now, and another one would do it. Knowing that the tanker's gunners had the range, the Japanese deserted their gun and disappeared below. Before the *Yamhill*'s gun crew could get away another shot, water was foaming around the submarine's nose as she made a hurried plunge toward the bottom.

Stepping up her speed as much as possible, the *Yamhill* endeavored to leave the submarine behind. Less than an hour later, however, the raider was again seen on the surface at a distance of several miles. A brief, long-range gun duel then developed. The tankermen had a near miss, but the submarine did not dive this time. Apparently, her commander was exasperated at the turn of events and chagrined that neither torpedoes nor shells had even dented the big tanker. The submarine kept company with the *Yamhill*. Constantly changing course and position, out of respect for the tanker's gunners, she fired steadily at her rich, oil-laden prey.

According to the *Yamhill*'s Captain Phillip Shinn, the raider fired sixty shells and was answered by at least thirty from the elusive "victim" that proved so unexpectedly hard to handle.

The Japanese finally gave up, and the *Yamhill* proceeded to her destination.

The hardy old vessel eventually finished out the war. Subsequently, she was laid up after 594 voyages across the seven seas.

An empty tanker often could take several torpedo hits without sinking. These ships are subdivided into many compartments, or tanks, in order to carry several kinds of fuel at one time. Unless the tanks contain a residue of gas from a previous cargo, there is little danger of fire in an empty tanker.

The tanker *Kittaning,* for instance, was hit by three torpedoes en route to Aruba in July 1944, but she did not sink. After abandoning ship, the captain and several officers reboarded the ship, which was towed to Cristóbal, Canal Zone, and salvaged.

Dramatic tales of heroism and action abound in the wartime annals of the tanker fleet. Among the more unusual is the story of the tanker *Brilliant,* bound in convoy across the Atlantic to England in November 1942 with 92,000 barrels of oil and gasoline.[8]

Submarines had been tagging the convoy. Early in the morning of 18 November, a U-boat targeted the *Brilliant* and torpedoed her on the starboard side amidships. The explosion was followed by fire that shot out of the tanks to the top of the aft mast. Fortunately, the tin fish had missed the gasoline.

The British rescue ship *Bury* dashed up from her station astern of the convoy and picked up men from a lifeboat that had been hurriedly lowered away. The captain, several officers, merchant crewmen, and Armed Guard gunners were in the boat. This was the only lifeboat that had left the ship because cool heads had prevailed after the first few moments of excitement and fear of explosion.

Shortly after the torpedo hit, Junior Third Mate J. C. Cameron, lowest in rank of all the deck officers, was ordered by the captain to stock his boat with cigarettes and navigating instruments, including the sextant and code book. After accomplishing these chores, Cameron suddenly remembered his new cap with the bright gold braid—the rightful pride and joy of any young ship's officer—and ran down to his cabin to retrieve it.

By the time he got back to the bridge, the lifeboat was gone and the sight of the falls dangling empty overside gave him a moment of feeling lonely and deserted. But this sensation was quickly dissipated when he ran toward the other side of the deckhouse and collided with Lt. (jg) John Borum, the Armed Guard gunnery officer. Both had the wind knocked out of them momentarily. Then they began to laugh because the situation seemed so ludicrous.

"Well," Borum said to the junior third mate, "It looks like you're in command. I don't see the captain or the other mates. What do we do? Leave her? You give the orders now."

The thought of being in command of a ship with a gaping hole in her side and flames roaring above the deck almost overwhelmed Cameron. But Borum seemed as unperturbed as though he might be standing there waiting for a streetcar. His calm demeanor was reassuring.

"I don't think so," Cameron managed to say. "I don't think we should leave her, at least not yet." The submarine still might be nearby, waiting to finish off the ship.

Dashing into the wheelhouse, he shut off the general alarm that had been clanging its wild summons for several minutes and called the watch engineer on the engine room phone. Third Assistant Sheaver answered.

"Sure," he said calmly, "everything is OK down here. Who left that crazy cowbell ringing? Do you want to scare the hell out of us?"

Cameron didn't take time right then to explain that he was now master of the *Brilliant*. He just said, "I'll call you back," and went on deck to determine the condition of his new command. The first man he met was radio operator Paul Yhouse, who was running to the bridge deck to fix the antenna that had been smashed by the explosion. He stopped to help Cameron turn on the automatic fire control system.

Chief Engineer Mathew Gutherz, after putting on all the warm clothes he could find in the expectation of leaving the ship in a lifeboat, came on deck to see flames shooting higher than the masts and balls of fire vomiting from the pump room skylight. The heat was so intense that he had to dodge back inside the deckhouse. He couldn't tell what was happening forward, but he went immediately to check the donkey boiler, which would supply steam for the pumps in case the diesel engine had been put out of commission. He found the boiler intact and, stepping into the engine room grating, looked down on the men on watch below. It was evident that Third Assistant Sheaver, First Assistant Wallace, and oiler Jamojski had full charge of the situation. There was no panic.

"It looked like another fire drill," he said later. The sight was so reassuring that he took off some of his excess clothing.

All this had happened in the space of a few minutes, while Cameron was turning off the general alarm and realizing the full portent of these amazing developments. Here he was, a young mariner making his first trip as an officer, in full command of a big ship that was burning and likely to be torpedoed again. Submarines seldom let a tanker get away with just one torpedo.

Bos'n Magne Nelson and some of the crew, meanwhile, had climbed back on board after the boat they tried to launch had capsized. No one was drowned, and the nearest to being hurt was able seaman John Peters, who had been on his way to the bridge to do a trick at the wheel when the torpedo hit directly beneath him. He had been dazed by a hail of rivets and was bruised around the face.

"Captain" Cameron, radioman Yhouse, and some others turned to with every available fire extinguisher, but the steam-smothering lines operating from the engine room soon had the fire under control. When one of the escorting corvettes signaled them to abandon ship, they replied that everything was "hunky-dory." The corvette was insistent and told them again to leave the ship and her cargo of fuel. Again, "Captain" Cameron and his

197

friends signaled that the fire was out and they preferred to stay on board and try to bring the *Brilliant* into port.

By this time, the tanker had developed a heavy list and two boats were prepared for launching; however, she righted herself after a while. When the corvette came by again, this time with official permission from the convoy commodore for Cameron to stay with the ship and head for Newfoundland, the battered *Brilliant* was on an even keel. "Captain" Cameron waved to the corvette and swung his wobbly ship slowly toward the west. They were off, torpedoes or no torpedoes. The ship's junior third mate was suddenly aware of the terrific responsibility thrust upon him, especially when he considered that a submarine was probably not far off and waiting for the convoy escorts to leave so she could finish the job.

Perhaps even at this moment, the U-boat skipper was studying the gaping hole in the *Brilliant*'s side and planning to make it even bigger. Despite the likelihood of another torpedo blast and the chance that, with it, might go all possibility of rescue, all hands had voted to stay with their youthful skipper and try to bring ship and cargo to safe harbor. As the chief engineer put it: "We're with you as long as the old tub'll float."

Even in a slight sea, the *Brilliant* creaked and groaned. The crew could not run her at anywhere near top speed for fear the strain would be too much for the weakened hull and she would come apart.

The torpedo had ruined the pump room, so pumpman Karelis teamed up with Chief Steward Russell Wilson to stand bridge watches. The crew was now considerably shorthanded after the departure of the lifeboat and a dozen or more of the crew.

Guns were kept ready and manned every minute. The *Brilliant* was soon far astern of the convoy as she plodded her wary and lonely course westward. Every man on board fully expected at any moment to hear the general alarm go off and see the white streak of a torpedo tracking toward them from an unseen submarine.

Despite this uncertainty, both merchantmen and Armed Guard gunners went about their jobs quietly and calmly. Cameron never left the bridge. The chief engineer sat sleepless in his room as he listened to the grinding hull plates and wondered whether he should suggest slowing her down or trying to keep the 8 ½-knot speed that the corvette had ordered them to attempt. He felt that even 1 more knot from the engines would tear them apart.

From the bridge, the men watched the stern of the *Brilliant* swinging in and out like a burlesque dancer doing bumps and grinds.

Fortunately, the submarine that torpedoed them either had been scared off by the escorts or had used up her last torpedo and returned to France; there was no sight of a U-boat. The sea held calm and fair. After several days, they sighted a small Canadian schooner and signaled for assistance. The schooner's skipper boarded the *Brilliant* and piloted her into Musgravetown, Newfoundland. The anchor chain had hardly gone through the hawse pipes and the tanker come to rest in safe harbor before all hands hit the sack, worn out and exhausted.

The *Brilliant* sat at anchor in Musgravetown for six weeks before getting orders to continue on to Halifax, Nova Scotia, for repairs.

The U.S. Maritime Commission had received word of the feat accomplished by the *Brilliant*'s crew in saving their ship and its valuable cargo. Captain Frank Rusk, head of the commission's Merchant Marine awards section, selected "Captain" Cameron as a worthy recipient of the Distinguished Service Medal of the Merchant Marine. A telegram, dispatched to Halifax, asked Cameron to leave his ship for a few days and fly to Washington, where plans had been made to make the award in the presence of high-ranking Merchant Marine and U.S. Navy officials.

Cameron never received this important message and never knew of the high honor bestowed on him for exceptional resolution, courage, and seamanship. Just a few hours before the telegram reached Halifax, the *Brilliant* had steamed out to sea, en route to New York, with a temporary patch covering the sixty-foot slash in her hull.

Fair weather had been predicted for at least twenty-four hours, but almost at once the weather changed for the worse, as it often does in that part of the world. Winds increased in force, and heavy seas built up. Changing winds, blowing now from one direction and then from another, created a mass of confused seas, the worst possible condition for a crippled vessel.

The tanker swayed so violently that the steering mechanism, which ran from the bridge to the steering engine room in the stern, snapped off. The emergency hand steering gear on the poop deck was hurriedly rigged and manned.

Captain Andrew Logan, who had taken over command of the vessel before it left Halifax, ordered all hands to don life jackets and the rubber cold-weather immersion suits carried by ships crossing the North Atlantic in winter. He realized that their situation was fast becoming desperate. The ship had become unmanageable, and it was impossible to steer her. The *Brilliant* soon began to break up with a loud grinding and tearing of steel hull and deck plates. As the men tried to lower the boats, the weakened hull collapsed with a crack like a cannon shot and the *Brilliant* broke completely in two.

The bow section and all the men on the bridge deck of the bow were soon lost to sight. The driving snow obscured them from those on the stern section, on which were thirty-one merchant seamen and Armed Guard gunners. The bow probably sank soon afterward, and all on it were lost—Captain Logan; Third Mate Cameron; First Mate Thomas Hickey, who had also joined the ship in Canada; radioman Yhouse, Lieutenant Borum; and seven more members of the merchant crew and Armed Guard.

Luck was with those riding in the derelict stern. They drifted for five days and were finally taken off by the Canadian minesweeper *Guderich* and the tug *Frijky*.

Cameron and the men of the *Brilliant,* said the Maritime Commission, had "lived up to the finest traditions of the American Merchant Marine."

The bombers would have been grounded, the tanks immobilized, and the factories starved for power without the tanker fleet. It was vital for keeping Britain in the war and, just as important, for fueling the great American war machine—the ships, planes and island-hopping armies—that moved relentlessly across the Pacific from Pearl Harbor to Tokyo.

In commending the tankermen for delivering the vital oil and gasoline to Pacific bases, Fleet Admiral Chester Nimitz had this to say:

> Our requirements were numbered in the millions of barrels of fuel to be transported thousands of miles to the scene of fleet operations. Our success in keeping the fleet properly fueled was dependent upon the delivery by these commercial ships. Not once did they fail.[9]

17
War in the Narrow Sea

THE WAR AT SEA had no theater of operations more hazardous to ships and men than the Mediterranean, the "narrow sea" where German and Italian air bases were within short flying distance from convoy routes and supply bases in North Africa. Bombers could attack a convoy anytime after it passed Gibralter and headed east. There was no way to deceive the enemy about a convoy's route; there was only one path—the shortest distance between two points. The Mediterranean was too small for alternate routes to a destination. Planes could attack, return to base, reload and refuel, and attack again before a convoy had traveled far.

The confined waters of the narrow sea were not as favorable for submarine operations as were the widespread waters of the Atlantic because submarines here were more vulnerable. German and Italian submarines were always a threat, however, and they exacted a heavy toll of merchant ships and their escorts while paying a great price themselves. Motor torpedo boats and Italian frogmen also sank some ships and damaged others. Especially

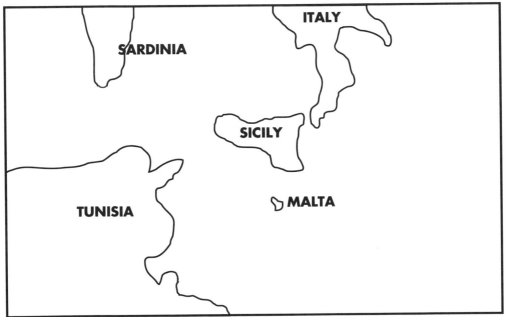

Map 2. The strategic location of Malta made it a British fortress in the Mediterranean: an air and submarine base threatening Axis supply routes to North Africa.

deadly were the mines, for thousands of them were planted by aircraft, submarines, and surface minelayers.

Probably few men who sailed this sea were history-minded, and those who were had more to think about than ancient battles and the ebb and flow of seaborne conquest on Mare Nostrum. As their ships cleared Gibralter and steamed to the east, they were traveling waters coursed by centuries of warriors and traders: great Roman triremes and slave-powered Algerian corsairs; Viking adventurers on the quest for trade and plunder; and fifteenth-century Venetian cargo galleys, outward bound on the long and dangerous voyage to England and Flanders, with holds full of glass and pottery, Greek currants, perfumes, spices, silks, and copperware. Few, if any, sailors in World War II convoys would know that the idea of protecting vulnerable merchant ships with escorting ships of war—of freighters sailing in convoy— had originated in Mare Nostrum hundreds of years ago.

Before the invasions of North Africa and Italy brought American freighters to the Mediterranean by the hundreds, a number of vessels flying the Stars and Stripes had undergone a baptism of fire in the fiercely contested reaches of the narrow sea.

In April 1942, German bombers delivered 4,082 day attacks and 256 night attacks on the island of Malta, the vital British bastion lying athwart Africa and Sicily and commanding passages east and west. It had become the most bombed spot on earth.

Reaching the island was only part of the challenge for ships with relief cargoes; staying there without being hit or sunk was equally challenging.

The hazards of the Malta run were evident in this report by Captain R. E. Barrera of the American Liberty ship *O'Henry*:

> 5 March 1942: A stick of four bombs hit the water close to a Dutch tanker right behind us. All our guns firing. No lack of targets. Next, a stick of bombs fell between us and the convoy commodore abeam of us.

The next attack was aimed directly at the *O'Henry*. As the bomber began his dive the aft 20-mm guns went into action and when the plane was about 2000 feet from the ship the two 20-millimeters on the bow joined in. The plane's starboard motor burst into flames. For a few moments it looked as though he was to crash into us. Our guns continued to pour shells into him. As he swooped over us, mast high, his plane began to come apart. He crashed into the sea just ahead of the ship.[1]

The value of ample guns and a well-trained gun crew was proved several more times in this battle when the ship's barrage of fire kept planes away or made them drop their bombs prematurely. Even so, a bomber dived through the defensive barrage and planted a bomb fifty feet off the port bow that sprayed the ship with shrapnel. During twenty-two minutes of action, the *O'Henry*'s gunners fired 2,118 rounds of 20-millimeter shells and 264 rounds from the shorter-range 30-caliber machine guns.

The hard-pressed defenders of Malta and the island's citizens lined the harbor front of Valletta when the ships came in. Captain Barrera wrote: "The cheers and the shouts of joy made us feel as though our effort had been all worth while."[2]

The American freighter *Chant* and the tanker *Kentucky* were part of Operation Harpoon in June 1942, in one of the Allies' desperate attempts to supply Malta. On June 14, this convoy, which included six heavily laden merchant ships, was attacked by no less than twenty-eight torpedo planes and ten high-level bombers flying from Sardinia. The Dutch freighter *Tanimbar*, with an American gun crew, was sunk and the British cruiser *Liverpool* badly damaged, both by torpedoes. Later the same day, the enemy attacked again with German JU-88 bombers based in Sicily. British naval historian Donald MacIntyre described this assault as "a wild, thunderous scene of diving planes, bursting bombs and a storm of gunfire."

The American ships survived this melee, but the *Chant* was hit and sunk by Stuka dive bombers the next day. The *Kentucky* was so badly damaged by bomb hits and near misses that she couldn't keep up with the convoy. She was a prime target for the next attack; without any tugs or other craft to take her in tow, she had to be sunk.

From then on, Operation Harpoon became a classic battle in which outgunned destroyers, with water screaming from their bows and smoke pouring from their stacks, dashed into battle against Italian cruisers that had arrived to destroy what was left of the convoy. Heroic action by these dauntless escorts helped two freighters to finally reach Malta with 15,000 tons of vital food, fuel, and ammunition. Two destroyers were sunk, and many men lost their lives in the attempt to get the cargoes through. This operation helped to make the story of the Malta run one of the most thrilling and heroic sagas of the war.

Malta was blasted day and night. With its defenders, as well as the local population, in dire need of fuel, food, bombs, ammunition, and other supplies, another massive effort was made to supply the island fortress in August 1942. The British government was determined that what Winston Churchill called "our unsinkable aircraft carrier" must hold out at all costs. Its strategic position in the narrow corridor between Sicily and North Africa made it the key to naval supremacy in the narrow sea.

Under the code name Operation Pedestal, a powerful fleet of battleships, aircraft carriers, destroyers, and auxiliaries was assembled to help fourteen merchant ships run the Axis blockade with vital supplies. The Merchant ships included the American freighters *Santa Elisa* and *Almeria Lykes* and the American tanker *Ohio,* manned by a British crew.

Most of the major escorting warships could not be risked beyond Cape Bon, on the North African coast less than one hundred miles southwest of Sicily, because they would be too close to Axis air bases. After they returned to Gibralter, the rest of the fleet suffered three days of unremitting assault from high- and

Battle action! This dramatic wartime painting by Lt. Carl Ruggiero of the U.S. Maritime Service shows a convoy, with a Liberty ship in the foreground, under air attack in the Mediterranean. The men on the raft narrowly missed being strafed by a plane. (U.S. Maritime Administration, 5303)

low-level bombers and torpedo planes, as well as from submarines and torpedo boats darting out from the African shore. Naval losses were heavy in ships and men. The carrier *Eagle* was sunk, and the carriers *Victorious* and *Indomitable* badly damaged. Many carrier planes were lost. The *Santa Elisa* and *Almeria Lykes* fought their guns gallantly, but both were sunk by bombs. Only five of the fourteen merchant ships reached Malta to deliver 32,000 tons of cargo.

In November 1942, a supply run to Malta from Port Said, Egypt, called Operation Stoneage included the American freighters *Robin Locksley* and *Mormacmoon*, along with one Dutch and one British ship, plus escorting warships. Fortunately, this convoy had fighter protection from airfields in North Africa, and

British fighters beat off one attack by JU-88s. The British light cruiser *Arethusa* was hit during a subsequent attack by torpedo planes, with the loss of 155 men. In an inspiring example of seamanship and bulldog determination, she was towed, stern first against heavy winds and sea, to Alexandria, Egypt, for repairs so that she could fight again. The *Robin Locksley* and *Mormacmoon* reached Malta, but during the seventeen days it took to unload cargo and wait for a return convoy, they underwent many air raids and near misses from bombs. The ships made a safe return to Port Said.

Stationary and floating mines presented additional hazards to the merchant fleet in the Mediterranean. On 1 January 1943, the *Arthur Middleton* was en route from New York to Oran with ammunition and hundreds of sacks of Christmas mail. She was three miles from her port of destination when the ship was blown apart by a violent explosion. The eleven-ship convoy was just getting into position to split up and enter the harbor in line. The weather was clear and the sea smooth. The escorts had no indication of a submarine. The *Samuel Chase* was on the *Middleton*'s starboard quarter, the *Bret Harte* off her port bow, and the *George Weems* following close astern.

An observer on the *Samuel Chase* said, "There was a sudden roar on the *Middleton*. An explosion sent water, steel plate and a myriad pieces of the ship flying hundreds of feet into the air. There was a great cloud of gray smoke and when it blew away there wasn't a piece of ship to be seen."

Everyone on the *Middleton* was lost except for three Armed Guard sailors who jumped overboard at the stern. They found a doughnut raft and clung to it until they were picked up and taken to the hospital ship *Oxfordshire*.

The consensus was that the *Middleton* had struck a mine. A French minesweeper had been blown up in the area just a few hours before the *Middleton* exploded.

The *Francis Drake*, under Captain Savillon Chapman, was one of several American Libertys chartered to the British Ministry of War Transport to carry gasoline in drums, ammunition, and other supplies from Alexandria to Tripoli, Libya. On each return trip, she transported hundreds of German and Italian prisoners. At Tripoli, the retreating Germans and Italians had scuttled ships to block the entrance to the harbor. Although the British had blown up the wrecks, every ship that entered the port scraped and ground over the shattered hulls. The *Drake* spent five months on shuttle runs between Egypt and Tripoli and survived numerous air attacks without major damage.

The Liberty ship *Samuel Parker* was also chartered by the British for the "milk run" between Egypt and Tripoli. Her master, Captain E. J. Stull, not only had a keen eye for exciting events but a way with words in describing them.

He recounted a voyage in convoy to Tripoli in 1943 with tanks, bombs, gasoline, and British troops:

> Dusk, March 15, low overcast. We hear a rumble of bombers from upstairs. Half of gun crews ordered to stand by the guns. The rumble died away. Some of our planes on the way to unload on Italy, I thought. Several minutes later three huge black bats swooped out of the low clouds to mast high. They were as big as ships—or so it appeared—like hawks diving on chickens. They had shut off their motors and swooped down on us in a surprise attack with torpedoes. The destroyer near us opened up with a swarm of bright red tracers. We soon joined in. One bomber got in the fire of a Greek destroyer and went in with a big splash. The other bombers zoomed up to cloud cover in a rain of shells. In those few seconds we had nine guns going. Then our air escort came streaking in from across the horizon dropping identification flares. Other bombers we hadn't seen joined the party. Bombs were dropping all around and the sky was full of tracers going in all directions. Our escorts spread smoke screens and we made emergency turns. After several minutes we

stopped firing to listen. All was quiet—like nothing had ever happened.

Ten minutes passed. Then a rumble of planes from another direction, with cloud cover. A high level bombing attack this time. All the ships opened up with everything on the menu. It was soon dark with a half moon. After shooting the clouds full of holes we stopped again to listen. No sounds. Half an hour passed. Then we heard that rumbling sound again. A wide, low cloud was drifting over us. From beyond it came a sudden, terrific roar like roaring of express trains, zooming down a celestial track. They were coming in low. The guns barked, snarled, and spat streaking hot metal into the sky. Red bullets from near-by ships streaked through our rigging. They were more dangerous than the bombs. We learned later that the convoy shot down four bombers.[3]

There was no rest in Tripoli. On the night of 16 March, thirty bombers raided the port. A hundred guns opened fire.

"There was a 4th of July–like luminous lacing of red tracers, with searchlights fingering the sky. The whole port was like a forge in hell going full blast," Stull said.

On 19 March, there was another surprise attack. A bomber just missed hitting a mast on the *Parker* and crashed into the British freighter *Ocean Voyager* berthed nearby. The freighter, as Stull described it, "became a roaring mass of flames, with drums of gasoline exploding like Roman candles."

The *William Coleman*, tied up next to the *Parker*, slipped her lines and steamed seaward to escape the conflagration. The *Parker* launched a lifeboat and rescued men who had jumped overboard from the *Ocean Voyager*.

"At exactly midnight," Stull said, "the harbor was shaken by a blast that would have put a volcano to shame. A wall of water and mud hit us and flying steel rained down on us. The *Ocean Voyager* had exploded."

During many months of duty in the Mediterranean, the battle-scarred *Parker* became known to her crew as the "Fightin' Sam." She later joined a select company of freighters honored as "Gallant Ships of the Merchant Marine."

On 8 November 1942, a massive Allied invasion force, operating in great secrecy and with almost perfect coordination, bombarded Vichy French defenses and landed troops on the Mediterranean coast at Oran and Algiers, Algeria; Casablanca, Morocco; and adjoining strongholds on the Atlantic coast. For the next six months, Field Marshal Erwin Rommel's Afrika Corps put up a stiff fight, but British, American, and Free French armies kept attacking and pushing the Germans and Italians into an ever-shrinking perimeter in northeastern Tunisia. All resistance ended on 13 May, and the entire coastline of North Africa, with its valuable ports, was now in Allied hands.

One of the unheralded achievements of the African invasion occurred after the capture of Oran, when twenty-five wrecks, including two dry docks, were raised and removed in less than three months' time. Oran then became the major port receiving U.S. war supplies for the African campaign. Bône (Annaba), Algeria, and Algiers were important later for staging and supplying the invasions of Sicily and Italy.

With North Africa in Allied control, plans could now proceed for these invasions, the Allies' first strike against Europe. Merchant ships, mostly American Libertys, were in the forefront of the invasions and later delivered the follow-up cargoes of ammunition, gasoline, food, trucks, tanks, guns, and the many other materials of war, including beer and cigarettes.

Sicily was the first target, with American forces invading on the west and British forces on the east. Most of the troops and supplies for the eastern force were ferried from Egypt by American merchant ships. D-day for the Sicilian campaign was 10 July 1943.

As the *Jonathan Grout*, carrying British troops and their equipment, steamed toward Avola, the invasion beach reminded those on board of travel folders advertising pleasure cruises to the Mediterranean: calm seas, soft breezes, and blue skies.

On the gun platform at the stern, the author talked with one of the Armed Guard gunners, who was patting the long, thick barrel of "Our Minnie," the five-inch gun that had come from the secondary battery of an old battleship. "Hell," he said, disgustedly, "ain't this somethin'. I've been waitin' to do some shootin' with Minnie for six months and now look what happens. The first big show we get in and the enemy gives up without a fight."[4]

An English corporal of infantry, who had been fighting the Germans and the Italians for two years in North Africa, shook his head. "This is too good to be true," he said. "This isn't like Jerry at all. Too bloody peaceful."

A few minutes later, HMS *Frebus*, a stubby monitor with twelve-inch guns, steamed close by and let go a booming salvo toward the beach. The shells kicked up dirt and dust in the hills along the shore. A cruiser and two destroyers moved in toward the beach farther up the coast and joined their throaty voices to that of the *Frebus* in silencing stubborn defense batteries.

As she moved shoreward, the *Grout* passed pieces of airplane fuselage and whole wing sections floating on the water. A tug had tied onto the tail of a half-submerged glider and was pulling it ashore.

"What do they want that junk for?" the gunner asked.

"It ain't junk," someone told him. "They want what's inside. There's bodies inside. That plane must have crashed."

Bodies soon could be seen floating in the water. Many planes had been shot down when "friendly" guns had opened up on the incoming paratroopers during the night in confusion over recognition signals. This was one of several "snafus" during the Italian campaign when Allied paratroops were shot down by their own forces.[5]

Even before the *Jonathan Grout* arrived at her designated anchorage and the chain clattered through the hawse pipes, British civilian stevedores on board had the booms rigged and

212

were lifting barges off their cradles on the foredeck. Within an hour, the barges were chugging ashore with tanks, trucks, gasoline, guns, and ammunition. Several large troopships soon came to anchor and debarked thousands of assault troops in landing craft.

The Germans were not long in responding. Stuka dive-bombers, with sirens in their noses that were intended to unnerve the gunners below, attacked but were driven off by intense fire from merchant ships and warships.

During the next five days, the invasion fleet underwent day and night attacks. On the afternoon of 11 July, three flights of high-level bombers swept over the anchorage and released bombs that shimmered like pieces of tinfoil in the bright blue sky.

A navy gunner on the Liberty ship *Colin Kelly* said, "The stark terror of watching them come down at you is indescribable."

After the raid was over, cooks on the *Jonathan Grout* salvaged big fish that had been killed by the bomb concussions and prepared an "air raid fish fry."

The Dutch ship *Bairn*, anchored just abeam the *Grout*, was damaged by close bomb bursts and went to the bottom.

On the *Colin Kelly*, as on the other ships, the Armed Guard, commanded by Lt. (jg) Vernon D. Ogren, slept and ate at the guns until the cargo was discharged and the ship departed. The *Colin Kelly* carried gasoline in drums, trucks, ammunition, and other equipment loaded in Haifa, Palestine, in addition to 260 British troops who had boarded in Alexandria.

In recollecting those eventful days, Third Mate S. G. Wonson described one of the many raids:

I was on anchor watch at 1310 when planes pounced on the anchorage through a gap in the hills. Two of them headed right for us. The heavy fire from our Oerlikons changed their minds and they dropped their bombs without hitting anything. It made us realize we had to be on the lookout all the time. The next

213

day our 3-inch 50 got off several shots at three low level bombers headed our way. A shell burst in front of the leading plane and it plunged into the sea. Our gunners yelled and shouted. Of course, other ships were firing, too.[6]

On the morning of 13 July, the Liberty ship *Timothy Pickering*, anchored off Avola, was discharging cargo and troops. Suddenly, without any warning of an air raid, two planes popped over the nearby mountain and roared down on the anchorage. Before the ship's gunners could go into action, the attackers planted bombs in number four hold, packed with ammunition.

"There was a tremendous roar," said an observer on a ship nearby. "Then a vast mushroom of smoke with huge tongues of red flames. Great gobs of liquid fire erupted from the ship high into the sky to a height of a thousand feet or more. The ship was destroyed and the attackers escaped."

More than 140 British troops, waiting to disembark, and 30 of the merchant crew and Armed Guard were killed. Those who survived were either blown overboard or were on the foredeck when the bombs hit.

One of the most spectacular action photos to come out of the war shows the Liberty ship *Robert Rowan* exploding in a violent eruption of fire, smoke, and bursting shells. The *Rowan* was part of the invasion fleet in the American sector on the West Coast of Sicily. Some thirty JU-88s attacked the anchorage at Gela, where the *Rowan* was unloading on the 11 July. She was bombed and caught fire. Fortunately, the ship was ordered abandoned before the ammunition exploded, or the death toll would have been high there, too.

The Liberty ship *Benjamin Contee*, bound for Oran, had just left Bône with two other merchant ships and two escorts on 16 August 1943. Besides her merchant crew and Armed Guard, the *Contee* carried eighteen hundred Italian prisoners of war and twenty-six British guards. The sky was clear, a full moon, and the sea was calm. Suddenly, torpedo planes, gliding in unseen and

214

The Liberty ship Robert Rowan *explodes after being bombed during the invasion of Sicily at Gela, July 1943. (National Archives, RG 357-G-230)*

unheard, with their engines off, jumped the convoy.

A torpedo exploded in one of the prisoners' quarters at numbers one and two holds and killed hundreds. Panic broke out among the prisoners, who overran the guards and took over the lifeboats. While they were trying to lower the boats, two Italian-Americans in the merchant crew ran among the mob and shouted, "The ship isn't going to sink . . . the ship won't sink . . . wait for life preservers."

This calmed the panic, and the prisoners formed up in lines to receive life preservers. The *Contee* stayed afloat and returned to Bône under her own power.

On both coasts, Liberty ships were used as assault transports, which put them on the front lines of action. A fleet of thirty freighters, mostly Libertys, were in the assault force on the east.[7]

After Sicily was secured, the next amphibious operation was directed at the Italian mainland, with the port of Salerno as the prime objective. Cargo ships, again mostly Libertys, supported the landings with vehicles, troops, fuel, food, and ammunition.

The *Hugh Williamson* arrived in the Gulf of Salerno on 11 September and was under frequent air attack until leaving on the 17th. Because she was fitted to carry a large number of troops, the *Williamson* also carried a larger gun crew, with twenty-eight men and three officers under Lt. R. H. McIlwaine.

Action began even before the ship arrived at her designated anchorage. The Armed Guard report reads:

> 11 Sept. . . . air attack at 0942 upon entering the Gulf of Salerno. All guns in action. No planes got close enough to bomb us. Second attack at 1715. Three planes. One bomb fell about fifty feet off our port beam. Our tracers bore right into him and he crashed on the beach.
>
> 12 Sept. . . . A British cargo ship near us was bombed and caught fire. USS *Biscayne* came by and asked for a party to help fight the fire. Sent S1cl Earl Snyder and several men.
>
> At 1400 attacked by five planes. Two headed for us. Opened fire with all guns. Our 20-millimeters poured shells into one that caught fire and crashed into the sea.
>
> At 1715 attacked by six planes. Three of them singled us out for a target and all our 20-millimeters opened up. The planes banked away from our barrage and dropped their bombs well clear of the ship.
>
> 14 Sept. . . . Anchorage attacked by five planes. One plane hit and became a ball of fire, plummeting into the sea astern of us. We did some good shooting.[8]

Gunners on the *John Howard Payne* claimed to have shot down two planes at Salerno. One entry in the voyage report states:

> 15 Sept. . . . 1825 . . . low level raid by eight planes. Several bombs fell nearby. Our 3-inch 50 made a direct hit on one of them and blew it to pieces.
>
> 16 Sept. . . . low level raid by ten planes. Our 20-millimeters put up a wall of fire. One plane headed right at us but caught our fire and crashed into the sea about one hundred yards astern.[9]

Quite often, the gunners on several ships shared in a kill. Evading the fire of one ship, a plane would fly into the fire from another. Ships also zeroed in on the same plane, so that a "team" effort accounted for many attackers, although it might seem to the gunners on one ship that they deserved credit for the kill.

The Liberty ship *Bushrod Washington* was carrying a typical—and highly lethal—invasion cargo when she arrived in the Gulf of Salerno on 11 September. Holds were packed with 105-milli-meter ammunition, hundreds of 500-pound bombs, and 7,000 five-gallon cans of aviation gasoline. On deck were army trucks and landing craft. The *Washington* was commanded by Captain Jonathan Wainwright IV, whose father had commanded American troops before their capture by the Japanese on Bataan in the Philippines.

Air attacks began soon after the ship dropped anchor and continued for three days, but the planes were beaten off by the gun crews. On 14 September, however, a plane, unseen against the glare of the sun, launched a glider bomb that hit on the boat deck, went down through the crew's mess room on the main deck, and exploded just above the engine spaces. The explosion blew a big hole in the ship's side and ignited gasoline in number four hold. The vessel soon caught on fire and was a total loss.

The *James W. Marshall* also arrived at a Salerno anchorage on 11 September. Four days later, she was the target for another glider bomb. It smashed through the bridge deck and then penetrated two decks below into the crew's mess room, where it exploded and killed thirteen men. The blast also killed and wounded soldiers who were working cargo.

The entire midships was soon a mass of flames, and the ship was abandoned. The fire was later extinguished, and a group of seamen led by Captain Wainwright volunteered to take over the *Marshall* and try to get her to a port for repairs.

First, however, came the task of discharging the rest of her cargo. The volunteers had to repair winches and cargo booms; pump out the engine room, which was under several feet of oily water; and get up steam for the winches and dynamos. Bodies of dead crewmen and soldiers were located and taken ashore for burial.

Always aware that the vessel might be bombed again, Wainwright and his men labored for nine days to repair the damage and off-load the ammunition. When the holds were finally empty, the *Marshall,* under Wainwright's command, was towed by another Liberty ship to Bizerte, Tunisia, for temporary repairs. Under command of Alfred Adams, a British captain, and with a volunteer crew, the ship then made a hazardous voyage to England for further repairs. The *Marshall* ended her career as a blockship on the Normandy beachhead.

Wainwright was awarded the Distinguished Service Medal of the Merchant Marine.

When the Italian campaign bogged down against stiff German resistance, the Allied command decided on a leapfrog operation with an invasion at Anzio, one hundred miles up the west coast, just south of Rome. This turned out to be a bloody and costly misadventure, and its conception and leadership have been debated ever since. For all hands involved, the operation became known as "bloody Anzio." For the merchant ships supporting the invasion, it was another Salerno.

The following is part of the voyage report for the Liberty ship *John Banvard,* which arrived at the anchorage on 22 January 1944:

22 Jan—1055; low level attack by eight ME 109s.
1250: low level attack by ten ME 109s.
23 Jan—1055; attack by 12 ME fighter-bombers;
1555, another attack by ten bombers.[10]

This was an especially violent attack by several groups of fighter-bombers. The first wave of fifteen came over just before dusk. The second group of forty-three, attacking in several waves, followed soon after. The assault was topped off by fifty-three planes in several waves. A 550-pound bomb hit the destroyer *Plunkett* and killed fifty-three men. The bombers also attacked three brightly lit hospital ships, as they had at Syracuse in Sicily, and sank the hospital ship *St. David.*

On 25 January, dive-bombers and low-level bombers again attacked the anchorage. On the 26th, the gun crews shot down a bomber during a raid in which thirty planes attacked the anchorage. A bomb hit the water ten yards from the *Banvard* and exploded. It shook the vessel and caused much damage. The voyage report continues:

29th: attack with glider bombs at dusk by about twenty twin engine bombers. British cruiser *Spartan* hit and capsized nearby. The Liberty ship *Samuel Huntington,* anchored off our starboard bow, hit by a glider bomb.

30 Jan 0340 hours. The *Huntington,* which had been burning most of the night, finally blew up. Shrapnel showered our ship.[11]

In a night attack, on 26 January, two glider bombs exploded close by the *Banvard* and all of her steam lines were broken. With the possibility of the boilers exploding, Captain John Lind ordered the ship abandoned. The crew later returned and got the vessel in operation.

According to the Armed Guard commander, Lt. (jg) Donald Peters, the *Banvard* went to general quarters for seventy-two alerts and twenty-five actual raids. "Our men lived at the guns,"

219

he said. "Shrapnel and shell fragments were a constant hazard during the raids, with so many ships around us all firing."[12]

The *Huntington* was at anchor a quarter of a mile off the beach when she was attacked with a glider bomb that exploded in the engine room. Although there were more than one hundred men on board at the time, there were only four fatalities.

Shelling from long-range shore guns and tanks was also a hazard for the ships at Anzio. The *Lawton B. Evans* was carrying ammunition and gasoline when she dropped anchor at "Peter Beach" on 22 January. The Germans welcomed her with shells exploding within fifty feet on the port side that holed the lifeboats with shrapnel and peppered the hull.

Deciding that this was definitely too close for comfort, Captain Harry Ryan shifted to another anchorage. The German guns followed, and the *Evans* had more near misses. When the ship went to a third anchorage, the shore guns shifted to other targets.

On 23 and 24 January, there were air attacks and more shelling, but the Germans did not get as close this time.

The Armed Guard report for 29 January reads:

> Bombers attacked with radio-controlled glider bombs that hit two Liberty ships and a cruiser. Shot down a dive bomber, which crashed on the beach. Shot down a glider bomb headed our way and another dive bomber which left us a souvenir. Its carburetor fell on the deck.[13]

For eleven days, Captain Ryan slept, when he could, in a chair on the bridge.

"I consumed an endless supply of coffee," he said later. "The bombs and the shells helped to keep me awake, too."[14]

The Armed Guard, assisted by the ship's crew, claimed five kills while expending 4,680 rounds of 20-millimeter shells and 80 rounds from the three-inch/50.

A German long-range gun planted three shells uncomfortably close to the Liberty ship *Hilary Herbert,* and her Armed Guard crew claimed credit for three kills during twenty-nine air raids.

One of these planes crashed into the starboard side of the ship just forward of the bridge.

Another target of the guided bomb was the Liberty ship *Elihu Yale*, hit on 15 February.

In his voyage report, Lt. (jg) Roger P. Wise stated:

> Two men on the after gun platform saw the bomb just before it hit. They heard a loud "swish"— like a gust of wind, then there was an explosion on the port side of number four hatch. Gunners and the gun tubs in that area were blown into the air. Fire broke out in the midships deckhouse and on an LCT alongside loading ammunition.[15]

Fortunately, neither the *Hilary* nor the *Yale* exploded, but both ships were total losses.

Action at the beachheads was only part of the sea war in the Mediterranean during 1943 and 1944. As long as the Germans had enough aircraft, they continued to challenge the convoys fighting their way to the beachheads and supply bases in North Africa.

The Liberty ship *Ann Bradstreet* was one of twelve merchant ships bound from Gibralter for Bizerte on 13 August 1943, when thirty-five Heinkel torpedo planes, followed by low-level JU-88s, launched a sunset attack. The *Bradstreet's* three-inch/50 bow gun opened fire first, followed by the 20-millimeters, as the planes came within range. A shell from the bow gun blew a Heinkel to pieces when it roared in on the port side to jockey into position for a torpedo drop. Within the next few minutes, there were targets for every gun on the ship. Gunners on the merchant ships and escorts splashed seven planes in this attack.

According to Captain Saamund Saamundsen, "It seemed as though the sea was full of torpedoes—like a school of porpoise. They came at us from all over. They missed us fore and aft, but not by much."[16]

Armed Guard commander John Gasnell reported:

A convoy of Liberty ships has terrific fire power. Every gun in the fleet was firing, but the German pilots didn't hesitate. They flew into a storm of steel. We filled the air with shells. One plane roared down on us in a shrill, terrifying scream. It looked like it was going to crash right onto us. At about two hundred feet the pilot pulled up, not much more than mast high. It seemed like we could reach up and touch the plane. Our guns poured shells into it. The pilot tried to get away but he wobbled, dipped a wing into the water, and crashed.[17]

Chief Steward Ralph Byers had a rather poetic recollection of the fight:

It was frightening, but it was fascinating. The planes came at us silhouetted against the setting sun— like a pack of greyhounds clearing the hurdle. They must have known that death was ahead of them, but they came on, boring right into us.[18]

The *William T. Barry* was in the same convoy. Ens. George C. Robbins, the Armed Guard officer, stated:

Our 20-millimeter on the port side of the bridge got a direct hit. The plane crashed in flames alongside of us as we steamed by. Our 3-inch 50 caught another one as it banked over the ship ahead of us. A wing came off and the plane nosed into the water and sank.[19]

Robbins received a Letter of Commendation from the U.S. Navy for the training and skill of his gunners.

"I would like to commend the merchant crew," Robbins said in his voyage report, "for their speed and willingness to assist at the guns and to help in passing ammunition."

O. P. Stender, captain of the *Barry,* also remembered this attack in a somewhat poetic way:

> The planes appeared on the horizon in front of
> the convoy. They came directly out of the sun. At first
> they appeared like so many blackbirds skimming over
> the water, their wings seeming to touch the waves.[20]

In a later voyage from Oran to Naples, Italy, in March 1944,
the *Barry* saw more action. Armed Guard Lt. James B. Ragland
was sure his gunners splashed at least two attackers. One plane
received several bursts from the three-inch / 50 gun and "was
blown to pieces," he said.[21] The *Barry* was more heavily armed
than most Libertys, with a pair of three-inch / 50s on the stern and
a gun crew of twenty-five.

The torpedoing of the Liberty ship *Paul Hamilton* in a torpedo plane attack on 20 April 1944 was a great tragedy. Besides
carrying a dangerous cargo of high explosives, the ship was a
troop transport. There were 498 men on board, including the
merchant crew and the Armed Guard.

Gunners on the nearby British tanker *Athelchief* fired at a
torpedo plane. Moments later, the plane launched its weapon at
the *Paul Hamilton*. Within seconds, according to the captain of the
Athelchief: "There was a tremendous explosion. Pieces of the Liberty ship were flung through the air in all directions. The ship
disappeared in a thick cloud of black smoke."[22]

Every man on the floating powder keg was lost.

An unexpected and unique job of salvage befell the Liberty
ship *William Meredith* after she discharged her cargo at Alexandria in April 1944. Captain L. G. Greene was directed to take
his ship and fifty British troops, in company with HMS *Captine*, to
the Gulf of Bomba, where the Liberty ship *Thomas G. Masaryk* had
sunk in shallow water after a fire that lasted for several days.
Earlier that month, the *Masaryk* and the *Meyer London*, together
with the *Meredith* and other ships, had been in a convoy attacked
by torpedo bombers off Algiers. The *Masaryk* and the *London*
were both hit.

Greene found a forbidding challenge when he anchored his
ship alongside the *Masaryk* and went on board to inspect her. The

entire midships and some of the cargo spaces had been gutted by fire. All of the steam lines on deck had been broken by the intense heat, so winches and booms could not be used.

The ship had been carrying much-needed valuable fighter planes, P-47s and P-39s. Amazingly, the salvagers found some of these planes untouched by the flames. In addition, they also recovered about 2,500 tons of vehicles, tires, guns, and canned meat intended for the Soviet Army. They were surprised to find a large amount of men's and women's clothing.

The crew of the *Meredith* were helped by Captain Sloane of the *Masaryk* and some of his crew. Operations were conducted in an area only 130 miles from Crete. The salvagers had the protection of British Spitfires, and a temporary radar post was set up on shore to provide warning of air raids. During the only air attack, which came on 6 June, a German bomber banked away from the barrage sent up by the ships and, much to everyone's amazement, made a bouncy but successful landing on the nearby shore. When the young pilot willingly surrendered, he said that he was not in sympathy with the war and did not want to fight any more.

"All during this operation," Green said, "none of the crew took out more than twenty minutes for meals. We worked sixteen hours a day in heat, slime, and muck."[23]

More than one hundred Liberty ships took part in the invasion of southern France, which began on 15 August 1944. Compared with the invasions of North Africa, Sicily, and Italy, this one was considered a "pushover," with few casualties to the invading troops and almost none to crews of the merchant ships.

Six battleships, twenty-one cruisers, and an armada of destroyers had bombarded the shore defenses. Planes from Corsica and Sardinia had carried out a saturation bombing of the beaches to destroy antipersonnel mines. Minesweepers paved the way for landing craft and transports. There were no longer German or Italian submarines in the Mediterranean: Germany had withdrawn its U-boats into the Atlantic, and the Italian Navy had surrendered in September 1943. The Luftwafte, as the Allies learned later, had fewer than one hundred planes to contest the landings. Many of these were destroyed before the assault troops went ashore.

The men of the Merchant Marine considered the invasion along the famous vacation beaches of southern France to be a peaceful anticlimax to the long and bitter war in the narrow sea.

18

When the Stukas Blasted Bari

O N THE EVENING OF 2 DECEMBER 1943, the harbor at Bari, Italy, was filled with freighters discharging cargo for the British Army, then battling its way northward along the Adriatic Sea. Among the fleet were a number of new American Libertys, the workhorses of the war.[1]

The docks were brightly lit up: lights on the cranes, floodlights on the ships, and headlights on the 8th Army lorries lumbering from the dockside with loads of ammunition, gasoline, food, cigarettes, and the myriad tools of war. Bari was a beautifully illuminated target.

This was the time of evening when cooks and messmen had hung up their pots and pans, swabbed out the mess rooms, and locked up their galleys for the night. Some seamen were writing letters home; others were playing cards or going about the regular routine of anchor watches on deck and below. In the harbor near the breakwater, the officers and men of the Liberty ship *Samuel J. Tilden* cursed a powerful searchlight that played directly on the ship as the anchor ground through the hawse and the propeller churned to a stop. Loaded with trucks, food, ammunition, and gasoline in drums, the *Tilden* had just come in from North Africa. Some two hundred soldiers on the freighter's main deck shielded their eyes as they tried to get a look at the city against the bright glare of the spotlight.

What carelessness caused a powerful light to be spotted on an ammunition-laden ship? That was one of the mysteries of that nighttime battle at Bari. The *Tilden*'s anchor had no more than struck bottom and the ship lost steerageway when all hands heard the first faint sound of aircraft engines. The drumming was audible throughout the harbor. The wind brought the sound of approaching planes to every lookout and every worker on the docks, but the lights were still bright and no air raid sirens sounded the alert. Like the wild Valkyries riding the night, the drum of engines grew louder by the second, their distance nicely camouflaged by a breeze muting the sounds until the planes were almost over the port.

Winches stopped as workmen glanced anxiously at the moonlit sky. Gunners on watch fingered their three-inch/50s, pom-poms, and Oerlikons and listened on the intercom for orders from the bridge of many ships. "Must be our own planes," they thought. "The shore guns are not paying any attention. The lights are still on. No sirens."

All ships at Bari had been instructed not to open up on aircraft until a master gun on shore gave the signal by firing tracers. Naval Armed Guard gunner Thomas Harper of the American Liberty ship *John L. Motley* was walking along one of the docks on his way back to his ship, which was anchored in the harbor while waiting for a berth. As he heard the sound of aircraft engines, he looked into a moonlit sky dappled with clouds. They were peaceful clouds—like the clouds in haying time—but behind them rode Stuka bombers, with veteran German pilots, speeding toward their unsuspecting quarry, with the bright harbor lights as their homing beacons. One moment, the planes seemed to be some distance away; the next, they were overhead with a thundering crescendo of attack.

"As I looked up," Harper recalled, "a bright light suddenly glowed in the sky. I soon realized it was a flare. In a few seconds there were more flares."

The floating lights illuminated the harbor and the shipping—every ship and pier clearly outlined by the guide plane for the bomb-laden Stukas to follow. The flare plane swept over the harbor, and then its engine was momentarily muted as it climbed for altitude.

Alarm bells rang on every ship. There were shouts of "Air raid . . . air raid," as merchant seamen and navy gunners ran to battle stations on twenty-three ships flying the flags of almost all of the Allied nations. The American ships were all Libertys. While the flares made their terrifying slow descent, the attacking aircraft swarmed down in mass assault.

Ens. Kay Vesole, Armed Guard officer on the American Liberty ship *John Bascom,* had just run up to the flying bridge, along with Captain Heitman, First Assistant Elin Nicholas, and Third Mate Allen Collins, when the bombers began their run.

"Captain," Vesole said, "It looks like it's time to open fire."

They couldn't see any aircraft against the maddening brilliance of the floating flares, but they thought a barrage of fire might help. It could divert the pilots and perhaps account for some planes as well.

"Fire away," Heitman shouted.

Vesole pressed the intercom phone to his mouth. "OK, boys," he said. "Start shooting."

The gunners on the *Bascom* opened up a second or two before half a hundred guns poured shells into the sky in a din that almost drowned out the roar of the planes. The 20-millimeter Oerlikons barked and spat their streams of tracer fire. Machine guns chattered. Heavier antiaircraft guns whomped and thundered.

The first stick of bombs hit a ship in the middle of the harbor. The bombs cascaded on her deck, one-two-three, in a brilliant Fourth of July–like burst of flame. During the next twenty minutes, the harbor of Bari witnessed a nightmare of death and destruction—a flaming, screaming, holocaust. Few of the survivors could later fully describe the complete and awful sequence of those hellish minutes.

Still spotted by the carelessly tended searchlight, the *Samuel Tilden* was a brilliant target. The soldiers and crewmen crowding her decks heard a plane, perhaps more than one, diving at them, but they could not see anything above the glare of the flares floating downward. The plane's dive was unhindered by a hail of 20-millimeter fire pouring from the *Tilden*'s guns, and the pilot planted his bombs from little more than masthead height. A 500-pounder plummeted down the *Tilden*'s stack. Exploding in the engine room, it wrecked the machinery and killed the men on watch. Several incendiary bombs then exploded on the deckload of canned gasoline and showered the vessel with fire. Soldiers jumped overboard to escape the flames.

In addition, shells started to crash into the ship, either from a shore battery whose fire control had gone awry or from another ship whose gunners were trying to blast the low-flying plane. Crewmen and troops were hit by shrapnel meant for the Stukas.

Within ten minutes after the first flare blossomed out over the harbor, every ship at Bari seemed to be on fire. A blazing tanker vomited red balls of oil that poured across the sky like comets.

Gunner Harper, meanwhile, stood helplessly on the quay watching the tracer shells streaking upward from the guns of the *Motley*. His shipmates were out there trying to shoot down planes they could not see, and there was nothing he could do to help. Other men, also returning from shore leave, watched the battle from the quayside, unable to reach their ships. Lucky for them that they couldn't, for the men on shore leave were the only survivors of some ships' crews that night.

While these sailors watched from dockside, the *Motley* and the Liberty ship *Joseph Wheeler* were blasted by direct bomb hits, the *Motley* taking two bombs in ammunition-laden holds and one directly down the stack. The ships soon became raging infernos. On the *Bascom*, which lay close to the *Motley*, crewmen ran fire hoses into the holds to keep ammunition and drummed gasoline from heating and exploding. Navy and Merchant Marine gunners stayed at their weapons and fired at the sound of Stukas diving and climbing and circling and diving again. The *Bascom* was hit with three bombs—on the stern, amidships, and on the bow. The first went down the hatch into number five hold. The second hit on the boat deck near the funnel, and the third plummeted through the hatch into number three hold, just forward of the bridge. Almost instantly, a shower of steel and flying splinters killed or wounded every man on board the ship. Tongues of flame shooting from the holds were higher than the masts. Amid the screams and cries of pain, there was no panic, no faltering at the guns or at other posts of duty.

Steam-smothering lines were turned on and flood lines opened into the after ammunition magazine. The crew who were not too badly hurt carried the more seriously injured to the boats and tended their wounds with bandages cut from sheets and blankets. Captain Heitman picked up the first assistant and carried him down to the boat deck before he realized that Nicholas was dead. The captain then hurried around the burning ship to see if any of the crew had been trapped below decks. Ensign Vesole, although sorely hurt, refused to join the badly injured and insisted on seeing how the others were faring. Third Mate Collins also ignored painful injuries to help get the one serviceable lifeboat over the side and then took a hand at the oars as the crew pulled it to the quay.

By now, the harbor was filled with floating wreckage and covered with thick bunker oil escaping from bomb-blasted tanks. This flammable mess caught fire from the blazing debris, and many men were burned to death as they tried to swim away from their battered ships.

Just as the *Bascom*'s lifeboat reached the quay, the *John Motley* exploded in a deafening roar. Fire and wreckage cascaded all over her section of the harbor. A dive-bomber blasted an Allied freighter carrying a load of mustard gas. As the vessel sank, her deadly freight spread over the harbor in a queer brownish vapor that added more terror to the pall of smoke and flame.

The explosions of the *John Motley* and the *John Harvey*, which erupted at the same time, were intense enough to lift the stern of the Liberty ship *Lyman Abbott* entirely out of the water and heel her over in a 38-degree list to port. Captain Carl P. Dahlstrom sent First Mate Grotevant on a fore and aft inspection, which revealed that the foredeck was blown open on the starboard side and the afterdeck had been curled up like the brim of a hat. There was also a ragged hole in the bridge deck where a bomb or fragment of the hull from an exploding ship had torn through the plating. Fire was now breaking out forward, but the crew could not fight the flames because flying shrapnel had punctured the hoses. Grotevant found a serviceable fire extinguisher and emptied it on the flames to quell the incipient blaze.

Other crewmen helped the steward attend the wounded. Lieutenant Brown, the army cargo security officer, had been hit by shrapnel. On deck, the third mate was found dead of a fractured skull. Others of the merchant crew and Armed Guard were hurt by bits of flying steel. Three battered lifeboats were filled with the wounded and lowered overside while Dahlstrom went through the ship, compartment by compartment, to make sure that no men were left behind. After the boatload was taken ashore and rushed to hospitals, the captain and several volunteers, including First Assistant Ledoux, Second Assistant Maury, Steward White, and able seaman Lan Lowry, pulled back to the bomb-shattered freighter, despite the fact that the *Harvey* and *Motley* were blazing wildly and threatening to explode at any moment. By the time they had boarded the *Abbott,* another burning ship drifted down on them and fouled the wreck. They fought the fire with equipment furnished by a detail of British soldiers. All that night, with help from the *Harvey's* and *Motley's* crews, they battled the flames on the abandoned ships alongside. Later, they were aided by Grotevant and a second party of volunteers that he had rounded up from members of the *Abbott's* crew who had been ashore at the time of the attack.

Early the next day, with messboys filling in as able seamen and with every man doing the job of three or four, the *Lyman*

231

Abbott got under way for the open sea. All navigating equipment was wrecked, and the rudder was sprung so far out of line that steering was difficult and erratic. Only five of the deck crew, several badly injured, reported for duty.

Able seamen Peter Hodak and Lan Lowry collapsed while standing wheel watches as the *Abbott* steamed toward Augusta, Sicily, where the captain had been directed to take the ship for emergency repairs. When she made port there, fourteen of her crew were rushed to an army hospital. Two of them died before the ship returned to Bari.

Throughout 3 December, search squads combed the wrecks and the harbor waters for survivors. From some ships, such as the *Joseph Wheeler,* the only men to escape had been those on shore leave at the time of the attack. When fourteen merchant seamen and navy gunners from the *Wheeler* left Bari on another ship, they saw her blackened hulk lying on the port side. The starboard side had been completely blown away.

Fourteen of the twenty-five ships in Bari on 2 December were sunk or otherwise destroyed. On the six American ships blasted by the bombers, thirty-eight bodies were found by search squads and buried in the military cemetery there. One hundred and fifty men were posted as missing, victims of the violent explosions that wracked their ships that terrible night. Violent though it was, the battle at Bari gets little or no mention in the histories of World War II, with their concern for the larger scope of conflict.

The American ships at Bari were all Libertys: *Joseph Wheeler, Samuel Tilden, John Bascom, John Harvey, John Motley, Lyman Abbott, Louis Hennepin,* and *Grace Abbott.* The first five listed were destroyed.

Their shattered hulks have been long since removed, and the docks at Bari have reverted to the use of peaceful trade and commerce. But long afterward, in the waterfront haunts where merchant seamen gather, veterans of the war would recall that night when the wild Valkyries rode the winter sky and Stuka bombs blasted the ships at Bari in one of the bloody but "unknown" battles of World War II.

19

The Indian Ocean War

CAPTAIN ROBERT SPEARING was uneasy as he paced the bridge of the freighter *Bienville*. He looked at the lifeboats swung out on the davits, ready for instant launching. A premonition of danger had haunted him ever since the *Bienville* had left Calcutta on 6 April 1942 and joined a convoy of unescorted ships at the mouth of the Hooghly River.[1]

"Convoy!" He almost laughed at the thought of it. Twenty-one ships steaming together for what meager protection their own guns could afford. Many of the ships, including the *Bienville*, didn't have any armament, not even so much as a rifle.

After entering the Bay of Bengal, the fleet had zigzagged to elude any submarines that might be waiting at this great confluence of shipping routes.

Official orders were to maintain a convoy formation until passing the tip of the Indian subcontinent, at which time the convoy was to break up. Some ships would then turn west toward the Red Sea or the Persian Gulf, others would strike out for Cape Town, with important war cargoes for the United States and Great Britain.

The *Bienville* had orders to stop at Colombo, Ceylon, and top off her cargo of sisal and manganese with rubber. She was also to pick up several Americans waiting for passage home.

For the third or fourth time since leaving Calcutta, Spearing went down to the main deck and checked the lashings of the two big life rafts that he had ordered especially built for the *Bienville*. Had it really been a premonition of disaster, he wondered, or just the ordinary precautions that any prudent captain would take under the circumstances? One raft had been placed on number one hatch, and the other was placed on number four hatch, aft.

Spearing climbed back to the bridge after finding the rafts secure and ready for launching. For a while, he leaned against the rail and stared at the Bay of Bengal, flat and windless, without the semblance of wave or swell. Smoke from the plodding ships streamed sluggishly into an almost cloudless sky.

The first mate broke into his reverie to tap him on the shoulder and hand him a pair of binoculars.

"Captain," he said, "take a look over to the sou'eastard there. Either there's a ship on fire or some old hooker is making an awful lot of smoke with her boilers."

Focusing the glasses on the spot indicated by the mate, Spearing saw a thick, black smudge on the horizon, with black smoke drifting into the morning sky.

"You're right," he said. "Too much smoke for anything but a ship on fire! Maybe a Jap sub. They warned us at the convoy conference about a Jap sub operating in these waters."

Spearing was still studying the distant smoke when a flag hoist was run up the signal halyards of the convoy commodore, a big British merchantman plowing a ten-knot path several ships' lengths ahead of the *Bienville*. The pennants hung listlessly on the halyards. It took several minutes to translate the coded message. The mate wrote it on a piece of paper and handed it to the captain.

"Disperse immediately," the message read. "Proceed independently to your destinations."

The officers looked at each other in dismay. Spearing crumpled the paper and tossed it over the side.

"This doesn't look good," he said. "That smoke on the horizon must mean trouble—big trouble. Check our position. Put us on a course for Colombo!"

"Aye, sir," the mate answered and headed for the chart room.

Within minutes after the signal to disperse, the convoy began to lose precise formation, every vessel attempting to leave the area as quickly as possible. Before an hour was up, the convoy had scattered like a blast of buckshot. The faster ships had drawn ahead and would soon be hull down on the horizon.

When Spearing had rung for full steam on the engine room telegraph, the black gang had pulled the burners and inserted small tips to spray finer streams of oil onto the fires for greater heat and utmost possible speed. But it would take more than hotter boiler fires and more steam to make the twenty-year-old *Bienville* exceed ten knots with her full load. At the most, they might get eleven knots if the engineers overlooked the red danger lines on the steam pressure gauges.

Just before six bells, they heard the first dull boom of gunfire. When the radio operator tuned in to find out what was happening, he discovered the air jammed with calls for help and reports from ships being attacked or sinking. They told of Japanese planes, destroyers, cruisers, and an aircraft carrier.

"Shelled by Japanese destroyer," said a frantic report from one freighter.

"Am afire from bomb hits," said another. "Going down by the head. Need assistance. Need assistance."

Captain Spearing knew immediately that an enemy task force had jumped the convoy—like a pack of wolves in a herd of sheep! An entire fleet of ships, full and down with a hundred thousand tons of war supplies, was steaming straight to slaughter.

And not a single gun for defense.

Continuing on the present course could only mean certain destruction. He ordered the helm "hard right," and the deeply

An engineer makes notations in the engine room log, a record of speed changes, steam pressures, and other data. At left on the bulkhead is the telegraph, by which the engineer receives orders from the bridge for "full ahead," "slow astern," "stop," and other commands. As the indicator turns to the desired command, the engineer acknowledges by repeating the order with the handle on the telegraph. The engine room is always the most vulnerable part of the ship, but the black gang cannot worry about submarines and torpedoes. (Art Holt)

laden ship swung slowly toward the Indian Coast, twenty miles away.

At 0715, the crew heard the drum of airplane engines. Seconds later, they spotted two aircraft heading toward them from the east, at about four thousand feet, one somewhat ahead of the other. Spearing studied the aircraft through the glasses, hoping they might be British planes responding to the convoy's SOS.

Not until he saw the first bomb drop from the belly of the lead plane was he sure that the aircraft were Japanese. For a second or two the bomb looked like a piece of sparkling tinfoil.

236

Then it took shape. It was black, with a yellow nose, and it was headed straight for the ship.

Spearing shouted to the man at the wheel, "Hard right. Hard right!"

But there was no chance for evasive action. The *Bienville* was a deep-laden ship, not a knife-bowed destroyer that could make a turn in her own length.

Watching a bomb drop toward him terrifies a person. His mouth dries, his bowels contract, his heart thumps, and he wants to run and hide—to cover his face and shut his eyes. The men on the *Bienville* could only clench their fists in desperation. The bomber lazied above them like a fat fly, a sucker shot for any gunner, but there were no guns on the *Bienville.*

Hitting in number two hold, the first bomb blew the hatch covers to bits and started a fire in the cargo of sisal. Seconds later, the second bomb smashed into the defenseless ship and exploded on the port side, forward.

Spearing ran into the wheelhouse and pressed the button for the general alarm, calling all hands to fire stations. Crewmen broke out the fire hoses and strung them along the open deck, even as the second plane started its bomb run at about three thousand feet. Both bombs were near misses. Columns of water flowered off the beam where the missiles hit a waveless sea.

As the planes roared away, Spearing told the radio operator to send out an SOS, with the ship's position, call number KDNE, and a report of the direction from which the aircraft had come.

The coast of India was still dim and distant.

By the time the fire was under control, a large vessel was approaching from the southwest. Hopes that she might be a British warship responding to the SOS were blasted after a check of the ship's official warship identification book. The strange ship had a silhouette that was undoubtedly Japanese. The cruiser was followed by an aircraft carrier and three escorting destroyers. They were soon less than a mile away, approaching fast and maneuvering to parallel the *Bienville*'s course.

The crew watched the enemy force approaching. They were tense, quiet, wondering what would happen next. There was no chance of flight, no means of offering resistance. The captain had only one course of action. He did not want the enemy to think the *Bienville* was trying, insanely, to make a run for it. All he could do was to abandon ship.

He rang "Stop" on the engine room telegraph and called the engine room on the telephone. "Shut down the plant," he said. "Hurry on deck. Don't waste any time."

Under Chief Engineer Paul Geisler, who had gone below to help the ship on her helpless flight, the black gang stopped the engine, put out the boiler fires, and made the machinery secure before going on deck.

There was no panic, no shouting. The four lifeboats were uncovered and swung on the davits.

"All boats ready for launching," the mate reported to the bridge.

Spearing checked the vessel's speed, reduced now to little more than a steerageway. If he had turned around, he would have seen the turret guns of the cruiser swing menacingly toward the *Bienville*.

With such a calm sea, it was possible to lower all four boats, two on a side. Crewmen stood by their assigned places. Spearing pulled the whistle cord, sounding the long blasts of abandon ship.

"Lower one and three," the captain called. The mate echoed the order, "Lower away!"

Number three boat was being lowered slowly down the side when one of the destroyers opened fire. Its first shell made a direct hit on the boat and blew men and boat into a thousand pieces. There were screams of pain. Shattered arms and legs and bits of bodies floated on the blood-stained sea.

Spearing stared at the slaughter unbelievingly. What command could he give? What could he do? He gripped the rail of the bridge in an agony of complete helplessness.

As number one boat lowered away, the cruiser opened point-blank from the other side of the freighter.

No one had expected anything like this. They had expected a warning shot—an order to heave to and abandon ship. They knew the Japanese would sink the *Bienville*, but who could have foreseen such a fiendish bombardment of an unarmed ship?

There was another blast of fire from the cruiser's turret. Moments later, a shell smashed into the freighter's side. It shattered steel plates and showered the decks with tiny fragments of metal. Number one boat was broken in two by the concussion.

"Lower number four," the captain shouted, hoping that the Japanese, at least, would not fire on a boatload of helpless men in the water.

But this boat was split by a shell blast. Most of its crew were able to climb out of it onto the deck. They huddled against the deckhouse to escape the rain of jagged metal and flying rivets. One man, sinking onto the deck, held the stump of a shattered arm. The steward and his men ran to the mess room and started tearing up tablecloths for bandages.

The cruiser's third salvo gashed the hull and ripped steel plates like so many tops of tin cans. Shells smashed the booms and cut down all the standing rigging. In a deadly hail of rivets, deck plates buckled and shattered. The rivets beat a deadly tune on the deck and superstructure—whang, zing, whang, zing! The sharp metal fragments sprayed the air.

Half a dozen men were lying in pools of blood along the deck. The captain saw one of his sailors sprawled face up on the boat deck, his fists clawing the air. A piece of shrapnel had all but disemboweled him. He shrieked for a few moments and then lay still.

Spearing was hit in the leg. He grabbed a signal pennant and tied a quick tourniquet to stop the blood.

There was nothing the men of the *Bienville* could do but listen to the screams of the shells and the screams of the terribly wounded and cry in desperation for guns—guns—guns. The Japanese ships were so close that they could see the officers, standing on the bridge, neatly attired in their tropic whites; the crew at the guns; the limpid signal pennants and the battle flags.

Survivors remembered a big wiper by the name of Pedro Cruz. While the ship was being ripped to pieces, Pedro sat on the stern and drank a cup of coffee.

"We didn't have guns," Spearing said, "but we sure had a lot of guys with guts. They took it like men. And big Pedro sitting there on the stern drinking his cup of jamoke. Just like it was the Fourth of July or something!"

To the crew of the *Bienville*, it seemed like an eternity before the ship began to sink. Little more than half of them were alive by this time, and the badly wounded had to be carried to the rafts. The steward and his men had tried to bandage the wounded, but shrapnel wounds need surgeons, not first aid.

What luck that the captain had had that premonition of disaster before leaving Bombay. Those stoutly built rafts were the crew's only chance of salvation. The rafts were too heavy to throw over the side, so the men lay down on them, grasped the grip ropes fastened to the sides, and waited for the ship to sink.

As part of her freight, the *Bienville* was carrying hundreds of monkeys and dogs consigned to experimental laboratories in the United States—a pitiful cargo that ships in the Indian trade had carried for many years. The final salvo from the destroyer blew open the after hatch and released a horde of monkeys. Terrified by the bombardment and sensing the imminence of death, these creatures ran wildly about the deck. They hopped onto the cargo booms and ran up the shrouds as they tried to escape.

Death here would be quick and merciful, compared with the torture in laboratories, but the monkeys, of course, didn't know that. Crying and whimpering, many of them clung to the arms and necks of the wounded men on the rafts. Their human-like eyes were full of shock and terror.

"Like little children," Spearing said. "Just like a bunch of little children—hanging onto us for help. We had to beat them off. We hated to do it. They cried just like humans, but we had to beat them off."

The dogs were unable to climb out of the holds. The sailors heard them barking and crying as the water poured through the shattered hull plates. Their cries were quickly stilled as the *Bienville* went down, sinking on an even keel.

Water poured through the freeing ports along the bulwark. In a second, the main deck was awash. "Hold on tight. She's going!"

The men grabbed the life ropes on the rafts as the suction from the sinking ship dragged them under the sea. They went down only a few feet, but it seemed like an hour before the buoyancy of the rafts overcame the downward pull of the ship. As the rafts shot to the surface, the men were gasping for breath.

Several monkeys had survived the downpull and they swam to the rafts, only to be thrown back into the sea. They struggled briefly and then disappeared.

The enemy task force, already far beyond the litter of wreckage, was heading toward the coast and a dim outline of several ships in the distance.

As the warships moved off, several men swam after the number two lifeboat, which had floated clear of the ship and was drifting several hundred feet away. Fortunately, the sea was calm, and they were able to reach the boat. They pulled it back to their shipmates on the rafts.

Meanwhile, the second cook, Arthur Chisholm, had died of stomach wounds. One of the able seamen lasted a few minutes longer. The others were trying to lift him into the lifeboat—a hard job, for he had lost both of his arms at the shoulders. He shook his head and tried to smile.

"Ain't this a hell of a shape for a sailor to be in," he said. They gave him a cigarette to help him on the "long voyage," and he died soon afterward.

By a strange coincidence, Second Mate Stultz had been born in the Bay of Bengal on board a sailing ship captained by his father. Badly torn by shrapnel, Stultz begged to be thrown over the side, but his shipmates refused.

"I'm making the round trip," he said. "This is where I started and this is where I'm ending." He died a few minutes later.

These men and a young engine cadet, who was making his first trip at sea, were consigned to the deep over the sunken *Bienville*, with Captain Spearing reciting the traditional burial service of the sea.

After recovering from the initial shock of the ordeal, they manned the long oars and pulled toward the coast. Many of them glanced back now and then to where so many of their shipmates had lost their lives. There wasn't much talk as they heaved on the heavy oars. They still couldn't believe that this ghoulish event had actually happened.

The sea held calm, and they landed at the village of Kdoput the next day, 8 April. Natives swam out to help them through the surf.

As soon as the nearest military post could be notified, the British sent stretcher bearers. They carried the worst of the wounded twenty-four miles to a hospital. Five of the survivors were mortally wounded and died during the stretcher trip or soon after reaching the hospital. Of the *Bienville*'s crew of forty-three, nineteen finally reached home.

Official government files list the *Bienville* as "sunk by enemy action, Indian Ocean area." This is not much of an obituary for a ship and her crew.

Somewhere off the coast of India, the gallant *Bienville* lies with the other shell-ridden hulks of that ill-fated fleet.

Another costly attack on merchant shipping in the Bay of Bengal had been made by the Japanese carrier *Ryujo*, six heavy cruisers, and several destroyers. They sank twenty-three Allied ships there, plus a number of freighters along the coast of India. Without losing a single vessel, the Japanese also sank several British warships.

The freighter *Exmoor* was a victim of this same task force while bound from Calcutta to Colombo on 6 April in a group of five ships. They were some 250 miles southwest of Calcutta when two Japanese cruisers pounced on the unescorted convoy and began shelling. A cruiser abeam of the *Exmoor* fired about twenty rounds before the vessel began to go down. No men were lost in the crew of thirty-six, but the vessel took with her a valuable cargo of jute and manganese.

U-boats haunted the shipping lanes along the East Coast of Africa, especially the Mozambique Channel between Madagascar and the African coast.

The *Alcoa Pathfinder*, a veteran of the prewar Merchant Marine, was plodding along thirty miles south of the port of Lourenço Marques, South Africa, on the morning of 23 November 1942, when a torpedo exploded in the engine room and killed the men on watch there. Within three minutes, the ship was going under, carrying with her 7,200 tons of hides; coffee; and chromium ore, used in making guns and armor plate. Radio operator Andy Tocco also went down with the ship while sending an SOS.

Ships assembling to await a convoy. In the foreground is a Liberty, with a typical large deckload. The photo shows the arrangement of guns, lifeboats, and life rafts on skids. (U.S. Maritime Administration)

A German submarine surfaced, and her captain ordered the survivors to bring the lifeboats alongside. Captain Fred Dumke and the crewmen were questioned about the vessel's ports of call and destination, but no attempt was made to harm the men. The survivors were rescued a few days later.

A dramatic and heart-wrenching ordeal followed the torpedoing of the *Harvey W. Scott* some sixty miles off the coast of East Africa on 3 March 1943. All hands abandoned ship safely, but the crews of several other ships in the area were not so fortunate. The British ship *Nirdura*, which was carrying eight hundred mules, was sunk with most of her crew.

At about 0300, the crew of a lifeboat from the *Scott* heard cries for help. Getting closer, they found a large group of men from the *Nirdura* in the water. Some had life jackets, and others were clinging to bits of wreckage.

"We took eighteen of them into our boat," Cadet Robert Clark said. "The boat was then badly overloaded, and we couldn't take anymore. We just had to leave them behind. We heard their cries for a long time as we rowed toward the shore. We reached the coast the next day."[2]

Just two days later, the *James B. Stephens* went down in the same area. She had been bound toward the United States with a strangely assorted cargo of empty beer bottles, shell cases, and damaged propellers.

After the Liberty ship *Richard D. Spaight* was torpedoed near Durban, South Africa, on 10 March 1943, an emergency operation was performed in a lifeboat. An Armed Guard signalman had two fingers smashed between the lifeboat and the ship's side. He was in terrible pain and asked a shipmate to cut off the finger. No anesthetic or surgical instruments were available but the operation was performed with a navy jackknife and a pair of scissors. Despite much loss of blood, the injured sailor was held up by shipmates and signaled the lighthouse at Cape Saint Lucia, South Africa. Twelve men were lost in this sinking.

The Liberty ship *William King* was also homeward bound from the Persian Gulf via Durban on 6 June 1943, when a torpedo hit in the engine room. The boilers exploded and the men below were killed. All but six of the crew abandoned ship in lifeboats and rafts. The submarine then surfaced and ordered the survivors alongside.

The following was written later by the Armed Guard officer, Lt. (jg) Gordon W. Baker, Jr.:

> An officer questioned us as to the name of the ship and its cargo and asked for the captain and naval officer to identify themselves. When there was no reply to this request the officer on the deck of the submarine ordered two of his men to spray the water around us with fire from automatic weapons. Upon seeing this, Captain Owen Reed got up and identified himself as the captain and was taken on board the sub, which then submerged.[3]

The submarine was U-51. The survivors were in the boats for six days. During that time, two more men died of burns and wounds.

A heroic tale of the sea followed the sinking of the Liberty ship *Henry Knox* on 19 June 1943. Rainsqualls from the southwest monsoon provided welcome relief for the crew of this Liberty ship, loaded deep with war supplies for the Russians, as she headed for the Persian Gulf. She was eighty days out of San Francisco, 850 miles southwest of India.[4]

All hands were at general quarters. The merchant crew and Armed Guard gunners kept the usual sunset alert, a precaution against attack during a time of day favorable to submarines. The sun was sinking in the golden brilliance so common in the Indian Ocean. In a half hour, it would drop over the horizon, darkness would descend over the waters, and the call would come to secure general quarters. The ship would then settle down for another night.

A few minutes before 1900, a torpedo exploded with a terrific blast on the port side at number two hatch. Rolling balls of fire erupted from the hold. Flames swept over the foredeck, then spread from bow to stern like a Fourth of July fireworks display, as 1,100 tons of smokeless powder topping off the cargo in three of the five holds was touched off.

Cadet Maurice Price was standing watch on the port side of the bridge about twenty feet from the impact of the torpedo. He recalled:

> A Navy gunner was standing almost beside me. He was blown clear off the ship. I was knocked flat on the deck. I got up dazed. There were flames all around me. I ran through a sheet of fire into the wheelhouse and into the passageway past the captain's quarters. He came out of his cabin as I ran past. He was scorched and his clothes were partly burned off. We groped through the smoke and found the ladder leading down to the boat deck. Men were trapped in the passageways because the blackout baffles at the exit to the deck were on fire. There was a lot of smoke, too. I wasn't about to be burned alive in there or smothered, so I dropped to my knees and crawled as fast as I could through the burning baffles. Except for burns on my hands and having some of my hair burnt off, I made it OK.
>
> The boat deck was scorching hot. There were several bodies lying around. They had gaping wounds, and it looked like they were all dead.[5]

Price had left the midships house by number one boat, which was still hanging on the falls. The paint on the hull was burning and peeling. Just astern of it was the motor lifeboat. The falls were on fire and some of the gear in it was burning. He was assigned to this boat, and his job was to insert the plug before launching. While he was doing this, the forward falls burned through and the bow dropped down, leaving the boat suspended. In a few seconds, the stern falls burned too, and the boat dropped into the sea. Caught around the legs in the scramble net,

Price dangled about fifteen feet above the water until he managed to free himself and fall between the lifeboat and the side of the ship.

The boat was made fast by the painter, and the ship's engine was still turning slowly. The heavy metal boat kept banging against the ship's side and hitting Price as it swung. The blows injured his chest and ribs and bruised his legs, but he managed to get into the boat before he fainted from the pain. By this time, a number of crewmen had jumped into the water and also climbed into the boat.

"When I came to," Price remembered, "the ship was roaring with fire and huge pillars of smoke were eddying into the darkening sky. We cut the painter and pulled away as fast as we could."

They used the bailing bucket to put out the fires in the boat's equipment, then sat at the oars for a while to see if any more survivors were nearby.

"We were all in a shock," Price said. "It had all happened so fast. While we were sitting there a sub surfaced about five hundred yards away. We saw sailors pour out of the hatches onto the deck. They were pointing at us and laughing."

They spotted several of their shipmates by the little red lights attached to their life jackets and pulled them on board. One of them was Captain Eugen Olson, and he took command of the boat.

There was a series of muffled explosions on the burning ship as ammunition lockers exploded. Bright tracer shells zoomed through the sky in a crisscrossing galaxy. At about 2200, number five hold exploded. Tongues of fire shot hundreds of feet into the air and generated enough heat to reach the lifeboat a quarter of a mile away.

For an hour or so, the men in the boat listened to the deep throb of diesels while the submarine prowled around the scene. Her skipper probably thought that an SOS had been sent and a rescue ship would come along. When the submarine headed toward their boat, the men lay flat and hoped they wouldn't be seen. The submarine passed close by but did not try to ram or shell them.

During the rest of the night, the men rode at a sea anchor. When daylight came, they pulled around and looked for other survivors. They picked up eight shipmates who had been clinging to pieces of wreckage and kicking their feet to scare away sharks. As they pulled a young gunner from a bit of flotsam, a huge shark jerked him from their grasp and carried him underwater. Several mangled bodies in the water indicated that sharks had been busy during the night.

The men also spotted the ship's mascot, a Scottish terrier, floating on a tiny cork life raft made for him by one of the crew. He died soon after they picked him up.

They sighted number four boat about noon and were also soon joined by number one boat in command of the chief mate. After a while, they found a life raft with the second and third mates and several crewmen.

The chief mate's boat had been intercepted by the submarine, whose captain had asked for the *Knox*'s master. Unhappy at getting no satisfaction as to his whereabouts, the submarine skipper had his men take the boat's mast, sail, and rations and break several oars before leaving them to what the Japanese supposed would be death by starvation.

After a roll call of survivors, the captain concluded that twenty-five merchant seamen and navy gunners had been lost in the sinking, in the explosion and fire, or from wounds or sharks during the night.

He decided that their best chance was to make for a group of islands about three hundred miles to the northeast toward the coast of India. It would be a long trip, and, thanks to the Japanese, their supplies and equipment were now meager. With an oar for a mast, a bit of flag for sail, and the men pulling at the four oars that were still usable, the boat started off under a brisk southwest wind, hopefully toward a distant landfall.

One of the gunners died a few hours later, and they dropped him into the sea with a short prayer by the captain. A badly wounded man died in each of the other boats that night—the second assistant engineer and a sixteen-year-old gunner they called "the kid."

The Indian Ocean sun was hot and merciless. Water rations were limited to two ounces for each man in the morning and afternoon.

"Everybody who was able had to take turns at the oars," Price said. "Nobody had the strength to pull very hard, but every stroke helped. We also took turns at the steering oar and the bilge pump. The boat had been damaged and it leaked all the time. We never stopped pumping."

On the second night, the weather freshened until it was blowing gale force. The seas were running so high that their boat was almost capsized while riding at sea anchor. The gale blew for twelve hours. When the skies cleared and the seas calmed, they could see no sign of the other boats. They decided their comrades had been swamped during the night.

The captain set the food schedule that would prevail throughout the voyage: for breakfast, three malted milk tablets; for lunch, two malted milk tablets and a graham cracker; for supper, an ounce of pemmican. Water rations were increased when frequent showers replenished the beakers.

Incapacitated now because of his injuries, Price lay in the bottom of the boat, unable to sit up, scorched by the sun during the day, and soaked by the rains at night.

Blistered by the sun and suffering from cracked lips, the men found it difficult to talk, but when they did the conversations were about juicy steaks, fried chicken, creamy mashed potatoes, luscious red tomatoes, and mounds of ice cream.

Although seldom mentioned in stories of long voyages in small boats, taking care of bodily functions was very important and eventually accomplished without embarrassment.

"It gets so you don't notice what other guys are doing," Price explained. "Staying alive is the first thing in your mind. The social niceties don't seem important."

Every evening at sunset, the captain conducted a prayer service, at which they offered thanks for their deliverance from the holocaust on board ship and reverently asked aid for their rescue.

After five days of fishing with lines that failed to draw even a nibble, they watched a squid tumble into the boat as though it had been dropped from heaven. Soon afterward, they caught a small shark and cut it up for dinner.

A few days later, they sighted palm trees, which they mistook at first for a mirage. When the trees stayed on the horizon and they saw a low-lying atoll, they rowed toward it with all the strength they could muster.

Seeing that a heavy current was setting against them, they pulled toward a point beyond the island and then let the current take them toward heavy breakers beating against a sandy shore. Chancing the breakers was a dangerous gamble, but the men voted to try it. With the wounded lying in the bottom of the boat, they rode the crest of a huge wave over the reef. Another wave broke over the boat and capsized it on the coral rock, but all hands made it to the beach.

The islet was uninhabited, but they found plenty of coconuts and feasted on them for hours. They made beds of palm fronds and finally slept, exhausted and unmindful of a warm night rain.

The next day, they discovered that their island refuge had provided haven for other castaways. They found ship hatch boards, a crude fireplace, and the whitened bones of some unfortunate sailors who had made it to the atoll but no farther.

About noon the next day, the men spotted a sail offshore. Their signals attracted a small craft manned by what Price called "strange little black men with abnormally large heads and spindly arms and legs, all of them in great need of soap and scrubbing."

Taking the castaways to their own island some miles distant, the little men hosted them to a sumptuous dinner. The crew later discovered that the entrée had been roasted dog.

"Pig or dog," Price said, "it tasted great. We ate every bit of it."

The next day, they were taken to still another atoll where they had a happy reunion with the crew of the third mate's boat.

A small sailing vessel came by several days later and took them to a much larger island six hours away. After a few days, they were picked up by a Royal Air Force patrol boat and taken to a British flying boat base. There, they feasted on bully beef, potatoes, butter, cheese, and apricots.

They were at the base for a week or so. The patrol boat then directed a small sailing ship to the island, and the survivors were taken to Colombo, where Price and several other injured men were hospitalized and eventually returned to the States.

The third boat was never found.

One of the most graphic accounts of a wartime torpedoing came out of interviews by Lt. (j.g.) Joseph C. Dea, USN, with survivors of the *Knox* while they were at Columbo.

On 14 August 1943, Lieutenant Dea reported the sinking to the Chief of Naval Operations:

> A torpedo struck in number three hold, some twenty feet forward of the deckhouse and fifteen feet below the waterline, blowing deck and cargo over a wide area. The explosion was instantly followed by a concussion and a dull, rushing sound. Some thought it might have been a second torpedo. It is also considered that it may have been the smokeless powder in the cargo blowing up. Immediately following the impact, a great sheet of flame shot upward, followed by a shower of debris, dunnage, tires, powder tins, and other material. There was a literal rain of fire as ignited capsules of cordite fell over the entire length of the deck and into the sea. The burning capsules gave off an intense heat that ignited the deck cargo. Handfuls fell on the steel deck, blistering and burning the dry paint and warping the hull in a few minutes' time. Life rafts, the cordage on the boat falls and rigging were set afire by the cordite. The main engine room controls jammed, the engine room telegraph was rendered inoperative, cargo was blown all over the ship and the

surrounding sea. The ship gradually came to a stop and at 1700 hours it sank bow first.[6]

On 10 July 1943, the *Alice F. Palmer* was hit by a torpedo that exploded in number five hold and broke the tail shaft. Twenty survivors in one boat were sighted by a Catalina flying boat. It landed and took them on board, but it was unable to take off because of the weight of so many passengers. The plane taxied seventy miles to Cape Sainte-Marie on the southern tip of Madagascar, where the survivors were put ashore.

Another *Palmer* lifeboat traveled under oars and sail for sixteen days before reaching an island off Portuguese East Africa.

Five men were lost when the Liberty ship *Robert Bacon* was sunk in the Mozambique Channel during the night of 14 July. The submarine had to fire a third torpedo to sink this ship, when she refused to go down after the first and second hits.

Another U-boat's career was almost ended when she dispatched a torpedo at the *Cornelia P. Spencer* on 21 September. The Armed Guard gunners were already at battle stations because all hands knew they were in hazardous waters. When the submarine surfaced to use her guns, she was greeted with half a dozen salvos. She crash-dived and then retaliated by torpedoing the *Spencer* in the stern. The magazine exploded, and the rudder and propeller were destroyed. Several gunners were killed. Again, three torpedoes were needed to sink the ship.

Crewmen lost no time in leaving the Liberty ship *Elias Howe* when a torpedo hit set her on fire shortly after midnight, 24 September. They were riding a powder keg. The ship, bound from Durban to Aden on the Red Sea for orders, was carrying a cargo of explosives. Fifteen minutes after the fifty-eight crewmen and Armed Guard gunners had abandoned ship, she blew up. According to the voyage report: "The ship had disappeared before the flash and smoke of the explosion had cleared away."

The year 1944 began with the sinking of the Liberty ship *Albert Gallatin* during the early morning hours of 2 January. Running alone from Aden toward Bandar-e Shāhpūr, Iran, she was carrying 7,000 tons of war supplies and 500 bags of mail. Gunners fired twenty-five rounds in the direction of a periscope track sighted by lookouts. Despite their vigilance, a torpedo hit the ship on the port side and blew up the boilers. An explosion broke the ship in two, and she sank shortly thereafter. Another violent explosion in the water after the *Gallatin* sank was heard by the crew of the British ship *Britannia,* some six miles away. Was the *Gallatin* carrying some especially powerful explosives, perhaps of which even her captain was unaware?

Much vital war freight went down when the *Walter Camp* was sunk on 25 January. She was carrying 9,500 tons of barges, truck bodies, cranes, and earth-moving equipment. Survivors were picked up by the HMS *Danae* and landed at Aden.

On 3 February, the *Richard Stockton* ran into a hurricane en route from the Persian Gulf to Mozambique. Winds of 125 mph blew paint off the stack and deckhouses; gun covers were torn to shreds. Lt. (j.g.) Jack Grode, the Armed Guard officer, reported:

> It looked at times as though we wouldn't make it. Seas were like mountains. If you had ventured out on deck you would have been blown over the side. But the ship was tough and she brought us through.[7]

The Liberty ship *Richard Hovey* was homeward bound through the Arabian Sea on 29 March when she was torpedoed by a Japanese submarine. Two torpedoes broke the ship in two, after which the submarine surfaced and shelled the wreck. Her crew then turned their attention to the lifeboats and machine-gunned them and tried to run them down. Survivors jumped into the water to escape the bullets. Purser James O'Connor told how the submarine deliberately rammed the boat in which he was sitting. As it turned over, the Japanese sailors laughed and took pictures of the men struggling in the water.

When the Japanese located the boat containing the captain, they ordered him and several others to board the submarine and took them away.

None of the crew of one lifeboat from the *Richard Hovey* might have survived if it had not been for John Drechsler, a junior assistant engineer. The machine-gun bullets had punctured the water beakers. Drechsler fashioned a still that provided each of the thirty-eight men in the boat with seven ounces of water a day for the sixteen days they were afloat under a blistering sun. He fashioned this lifesaving device from an air tank taken from a raft, bits of pipe, and a rubber hose.

Drechsler's ingenuity in saving the lives of his shipmates was rightfully described by a War Shipping Administration news release as "one of the truly heroic deeds in the war at sea."

Even the brutal attack on the *Bienville* paled in comparison to the fate of the Liberty ship *Jean Nicolet*, when she was torpedoed by the Japanese submarine I-8 on 2 July 1944, about six hundred miles from Ceylon.[8]

The *Nicolet*, bound for the Persian Gulf, was carrying 10,000 tons of machinery, steel plate, and other war cargo for the Russians. On board were forty-one merchant crew, twenty-eight Armed Guard, nineteen U.S. Army personnel, and twelve civilian construction workers.

At about 1900, a torpedo exploded in the engine room. A second tin fish smashed into number three hold a few seconds later.

When the vessel began to take a heavy list, Captain D. M. Nilsson ordered the ship abandoned and all hands, except those who had been killed in the engine room, got safely away on boats and rafts. When it appeared that the *Nicolet* was not going to sink right away, they rowed back to her with the idea of boarding and awaiting help, for an SOS had been sent out. They soon changed their minds, however, when the submarine, unseen in the gathering darkness, began shelling the vessel and set her on fire.

An hour or so later, the submarine came up to the boats and rafts where they had congregated. An officer, speaking good English, ordered them to the side of the submarine. One raft was able to slip away in the darkness.

The men were then commanded to board the submarine, one by one. After that followed a night of mayhem seldom seen in modern annals of the sea. The victor usually treats the vanquished with humanity and respect, but not in this case.

As soon as the men climbed onto the submarine's deck, they were stripped of their watches and money and ordered to kneel down. Their wrists were bound together with wire or rope. All of them sensed that something terrible was about to happen.

With the Japanese crew lined up on each side of the deck, the captives were forced to run the gauntlet. They were clubbed with pieces of pipe and prodded by knives and bayonets. Most of them, bleeding and unconscious, fell or were pushed overboard.

At about midnight, after some fifty of the men had been wounded and pushed into the sea and about thirty were still sitting on the deck awaiting their turn, there was a hum of airplane engines—a plane responding to the *Nicolet*'s SOS. The Japanese scurried below, and the I-8 quickly submerged, leaving the wounded to flounder in the sea with their hands tied.

Fortunately, it was calm and some of them were able to dog paddle or float while struggling to free their wrists. A few bound with rope were able to get free, and several later reported that they hadn't been tied too tightly. Perhaps one or more of the Japanese sailors had been somewhat compassionate.

A few men were still afloat the next morning when another plane dropped life preservers. It also directed a ship of the Indian Navy to the scene. Twenty-three of the men survived, including those who had escaped the mayhem by drifting out of sight on the raft.

A rich treasure went down with the Liberty ship *John Barry*. She was torpedoed on 28 August, while en route from Aden to Rā's at Tannūrah, Saudi Arabia, on the Persian Gulf. The night was bright with moonlight and the seas were rough when the tin fish exploded on the starboard side forward. Seven crewmen were injured, but there were no fatalities. The steamships *Sunetta* and *Benjamin Bourn* picked up the survivors.[9]

The *John Barry* turned out to be a mystery ship as well as a treasure ship. Although the War Shipping Administration revealed after the war that she was carrying $25 million in silver bullion, more recent developments indicate that the *Barry*'s treasure consists of 3 million silver coins minted for Saudi Arabia, plus two thousand tons of silver ingots.

The U.S. government has never relinquished ownership of the vessel and cargo, but, according to the U.S. Maritime Administration, salvage rights were sold to a group in Oman. This group, in turn, sold the rights to another group, which began salvage operations several years ago. Special technology had to be developed to tap the ship's cargo, which lies in eight thousand feet of water. About 1.5 million coins have been recovered so far. The salvagers believe that the Barry's treasure is worth more than $300 million.

The mystery still remains. Why was such a treasure dispatched to Saudi Arabia via Iran in a ten-knot freighter, rather than in a cruiser or destroyer, through submarine-haunted waters?

20
The Long Haul

S HIPS OF ALL ALLIED NATIONS supplied the war in Europe, but transporting war material to the Pacific theater was almost entirely an American effort. Hundreds of ships, at first the famous Libertys and then the faster Victorys supported the island-by-island march from Australia back to the Philippines and thence to Okinawa and Japan.

Until the Japanese invasion of the Philippines, most voyages were made without incident. The Japanese, with few exceptions, did not use their submarines effectively to contest the American line of supply. Merchant crews and navy gunners eager to see action found most trips unexciting. "From Monotony to Boredom to Ho-Hum," one bit of wartime verse expressed it—no enemy action within hundreds of miles, no embattled convoys, few prowling U-boats, no submarine wolf packs. Many laden ships waited days or even weeks to unload part of their cargoes at some island base and move on to another island to discharge, move again, or sometimes sit at anchor for what seemed like eternity to the crews. Often, they waited for orders to discharge

The sleek freighter United Victory *was one of many Victory-type ships employed for the "long haul" between U.S. West Coast ports and distant supply bases and battlefronts in the Pacific. (U.S. Maritime Administration, 3969)*

or up-anchor and then headed for another island without having unloaded a single bomb, barrel, or bale. It was joked about, and not without some element of truth, that ships with beer in the cargo got priority in discharging.

One ship spent weeks steaming from base to base, as her captain tried to get rid of a cargo of barbed wire. Finding no one who wanted it or knew anything about it, the disgusted captain took it back to the West Coast where it had been loaded. The barbed wire, it was then learned, was supposed to have gone to the Aleutians.

Another classic snafu involved the Liberty ship *James Buchanan* in 1943. Her cargo included PT boats and complete equipment for a PT boat base, plus two hundred men of a PT boat squadron. Men and cargo were to be unloaded in Pago Pago, but no one there would accept it. They claimed they had received no orders for any such men or material.

"We don't want it," said the local commander. "Do whatever you want with it." So the exasperated captain, with the help of his crew, navy gunners, and disgusted passengers, unloaded the cargo on the beach. It stayed there throughout the war—testimony to wartime waste and bungling. The *Buchanan* continued on to New Caledonia to unload bombs.

Many Liberty ships were used by the army for inter-island shuttle runs. One voyage of the *Jose C. Barbosa*, for example, lasted nine months. Starting at San Francisco, she made stops at Espíritu Santo, New Hebrides, Milne Bay, and Lae, New Guineau; Buna, Papua New Guinea; Hollandia, Seadler Island, the Admiralties; and a number of other island bases. The crew had a grand tour of the South Seas. They saw plenty of soldiers and marines but were disappointed not to see any native girls. During the entire voyage, the *Barbosa* never had a chance to evade a submarine or shoot at a plane. The crew were sure the *Barbosa* had become the forgotten ship of the South Seas and probably would float from island to island forever.

Although few histories of the naval war in the Pacific even mention it, Japanese submarines made a bold but mostly ineffective foray against American shipping along the coast of California in December 1941.

The tanker *Emidio* was twenty miles off Cape Mendocino, about two hundred miles north of San Francisco, when lookouts were amazed to see a submarine come to the surface a quarter of a mile astern. Any doubts about her being friendly or unfriendly were quickly dispelled when the submarine's deck gun began firing. Captain Clark Farrow ordered full speed and tried to outmaneuver the attacker, but she was too fast. The first shot missed, but the next five were hits. Finally getting into a good firing position, the submarine launched a torpedo that hit the tanker in the engine room and killed the men on watch. An SOS brought two U.S. Navy bombers to the scene, and the submarine submerged. After the war, she was identified as the I-8, which later saw action against American forces in the South Pacific. Six men of the *Emidio*'s crew were killed and five injured.

A submarine attacked the tanker *H. M. Storey* on 22 December only two miles off Point Arguello, California, twenty-five miles north of Santa Barbara. The *Storey* escaped. The tanker *Agriworld* was stalked for half an hour by a submarine but made it safely into Santa Cruz.

Shortly before dusk on 23 February 1942, a submarine surfaced off the coast near Santa Barbara and bombarded the oil fields at nearby Ellwood. No one was injured and no damage was done, but the fact that the enemy could shell such an important area at its leisure showed the utter lack of sea defenses along the coast.[1]

These attacks sent shock waves up and down the West Coast and heightened fears of an impending invasion by the Japanese, or at least an attempt to land saboteurs. They even prompted the Mexican government to dispatch 1,500 soldiers to patrol the shores of its state, Baja California. The Japanese could have effected a much greater psychological impact and done more damage to shipping if these forays had been better planned and carried out. Submarines lying even briefly off the ports of Los Angeles and San Francisco could have exacted a considerable shipping toll.

So nervous was the military at its land-based coastal defenses that, during the early morning hours of 25 February, army antiaircraft batteries around Los Angeles fired 1,430 shells into the sky. Later, no one explained the nature of the target.

One of the most amazing voyages of the war began in January 1942, when the U.S. Army commandeered the freighter *Coast Farmer*, then lying at Brisbane, Australia. Unknown to Captain John Mattson or any of his crew, the *Coast Farmer* and several other vessels had been picked by the army to rush ammunition, food, fuel, and medical supplies to the hard-pressed American forces fighting in the Philippines. They were to sail, unarmed and unescorted, through hundreds of miles of enemy-held waters.

In a few days, the ship was crammed full of cargo. Then, in a typical example of wartime snafu, the cargo was unloaded and put back on the dock because, as an Army officer explained to Captain Mattson, "Your ship is too slow. We need a much faster vessel." When no faster ship could be found after a week or so, the cargo was reloaded and the old *Coast Farmer* dispatched to tiny Thursday Island off the northern tip of Australia in the Torres Strait. There, Captain Mattson was given his orders—to proceed at full speed to a designated spot on the coast of Mindanao in the Philippines, where American troops would be waiting for him and the cargo would be unloaded. Somehow, the *Coast Farmer* was to sneak past Japanese bases, elude enemy planes, and hope that no Japanese patrol ship became suspicious enough to stop her and ask questions. The captain's revolver, the only firearm on the ship, was hardly enough to defend against anything, "not even a seagull," as Mattson said later.[2]

He also learned at Thursday Island that another ship bound for the Philippines had not been heard from and probably had been bombed or torpedoed.

During her hair-raising run, the *Coast Farmer* passed a chain of islands held by the Japanese and, at one time, was only forty-five miles from the busy Japanese base at Amboina, Netherlands Indies. The crew saw Japanese planes and spotted small vessels that might have been patrol boats on the horizon, but the *Coast Farmer,* making as little smoke as possible and going full speed mainly at night, finally was within sight of the mountains of Mindanao. As the ship approached land, all hands waited nervously to learn what they would encounter. Would American forces still be there, or would they be greeted by the Japanese? Would they be shelled or sunk and taken prisoner? The ship slowed to a crawl while lookouts scanned the shore of Gingoog Bay with binoculars.

"I never want to live through that kind of uncertainty again," Mattson said. "We couldn't see any sign of life along the shore, which was forested and seemed to be indented with a bay or river. I double-checked the charts and my orders, but according to them we were at the right spot."

Mattson was trying to decide whether to drop anchor when a launch put out from the shore. In it were men in khaki uniforms. Were they Americans or Japanese? The Japanese wore khaki, too.

It was hard to identify them as fellow countrymen because they were tanned and bearded, "kind of scroungey looking," Mattson said. The launch approached the *Coast Farmer* warily and circled the ship before coming up to her boarding ladder. The first man to climb on board was an officer with a pistol in his hand. After a quick look at Mattson and the crew, he shouted to the others to follow.

"OK, boys," he shouted. "This is it. They made it."

"We've got to get the ship close to shore before any planes spot you," he told Mattson. "There's deep water there and the mountain will help to hide you."

Even while the anchor chain went clattering through the hawse pipes, the crew were uncovering the hatches. Barges manned by soldiers came out from shore to receive the cargo.

Getting to the Philippines was one thing, but getting back was another. During the return trip to Thursday Island, the *Coast Farmer* had several narrow escapes from detection by other ships. The very audacity of the voyage probably kept the enemy from being suspicious, and the ship made it safely back. Ironically, she was torpedoed and sunk some weeks later by a Japanese submarine off the coast of Australia.

America's counteroffensive in the Pacific would have been impossible without the vast quantity of goods delivered by the Merchant Marine. A typical ship's cargo could include bombs, trucks, bulldozers, canned Spam, Quonset huts, gasoline in drums, small arms ammunition, clothing, tents, cots, lubricating oil, and, of course, beer and cigarettes. Watching slingloads of beer being unloaded from his ship, one captain wondered if the far-flung island bases in the Pacific were not "floating on beer."

To lonely troops on isolated bases and to thousands of soldiers, sailors, and marines training for invasion operations, mail was almost as important as food. The Merchant Marine delivered tons of it.

Compared with the Atlantic, Mediterranean, Indian Ocean, and Atlantic-Arctic theaters of operation, most of the Pacific might have seemed calm and unexciting to merchant seamen. As the tide of battle moved westward, however, many saw all the action they could want. Merchant ships took part in all of the invasions after the initial landings on Guadalcanal.

The first Liberty ship to be sunk in the Pacific was the *John Adams*, torpedoed on 5 May 1942 near New Caledonia. Five navy gunners were killed. Fortunately, the torpedo missed the two thousand tons of gasoline in the holds or there might have been no survivors.

The Liberty ship *William Dawes* was en route from Adelaide, Australia, to Brisbane on 21 July 1942 when a torpedo blew off the stern. Three men were killed and several wounded. Like most Liberty ships, the disabled *Dawes* was hard to sink and had to be sent down by gunfire from HMS *Southampton*.

The American West Coast had feared an invasion after the visit by Japanese submarines, but the invasion of America actually took place in the far-off Aleutians, the island chain extending westward from the Alaskan mainland to within a thousand miles of the northern islands of Japan. The Aleutians were known to mariners as having the world's worst weather, with rain, snow, mist, fog, strong currents, vicious storms, and almost continual overcast. The islands were a "cold hell" for the invading Japanese, for the defenders, and especially for U.S. Army and Navy pilots who had to fly in such abominable weather. Many were lost.

The war in the Aleutians began on 3 June 1942, when Japanese planes made successful attacks on Dutch Harbor. It eventually involved more than 100,000 American and Canadian troops, a large fleet of warships and submarines, and hundreds of aircraft. Huge amounts of food, fuel, ammunition, bombs, and construction equipment for this northern war, as well as troops, were delivered to Alaskan and Aleutian bases by the Merchant Marine. A voyage from Seattle, Washington, to Kodiak, Alaska, a main supply depot, covered some two thousand miles.

The Japanese occupied Attu and Kiska islands on the end of the Aleutians in June. American forces did not retake the bleak and fog-swept island of Attu until May 1943. The cost was considerable, with more than 1,800 casualties.

In a masterful coup involving speed and deception, the Japanese completely evacuated 5,000 troops and civilian construction workers from Kiska in July, but the abandoned island endured a merciless saturation bombardment by American warships and planes. When 34,000 U.S. and Canadian troops stormed ashore, they found nothing but a few hungry dogs. This pointless and unopposed invasion, unfortunately, was not bloodless. Many troops were drowned or killed or wounded in accidents, trigger-happy shootings, and incidents of mistaken identity.

A Japanese submarine scored one hit on merchant shipping during the Aleutian campaign. The small freighter *Arcata* had left Bethel on the west coast of Alaska on 11 July 1942. She had cleared Unimak Pass and was steaming south toward Sitka on 14 July at 2000 when the lookout sighted a submarine surfaced quite brazenly a mile away. Any thought that she might be American was soon dispelled when she opened fire. The first four shots were misses, but the fifth hit near the starboard bow. The enemy gunners were not very adept, for the next six shells missed the ship. The attacker then stopped firing and kept pace with the fleeing freighter. She gradually closed the distance.

At 2230, now within closer range, the submarine opened fire again. The shells hit a wing of the bridge, the radio shack, and the chart house and carried away the rudder. Captain Christian Evenson then gave the order to abandon ship.

When one of the boats was lowered overside, the discharge from the condenser filled it with water and rendered the boat useless. The captain and two seamen then launched a raft. Another raft was successfully launched, and fifteen men were able to climb onto it. Soon after, the submarine focused a searchlight on the raft and a sailor opened fire with a hand-held machine gun. Fortunately, the raft fell into the trough of a sea and the bullets passed over the men. The other raft was also the target of machine-gun fire. During the next day, a plane flew over but did not see the rafts. When the survivors were picked up by a de-

stroyer three days later, eight men had died of wounds or exposure. Fourteen survived.

A number of other sinkings were the result of sporadic
Japanese submarine activity in the Pacific. The *Edgar Allan Poe*,
bound for Espíritu Santo, was fifty-six miles southeast of Nouméa,
New Caledonia, on 8 November 1942 when she was torpedoed in
the engine room. Despite a hole more than forty feet long in the
hull, the ship did not sink and was towed to Nouméa for salvage.

A torpedo plane targeted the *John H. Couch* at Koli Point,
Guadalcanal, on 11 October 1943. The ship was beached, and
three men were killed. On the same day, the *George H. Himes* was
torpedoed by a plane at Koli Point and beached with her cargo of
lumber, ammunition, food, and other material. There was no loss
of life.

The ability of Liberty ships to sustain extensive damage and
still stay afloat was evidenced when the *Matthew Lyon* was torpedoed in August 1943 while en route from Guadalcanal to Espíritu
Santo. Despite a huge hole in the hull, she continued under her
own power to her destination.

Although the chance of meeting an enemy submarine in the
Pacific was not as likely as it was in the Atlantic and other areas,
ship captains were wise to be on the alert, with sharp lookouts
and guns ready for action. In 1944, the tanker *W. W. Rheem* was
saved from destruction by the alertness of captain and crew.

Captain G. A. Johnson, who had survived a torpedoing earlier in the war, was on the bridge at night when he sighted a
suspicious disturbance in the water about two miles off the port
quarter. With a quick look through the glasses, he saw that the
ruffled action on the surface of the sea was no gamboling fish but
a torpedo track pointing straight toward his ship. Instantly, he
ordered, "Starboard you helm; hard over," and all hands on the
bridge watched anxiously to see if the explosive missile would
miss. As they followed its telltale track, lacing through the sea in
clear outline against the darkness, a second torpedo, previously

unseen, passed within a few feet of the stern. The gunners there said they could almost have reached out and touched it. After the first torpedo had also slid safely by, there was an earsplitting explosion.

The vessel careened as though another ship had rammed into it—a third torpedo had struck home on the port side, forward. The explosion sent a pillar of flame shooting skyward higher than the masts. Bits of steel and debris rained down on the decks. Plates buckled, and the vessel listed as water poured through a hole in the side. Fortunately, this surge of water put out the fire. Plans to abandon ship were canceled when a quick survey of the damage convinced Captain Johnson that his ship could still float. Because the oil carrier had been built with a honeycomb of tanks, such a blast could occur without the vessel sinking or being made a complete derelict. The crew of the *Rheem* stayed with their crippled ship and shifted cargo so as to lighten the forward tanks.

The ship crept precariously on. All hands expected that a fourth tin fish would slice into them and complete the job at any moment, but no torpedo came. Nor did the submarine surface to finish them off with gunfire. For some reason there was no follow-up; perhaps the submarine commander assumed that the crew would abandon ship and she would sink anyway. Or maybe he preferred to save his remaining torpedoes for other targets lured to the scene by the tanker's SOS. The *Rheem*'s crew were not intimidated by the serious damage to their vessel. There was no rush to the lifeboats, no thought of abandoning ship, if they could possibly bring her in with her vital cargo of fuel for the navy.

Regardless of the possibility that the submarine was still lying in wait close by, Johnson held to his course and the *Rheem* arrived a few days later at her destination, an island supply port in the Western Pacific. No repair facilities were available, so she put to sea for California in her damaged condition. Slowly, at a speed of a few knots, she crawled toward her home port more than five thousand miles away. The hardy old ship eventually finished out the war and was finally laid up after 594 voyages across the seven seas.

At a time when no Japanese submarines were thought to be active in the eastern Pacific, a lone prowler bagged a Liberty ship and sent her to the bottom with 10,000 tons of cargo.

On 30 October 1944, the *John A. Johnson,* running without convoy, was bound from San Francisco to Honolulu, with holds full of food, trucks, ammunition, high explosives, and construction equipment. In the early morning darkness, a torpedo exploded just forward of the deckhouse in number three hold and hit at the turn of the bilge when the ship rolled in heavy seas. Within ten minutes, the vessel broke in two and the order was given to abandon ship. All hands got away in two lifeboats and a raft.

The submarine then surfaced and began shelling both sections of the severed ship, the forward and rear parts having drifted about a quarter of a mile apart. The shells set both sections on fire. Within an hour, the front part, which contained explosives, blew up and flames shot hundreds of feet into the air.

After shelling the ship with both deck guns, the raider centered her attention on the lifeboats. Number two boat, with twenty-eight survivors, was the closest one. The submarine bore down with the obvious intent of ramming and sinking it; when she was less than a hundred feet away, the survivors jumped overboard. The bow of the submarine hit the empty boat, but it was not damaged. A wave lifted the little craft free of the impact, and it bounced harmlessly along the raider's hull. Meanwhile, Japanese sailors were shooting at the floundering survivors with pistols and rifles as a spotlight targeted them in the water. After the submarine moved off in search of the other victims, the remaining survivors climbed back into the boat.

The submarine then rammed the raft, which had seventeen survivors, after firing on it. Three men were killed and others wounded. The raider then submerged and disappeared. A Pan American Airways flying boat, spotting the survivors at 1000, radioed for help and directed the USS *Argus* to their rescue. A total of ten men were killed in this wanton shelling of the lifeboat and the raft: four of the merchant crew, five of the Armed Guard, and the army cargo security officer.

A new and terrifying kind of warfare from the air greeted invasion forces during the battle for Leyte in the Philippines. Its weapon was the kamikaze—the "divine wind," the suicide plane—whose brave young pilot, eager to give his life for the emperor and knowing that he would be blown to bits, deliberately crashed into a ship.[3]

The first kamikaze attacks came on 25 October 1944, about forty-five miles off Singao Island, when a suicide plane exploded on the flight deck of the aircraft carrier *Santee* and continued down into the hanger deck. There were forty-three casualties, sixteen of them fatal. Also hit were the carriers *Suwanee* and *St. Lo,* which sank after a violent explosion of bombs on the hanger deck.

After these successes, the kamikazes turned their attention to the supply ships in Leyte Gulf.

Kamikazes were named for the divine wind that, according to Japanese legend, the sun goddess sent to wreck the invasion fleet of Kublai Khan in 1281. Two types of kamikazes were used. One was a small piloted plane with 250 pounds of explosives set to go off on contact. The other was a glide bomb launched from a bomber and carrying 2,640 pounds of dynamite. It was guided to its target by the pilot. At Okinawa, kamikazes sank 34 warships and damaged 288, including 36 carriers, 15 battleships, and 87 destroyers. They sank or damaged about 30 merchant ships.

There was no lack of action for merchant crews and navy gunners when the invasion of the Philippines began at Leyte in October 1944. In just two weeks, the Merchant Marine delivered 500,000 tons of food, ammunition, and other supplies, plus 30,000 soldiers. The Army credited the gunners on these merchant ships with downing more than one hundred planes during the ten weeks after D-day.

The Liberty ship *Adoniram Judson* saw action even before her anchor hit the bottom of San Pedro Bay on 22 October. Fighters and bombers, attacking under the light of a full moon, were beaten off by intense fire from her three-inch gun and the 20-millimeters. The following is a typical entry from the Armed Guard commander's report:

> Jap Zero making a run on the stern. Aft 3-inch gun opened fire and forced him away at 1,500 yards ... Jap plane coming in on the stern. At 3,000 yards opened barrage and plane swerved off to starboard ... two Jap bombers overhead at medium altitude. Poor visibility. Two Jap bombers on port side at 5,000 yards. Our barrage diverted them. Almost constant alerts.[4]

The *Judson* had the makings of a volcano ready to erupt. In the holds were 3,000 barrels of high-octane aviation gasoline. One good hit from bombers would have taken ship and crew to "kingdom come."

The Liberty ship *Marcus Daly* was credited with shooting down several planes, as did the gunners of *David Dudley Field*.

General MacArthur, in lauding the *Daly* for helping to defend the dock area, noted in an official commendation that "for six days and nights her merchant crew and Navy gunners defeated vigorous attacks by enemy planes in a series of heroic actions." The ship also saw heavy action on returning to Leyte in December with another cargo, plus more than 1,000 troops.

The Liberty ship *Augustus Thomas* was carrying 3,000 tons of ammunition and 1,000 barrels of aviation gasoline—as lethal a load as one could imagine—while she waited to unload at San Pedro Bay in October. Alongside lay the small Navy tanker *Sonoma*. Four Japanese planes attacked the anchorage. One of them, with fire streaming from its engines and seemingly out of control, bore through an intense barrage. It hit the stack of the *Sonoma* with one wing, then spun around and crashed into the *Thomas*.

The plane's bomb load fell into the water between the ships and detonated, blowing big holes in both hulls.

A miracle must have occurred in San Pedro Bay that night. On board the *Thomas* were 548 men; 41 in the merchant crew, 27 in the Armed Guard, and 480 soldiers waiting to disembark. All survived.

The Liberty ship *Thomas Nelson* was a fighting freighter, but her steel-spitting guns were unable to ward off the fury of a Japanese kamikaze attack. On 20 November 1944, the *Nelson* was anchored at Dulag Bay in the Philippines with twenty other ships carrying troops and supplies.

The *Nelson* had 633 Army troops on board and a large cargo of ammunition when a suicide plane, which had been hit and disabled by the ship's gunners, was still able to crash onto the deck. Its bomb exploded on impact, setting the ship afire and killing some 140 soldiers and gunners. More than 80 soldiers were wounded. There were no more dangerous front lines than the beachheads served by the Merchant Marine.

Three hundred troops were starting to disembark from the *Benjamin Ide Wheeler,* anchored at Tacloban, Leyte. They were greeted almost immediately by an air attack. The next day a bomber appeared out of the clouds at about 1,500 feet, some four miles away. As soon as it came within range, all guns bearing on the target threw up a curtain of steel that tore off one wing. Careening out of control, the plane crashed into the *Wheeler* at number five hold. So many plates were blown loose in the hull that the ship settled to the bottom and sat there until she could be salvaged several months later.

The *Wilbur C. Atwater* survived 165 air raids and alerts without casualties during her stay in Leyte Gulf. The *Gilbert Stuart* was not so fortunate. A 20-millimeter gun crew stayed heroically at their post and fired at a kamikaze headed directly for them. The gun crew were killed, but the *Stuart* was able to deliver her cargo.

The *Mathew P. Deady* had 900 soldiers on board when she arrived at Tacloban on 29 October. She was a rich target for any pilot hoping to exact a heavy toll on the enemy before he rode to heaven on the "divine wind."

The ship had hardly come to anchor before a plane attacked, but its bombs were near misses. The pilot, perhaps gathering courage, then circled the anchorage for the supreme sacrifice. Breaking out of cloud cover and undeterred by the *Deady's* intense stream of antiaircraft fire, the pilot crashed his plane into the number two 20-millimeter gun platform located at number one hold. The resultant fire created such intense heat that the 20-millimeter ammunition exploded in the ready boxes and sprayed the foredeck and bridge with jagged shrapnel. Despite this rain of lethal steel, the merchant crew ran fire hoses along the deck and brought the flames under control. While the ship was fighting for her life, five more planes came in, bombing and strafing. One was splashed by the *Deady's* gunners. About 750 soldiers were waiting to disembark; 22 were killed, some by being blown overboard. Two of the Armed Guard were killed.

During her stay in Leyte Gulf, from 4 to 27 November, the *Alcoa Pioneer* experienced 103 air raids and alerts and survived fifty direct attacks by bombers and kamikazes. At 0700 on 19 November, three suicide planes dived out of cloud cover and headed toward the ship, but two were diverted by the intense ack-ack fire and selected other targets nearby. The third pressed its attack through the barrage and crashed into the bridge; Armed Guard Commander Howard Jersild and four of his gunners were killed. Fourteen more men, gunners and merchant crewmen, were seriously wounded when the plane blew up and doused the deck with flaming fuel.

There were numerous incidents of heroism that day, as badly wounded navy gunners stayed by their posts and merchant crewmen ran fire hoses into a hold filled with drums of gasoline to put out a fire before it could ignite this lethal load. Navy gunner Patrick Stevens stayed at his post, although his arm was almost severed. Temporary repairs were made to the ship by the merchant crew during the next several days, and she continued to discharge her cargo.

Countless other incidents of dramatic action and heroism took place during the battle for Leyte.

The Liberty ship *Antoine Saugrain* fought off a dozen kamikazes. In one raid, during which twelve Armed Guard gunners were seriously wounded, merchant seamen took their places at the guns. The ship was hit and sunk several days later by an aerial torpedo.

The *Morrison R. Waite,* a veteran of the landings at Anzio, where her gunners had shot down a German bomber, was attacked at Leyte. Bullets from strafing planes started fires in a hold containing ammunition and gasoline, and Captain F. F. Boyd ordered the hold flooded. While crewmen fought the fire, gunners continued to beat off the bombers. Able seaman Anthony Martinez went into the hold, which might have exploded at any minute, to help several injured men reach the open deck. After that, he dove overboard to help rescue injured soldiers.

Bombs started fires on the *William S. Ladd* at Leyte and the ship was sunk, but gunners had the satisfaction of splashing one of the attackers.

Gunners on the *Edward N. Westcott* blew an attacker to bits with their three-inch guns during the ship's approach to an anchorage off Luzon. So close was the plane when it blew apart that its careening engine, narrowly missing crewmen and gunners, smashed two cargo booms and crashed into the deckhouse. Six merchant seamen and seven of the Armed Guard were wounded by flying pieces of the shattered plane.

A bulls-eye by gunners of the *Floyd Spencer* saved that Liberty in a convoy en route to Leyte. Captain Simpson Blackwood said:

> It was a surprise attack. There had been no alert.
> One plane came up from the rear of the convoy and
> headed right for us at an angle. At about 1,800 yards

he dropped a torpedo. All our guns that could bear blasted away at him. When it was 100 yards away it came apart and crashed. The torpedo missed our stern by a few feet.[5]

Lt. (jg) William S. Birdwell, Jr., commanded the gun crew.

When the *Charlotte Cushman* (Captain Ellsworth Bush) returned home, she had five Japanese flags painted on her deckhouse. The flags represented the five planes shot down by her crew at Leyte.

During fifty-five hectic days at Leyte, the *Cape Constance* shot down two planes and kept others far enough away from the ship so that they couldn't drop their bombs or torpedoes. The *John Foster, Mary Kinney, Sidney Short, Laurence Gianella,* and *Clarence Darrow* shot down a total of fifteen planes.

Along with blazing guns and death-dealing kamikazes, there were other dramatic events in Pacific waters that, though less spectacular, were quietly heroic.

In November 1943, for example, the Liberty ship *Edwin T. Meredith* had teamed up with the destroyer *McCall* and a Pan American Airways seaplane to save 1,429 soldiers, merchant seamen, and navy gunners from the torpedoed troopship *Cape San Juan.* The *Meredith* won the praise of Adm. Chester W. Nimitz for expert handling and the willingness of her crewmen to jump into shark-infested waters and help the floundering survivors to reach boats and rafts.

The Liberty ship *John Howard Payne,* named for the author of "Home, Sweet Home," combined pinpoint navigation and skillful seamanship to rescue the crew of an Army bomber that had crashed in the western Pacific in 1945. Although the *Payne* was seventy-five miles from the crash site when she received a radio request to hunt for the downed fliers, Captain Orion A. Larson and his mates plotted a course that put the *Payne* within a few miles of where the plane reported ditching. With all available crewmen scanning the sea, the *Payne* proceeded at full speed to hunt for the proverbial "needle in a haystack" among the tumbling waves.

After several hours of searching, a lookout on the bridge reported lights off the starboard bow. The *Payne* headed toward the weak, glimmering light and came upon two men in a tiny inflatable yellow raft. A lifeboat was lowered, and the two fliers, both injured, were brought safely aboard. A radio message summoned a navy ship with medical facilities to pick up the fliers. Had the officers of the *Payne* been slower in response to the call for help or less skillful in navigation, two more names would have been added to the list of men lost when their planes went down in the Pacific.

The invasion at Mindoro in the Philippines was even more costly to merchant ships and their crews than the battles at Leyte. On 27 December 1944, a convoy bound from Leyte to Mindoro was attacked by kamikazes. One crashed into the ammunition-packed Liberty ship *John Burke;* the ship and all on board were blown to bits. The *Lewis L. Dyche* survived this attack but suffered a similar fate soon after reaching Magrin Bay when all of her seventy-one merchant crewmen and Armed Guard gunners were killed instantly in an explosion after a kamikaze hit. Another ship in the convoy, the *Francisco Morazon,* fired ten tons of shells in repelling suicide attacks. In a tremendous display of determined defense, the navy gunners, aided by the merchant crew, shot down six of the planes attacking the convoy.

The Armed Guard report from the *Morazon* gives a brief but dramatic account of this kamikaze raid:

> 1015 hours. Three planes attack the convoy. One plane shot down. Another plane dove into the Liberty ship *John Burke.* Two minutes later the ship blew up. No evidence of it remained. The blast shook the entire sea. Heavy shrapnel littered our deck. The *Burke* had completely disintegrated.
>
> A number of men in nearby ships were killed or wounded by debris from the exploding ship.[6]

Navy gunners on the bridge of PCE-851 search the sky for Japanese kamikazes as LST-472, a kamikaze victim, burns behind them. This action took place off Mindoro 15 December 1944. The photo was taken by Yn3c Daniel B. Murphy, USNR. (National Archives, 80-G-294573)

At the same time that the *Burke* was hit, another kamikaze, flaming and seemingly out of control, dove into the *William Sharon*. Its starboard wing clipped the funnel, and it swerved into number four gun tub, killing the gun crew, and crashed into the flying bridge, where the Armed Guard officer, Lt. (j.g.) Erick Gerhardt, was directing the fire of the guns. He was among several men killed on the bridge. Fires swept the midships section, but they were brought under control and the vessel returned to Leyte for repairs.

During a suicide plane attack later that same day, merchant ships and naval escorts shot down several attackers. The *Morazon*'s Armed Guard report continues:

> Our 5-inch gun secured a direct hit. The burning
> plane looked like the tail of a comet as it narrowly
> missed us and plunged into the sea.[7]

Action could come hot and heavy and often ended in tragedy for ships supplying the invasion forces. The *Hobart Baker*
was carrying 3,000 tons of steel airstrip landing mats when she
dropped her hook in an open anchorage off Bug Bay, Mindoro, on
28 December 1944. Soon after lunch, red tracer shells streaked
into the sky from a master antiaircraft battery ashore, a warning
that enemy planes were headed toward the area. Armed Guard
gunners and merchant crewmen ran to battle stations, but, after a
few minutes, when no planes appeared they decided it was a
false alarm and felt cheated out of "seeing some action." Their
appetite for action had been whetted at Leyte a few days before
when they had shot down a kamikaze.

They saw plenty of action after 1900. A plane was spotted
approaching the ship from the north at about 3,000 feet, and they
were called to battle stations again. Then the plane turned and
headed out to sea. Perhaps the pilot was giving himself a few
more minutes to breathe the air of life or to exult in the beauties of
a gathering twilight, or perhaps he just wanted a better angle for
attack. Five minutes later, he roared down toward the anchorage
and headed for the *Baker* at masthead height. There was no time
to even aim the guns. He had taken them by surprise—coming in
from the starboard beam and dropping two bombs into number
three hold. There was a terrific explosion that blew out the bulkhead between the hold and the engine room and tore holes in the
hull. The entire midships section was a mass of flames as the
Baker settled to the bottom of the shallow anchorage. The chief
engineer was killed, but all others on board the *Baker* survived.
The kamikaze pilot flew on to dive on another ship and ride the
"divine wind" to a flaming crash into the bay.

During the invasion at Mindoro, the Liberty ship *Juan de
Fuca* was caught in the shelling from a Japanese task force. She
was strafed by enemy Zeros, received a near miss from a high-

level bomber, was hit by a kamikaze, and was then blasted by a torpedo bomber. After Captain Charles Robbins beached his ship, he helped to salvage the Liberty ship *John Clayton,* which was first torpedoed, then blasted by a bomb that set her on fire. She was also beached.

The full potential of the kamikaze was demonstrated during the invasion of Okinawa, where thousands of American sailors died in air attacks, mostly by Japanese suicide pilots who put love of country above their own lives and crashed their planes into ships of the invasion fleet. Warships were their prime targets, but freighters supplying the invasion forces were targets, too.

A vast fleet of 1,300 ships and smaller craft launched the invasion in March 1945. Troops and supplies came from Leyte, Guadalcanal, Guam, Tinian in the North Marshalls, Espíritu Santo, and other island bases, as well as from U.S. ports on the West Coast. Several hundred Liberty ships, the faster Victory ships, and other types of freighters and tankers carried the bulk of ammunition, food, fuel, and other supplies.

Because their navy had been so greatly decimated by this time, the Japanese had no battle fleet or air force capable of contesting the invasion. Their last desperate hope lay in the fanatic devotion of kamikaze pilots eager to die for their emperor.

From the time they arrived at the invasion beachheads, the merchant ships were under almost constant alert. The approach of enemy aircraft was sounded by a line of radar picket ships strung out to the north of Okinawa, and many of these vessels also were kamikaze victims. A suicide plane could dive out of the clouds at any moment. Guns were always ready for action.

At one time, the gunners of the Liberty ship *Uriah M. Rose* were at general quarters for fourteen hours without a break. During a month in Okinawa waters, the *Rose*'s gunners, aided by the merchant crew, shot down two kamikazes and assisted other ships in splashing six more. Ships fired on any attacker within range. One of the *Rose*'s victims fell into the sea within fifty feet of the ship, a hairbreadth from disaster.

As with most Libertys and Victorys, the *Rose*'s antiaircraft defense included a three-inch/50 multipurpose gun on the bow and eight 20-millimeter Oerlikon guns. The Oerlikon was a Swedish make that performed tremendous service for the Merchant Marine, as well as warships of the Allied navies. For surface action, the *Rose* also carried a four-inch/50 gun on the stern.

The accuracy of her defense probably saved the ship from explosion and fire. One attack was chronicled in these words by the Armed Guard commander, Lt. John C. Landis:

> Enemy plane appeared out of clouds astern. Plane circled around to our starboard side and started toward us at about 1,500 yards. Several nearby ships opened up with their guns. Our 20-millimeters started firing at 1,000 yards. Our shells poured into the plane. It roared over us at about sixty feet and then crashed into the water with a loud explosion less than 100 feet away. We fired 450 rounds of 20-millimeter shells to bring it down. Shells well spent. . . . Merchant marine gunners and loaders did a splendid job.[8]

For some unexplained reason, Landis had only thirteen men in his gun crew and had to rely on the merchant crew to maintain a full complement on the guns.

Reports by Armed Guard officers, with a few exceptions, were short and factual. There were no dramatic elaborations, no hints of the stark fear that gunners could feel as they faced a bomb-laden suicide plane roaring toward them, closing in on them second by second until, many times, they saw the enemy pilot in his death-seeking dash.

On 6 April, the *Logan Victory* was one of several ships loaded with ammunition at anchorage at Kerama Retto when three kamikazes roared in to attack. The first pilot dove into LST (landing ship tank) 447 and caused many casualties. The second plane made a run on the nearby *Pierre Victory,* but it was blown to pieces less than fifty yards from its target. The third plane evaded intense ack-ack fire and crashed into the *Logan Victory* amidships.

An intense fire resulted, and the vessel was abandoned. She drifted for several hours, with ammunition exploding, until she was sunk by gunfire to prevent danger to other vessels. Captain Edson B. Cates, although seriously wounded by shrapnel, was the last to leave his ship. He died two days later on a navy hospital ship.

The nearby, ammunition-packed *Hobbs Victory* was also a kamikaze victim. The following is from the postvoyage Armed Guard report:

> At 1600 hours. Attack on anchorage by several planes. One selected the *Pierre Victory,* near us. Shot down by the *Hobbs Victory* when it was less than 100 yards from its target. Soon after, a Zero made a low level attack on the *Logan Victory,* anchored about 1,000 yards off our port bow.
>
> We opened fire with the 3-inch/50 but the plane smashed into the *Logan,* creating huge fires. Stayed at our guns. At 1845 hours two Zeros began an attack on us. One plane shot down by our gunfire and that from several other ships. Second plane swerved, then headed directly for us about forty feet above the water. All guns firing. Crashed into us just forward of midships at deck level. Just missed number four gun tub. Terrific explosion. Flames swept the deck. Gunner Russel Evjen at number six gun blown overside. Rescued but died later. Gunner Chester McNealy blown overside and lost.[9]

Lt. (j.g.) Emil Spierling, the Armed Guard commander, was also killed. The survivors abandoned ship before she sank.

On 27 April, the *Canada Victory* was attacked while at anchor off Green Beach, Okinawa. A suicide plane, with its engine cut out, used the cover of darkness to glide in to the target unseen. Because its approach was undetected, no guns opened fire and it crashed against the aftermast, fell into number four hold, and exploded. Fire soon spread throughout the after part of the vessel. Two Armed Guard gunners were killed. The ship had to be abandoned, and she sank soon afterward.

Despite the fury of the kamikaze onslaught on Okinawa, only three merchant ships were sunk, although many saw action.

The navy suffered heavily in ships and men. Some 30 ships and small craft were sunk and 368 damaged. More than 5,000 sailors were killed and hundreds wounded. Approximately 700 were killed on the aircraft carrier *Franklin* and 396 on the carrier *Bunker Hill*.[10]

A total of 44 merchant ships, most of them Libertys, were sunk in the Pacific. Japanese suicide pilots were responsible for the majority of the sinkings; aerial and submarine torpedoes and regular bombers accounted for others.

General MacArthur paid this tribute to the Merchant Marine:

> They have brought us our lifeblood and paid for it with some of their own. I saw them bombed off the Philippines and in New Guinea. When it was humanly possible, when their ships were not blown out from under them by bombs or torpedoes, they have delivered their cargoes to us. In war it is performance that counts.[11]

When the bloody battle for Okinawa finally ended and the island was secured, the Merchant Marine had completed its part in the war of the Pacific. Because of the Merchant Marine's "long haul," U.S. victory throughout the islands of the Pacific had been possible.

21
The Great Invasion

THE MOST FORMIDABLE ARMADA OF FIGHTING SHIPS that the world had ever seen launched the invasion of France on 6 June 1944. Hundreds of troop-packed landing craft crossing the English Channel were preceded by a bombarding fleet of battleships, cruisers, destroyers, gunboats, and rocket launchers. Close behind the assault forces were the troop and cargo transports.[1]

To one captain, the great miracle of the invasion was that such a vast movement of ships could take place without half of them being sunk in collision. From the ponderous battleships to the minesweepers, patrol boats, LSTs, small coasters, and Liberty ships, more than four thousand vessels jammed the channel on that historic day.

Correspondent Richard Strout, in a June report for *New Republic* magazine, says: "The English Channel was choked with traffic of every kind, including craft big and little, new and old. Suddenly, I realized what it meant. This was Dunkirk in reverse. We were going back."

Captain Heinrich Kronke, master of the Liberty ship *Cyrus McCormick,* said it was hard to believe that there could be so many ships. He wrote:

> Every ship in the world seemed to be there. The Channel is the busiest thorofare on the globe. Ships and small craft throng it day and night. There wouldn't seem to be enough room to squeeze in another ship. You have to be constantly alert to avoid hitting somebody, or being hit. There are some enemy planes but they don't seem to be hitting anything. Constantly overhead are hundreds of our own bombers and fighters, headed for the coastal defenses or for enemy troop concentrations farther inland. Air power is overwhelming.[2]

The support ships, including a large fleet of Libertys, headed for the Normandy beachheads with troops, trucks, shells, gasoline, K-rations, and every other conceivable requirement for the invasion forces.

The following dispatch was sent from London to *The New York Times:*

> Undaunted by the threat of air attacks, sea mines, surface fire, submarines, or coastal batteries, the merchant ships fulfilled their mission according to schedule and returned to Britain's shores to start a shuttle service that will not end before Germany's unconditional surrender. The ships that went to France were of every conceivable type of transport, from one-time luxury liners to seagoing tugs.

The Liberty ship *Francis C. Harrington,* steaming toward Omaha Beach close behind the initial assault waves, struck a mine that blew a hole in the port side, disabled the pumps and other machinery, and sprang the shaft bearings. For five days and nights, Chief Engineer Leonard Valentine and his black gang crew, often working in water up to their waists in the shaft alley, removed the damaged bearings, straightened the shaft with hydraulic jacks, made and installed wooden shaft bearings, and repaired the pumps sufficiently for the ship to return to England after the cargo had been discharged.

"Chief Valentine's skill and determination," the U.S. Maritime Commission said in a news release, "represented service of the highest order."

During the war, there were many instances among men of the black gang, far and beyond the call of duty, that were typical of the mechanical skill and ingenuity displayed so often by veteran marine engineers.

The *Collis P. Huntington* left Cardiff, Wales, for France on the morning of 6 June and arrived at Omaha Beach that afternoon. On the night of 7 June and during the morning of the 8th, she was shaken by several underwater explosions. A German ME 210 dropped a bomb that exploded about six hundred feet away on the starboard side.

Armed Guard Lt. Walter Flowers reported:

> Our 20-millimeters poured shells into the plane. Smoke poured from it, then it burst into flames and crashed about 1,500 yards astern.[3]

The Liberty ship *Park Benjamin* loaded in London and arrived off Caen, France, on 7 June. The voyage report commented on her arrival:

> Spitfires were giving us constant cover. We passed several mines. There were ships as far as the eye could see. The sky was filled with planes going to France and returning.[4]

The *Benjamin* unloaded trucks, tanks, and Bren gun carriers into LCTs (landing craft tanks). She made seven trips to the beachheads during June, July, and August.

On 7 June, the *Jedediah Smith* struck a mine en route to Omaha Beach but did not sink. She continued on to discharge her cargo. Mines, rather than planes and shore guns, became the greatest hazards to the invasion fleets, although there were some exceptions.

The *Robert Peary*, the Liberty that made shipbuilding history by being assembled in four days and fifteen hours, made several trips to the beachheads. She narrowly missed a mine at the same time that the mine exploded under the *Jedediah Smith*, which was nearby. At Omaha Beach, a number of large-caliber shells from shore guns also made life uncomfortable on board the *Peary*.

On 8 June, a convoy of seventeen Liberty ships brought the 90th Division to Utah Beach. All men and equipment were unloaded in twenty-four hours. Between 7 and 30 June, 570 Liberty ships, 788 small coasters, 372 LCIs (landing craft infantry), 1,422 LCTs and 905 LSTs discharged men and cargo at the Normandy beaches. These figures include more than one run by each type of vessel.

The *John Merrick* was in the initial landing and followed up with eleven round trips to the beachheads.

Captain D. A. Aannevik reported to the vessel's operators, The Calmar Steamship Company:

> 10 June. Today we are at an English port loading a vast amount of equipment for the great expedition. Many troops are coming on board. I am proud of my officers and crew and proud to be part of it all. We are doing everything possible to accommodate the officers and soldiers. We are confident that it will be a great success.[5]

His pride and enthusiasm must have been shared by hundreds of other captains on ships loading at every British port that had cargo-handling facilities.

The *Casamir Pulaski*, under Captain Vincent Poirer, received a hot reception when she dropped anchor off the French coast on 11 June.

Lt. (j.g.) Herbert Hurst, the Armed Guard commander, reported:

At about midnight a JU-88 glided down on our stern and dropped a torpedo. It was a near miss. Five minutes later another plane dropped a torpedo. It was a near miss, too.

Our 20-millimeters opened fire and the plane splashed just off the bow. A very bright pistol flare was shot off ahead of us and we heard several people calling for help. A small life raft was tossed overside for them but we couldn't tell what became of them.[6]

The *H. G. Blasdell* left Southampton, England, on 29 June for Utah Beach with 413 soldiers on board, plus 60 merchant crew and Armed Guard. At 1700, the *Blasdell* hit a mine. Most of the troops were in number five hold; 68 were killed and 180 wounded. The *Blasdell* was towed to Southampton.

Through the month of June, Omaha Beach received 197,444 troops, 27,340 vehicles, and 68,799 tons of supplies.

The War Shipping Administration later released the names of some 150 American merchant ships, mostly Libertys, that were part of the invasion and follow-up supply fleets.

The *Samuel Colt* spent fourteen months away from the States, a good part of that time on shuttle runs between England and the continent. As she crossed the channel on one trip, a flight of British Spitfires, headed for England, flew over the vessel. One of the planes dropped out of formation and fell into the sea. The pilot floated down in a parachute. Captain Robert Patterson changed course, headed for the spot several miles away over which another plane was circling, and rescued the pilot.

As a "Johnny-on-the-spot," the *Colt* later received an SOS from an English collier that had been rammed in a fog about eight miles off Milford Haven, Wales. Hurrying to the spot through drifting fog banks, the *Colt* picked up the collier's skipper and most of the crew.

More than once, routine shuttle runs were spiced with adventure.

Allied destroyers, destroyer escorts, and other craft patrolled the English Channel and its sea approaches against the expected forays of German submarines, destroyers, and E-boats. A fleet of submarines based at Brest, Lorient, and other French ports were a threat that never developed. A large fleet of 110-foot E-boats, much like U.S. motor torpedo boats, was based in Rotterdam, Holland. These boats were used to attack convoys. They scored some successes but were not the threat that the Allies thought they might be. The Germans also used "human torpedoes," or one-man (midget) submarines, but their effect was almost nil and many were lost.

Artificial harbors were created off the beachheads to protect freighters and landing craft from winds and sea surges while they unloaded. In what were called "Mulberry" harbors, huge concrete caissons were used to form breakwaters. Each harbor was large enough for seven Liberty ships and twelve smaller vessels to moor at one time.

Other harbors, called "Gooseberries," were formed by sinking a fleet of seventy freighters, twenty-five of which were American, to form breakwaters. They were towed to the designated locations, where they were scuttled by their crews.

Among the American ships were some dating from the World War I mass shipbuilding program, among them the *West Cheswald*, *West Grama*, and *West Honaker*. A number of Libertys, including the *Benjamin Contee*, which had been torpedoed in the Mediterranean with Italian prisoners on board, were also used. Other ships assigned to this rather ignominious fate were the *Artemus Ward*, *James Iredell*, *James W. Marshall*, and *Matt W. Ransom*, which had survived much battle action in the Mediterranean. Two new concrete ships built at Tampa, Florida, the *David O. Saylor* and the *Vitruvius*, were also scuttled.

These ships served their purpose well, for during the great storm of 20–21 June, which wrecked the Mulberries, the scuttled ships kept their places, withstood the waves, and, as historian Samuel Eliot Morison relates, "protected several hundred landing craft from destruction."

The French port of Cherbourg was captured in July. After the harbor was cleared of mines, sunken ships, and other debris, it became second only to Marseilles, France, as a delivery point of supplies for the liberation armies.

Four Liberty ships entered Cherbourg and began discharging cargo on 16 July. By the end of July, the port was able to accommodate fourteen Libertys, plus small vessels, at one time.

To obtain a greater flow of supplies for the armies driving through France, more port facilities were needed. The Allies decided to capture the German-held port of Antwerp, Belgium, one of the largest in Europe, with ten square miles of docks and the capacity in peacetime of berthing 1,000 ships at a time.

Capturing Antwerp was largely a British and Canadian effort, with the help of U.S. and Polish troops and members of the Dutch and Belgian resistance groups. Casualties were heavy, but the city was finally captured on 4 September. Because adjoining areas had to be cleared out, it wasn't until 28 November that the first convoy steamed up the Scheldt River, through the locks, and into the port.

Before Allied ships were able to use the port, courageous crews of little minesweepers had cleared the river and the harbor area of some 250 mines. This dangerous work was one of the lesser-known naval activities of the war. The crew of a minesweeper never knew when they might be blown to pieces.

Every ship unloading at Antwerp faced two of the most terrifying weapons of the war, the V-2 missile and the V-1 flying bomb. Introduced in June 1944, these weapons were devised to blast Britain into accepting a peace on Hitler's terms.

The V-2s were the most terrifying because they plunged from 50 miles above the earth into their targets without a sound. Each rocket weighed twelve tons and carried a ton of explosives. Traveling at a speed of 2,000 miles an hour, there was no way to intercept it with planes or antiaircraft fire. Some 1,300 V-2s fell on England and killed thousands of people.

Equally destructive were the V-1s, better known as "buzz bombs" because of the loud buzzing noise made by their engines as they cruised toward their objectives. Unlike the V-2s, they were visible by day and could be spotted at night by the red flames from their engines. They had a speed of 400 miles an hour. Of 8,000 V-1s launched against England, 2,400 hit and killed or wounded 24,000 people. The others were shot down by fighter planes or antiaircraft fire or snared by a net of balloons.

On 12 October, a V-2 missile, plummeting into the Rex Cinema in the center of Antwerp, killed 500 soldiers and civilians and wounded more than 400.

Dock workers and ship crews carried on despite this unnerving barrage. They paused when they heard the "buzz" of an approaching bomb. If the buzzing suddenly stopped, it meant that the bomb's engine had run out of fuel and it would be dropping somewhere nearby. People on the ships or docks could do nothing but listen and hope. Altogether, more than 1,200 V-1s fell on and around Antwerp and killed thousands. Many ships were blasted in the port area. For a while, no ammunition ships were docked in Antwerp because of the possibility of a V-1 hit and a devastating explosion.

As a member of the black gang on the *Bayou Chico,* the author was working with other crewmen on engine room repairs during one of the many German buzz bomb attacks. When we heard the persistent hum of an approaching bomb, we stopped our work and put down our tools to listen. There were tense moments as the sound became louder. No one spoke. The flying missile came closer . . . closer, until it sounded like it was overhead. As the buzzing continued, we knew it had passed on. With a collective sigh of relief, we took up our tools and went back to work.

The *Bayou Chico* had been the first American ship to transit the canal from the Scheldt River to the port of Ghent, Belgium. Hundreds of people lining the canal welcomed the ship and waved Belgian and American flags.

A number of ships transiting the North Sea to ports in Holland and Belgium were damaged by mines. These floating weapons were a hazard to shipping until long after the war.

The *Colin Kelly*, a veteran of the invasion of Sicily, hit a mine en route to Antwerp and was badly damaged. The explosion blew a hole in the engine room which, as oiler Henry Odom put it, "was big enough to drive a truck through." The ship did not sink and was salvaged. The *Kelly's* stack had nine swastikas painted on it for the number of German planes that she had shot down during her Mediterranean adventures.

The *Robert L. Vann* sank after hitting a mine in March 1945. A number of British ships were also victims of mines.

The Liberty ship *Francis Asbury*, commanded by Jean Patrick, at age twenty-four one of the youngest shipmasters in the Merchant Marine, hit a mine while approaching the Scheldt on 3 December 1945. The explosion blew up the boilers. No lives were lost, but men in the black gang were seriously injured.

After making many shuttle runs to the Normandy beaches, the *Dan Beard* was finally homeward bound when she hit a mine near the coast of England. The resulting explosion, which was typical of contact with a mine, was so severe that it broke the ship in two. Six merchant seamen and twelve members of the Armed Guard were killed. Captain William R. Wilson was among those rescued.

22

Lost Ships and Other Strange Tales

THE U-BOAT SKIPPER had the unsuspecting tanker squarely in the cross hairs of the periscope. She was a perfect target. He read the bearings and checked the course.

"Gut," he muttered. "Gut."

The ship was big, loaded deep, and proceeding alone on an empty sea. The skipper swung the periscope around for another sweep of the horizon to check again for enemy warships, but there was no vessel in sight.

He smiled and gave the order to fire, "Feuer eins!"

"Feuer zwei!" A second torpedo streaked from the tube toward the plodding tanker.

The submarine skipper hung on the arms of the periscope, his eyes glued to the glass. He counted the seconds by tapping his foot on the metal deck plates.

"Sunf . . . zehn . . . dreissig . . . funfzig . . . sechzig."

There wasn't much longer to wait.

The first torpedo hit with a geyser of spray that shot high above the tanker's deck. It was followed by a huge sheet of yellow flame as the explosion ignited the cargo. Moments later when the second torpedo struck, the ship was flaming like the fires of Vesuvius. Billowing clouds of smoke rolled into the sky.

The skipper took another look at the horizon and then gave the command to surface, "Auftauchen!"

But when the U-boat reached the surface and the crew poured onto the open deck to man her guns, the tanker was no longer there. Only the billowing smoke remained. The ship had exploded. The ship and crew had completely disappeared.

There was no way to tell what ship this had been—no lifeboats, no life preservers floating about with the vessel's name, not the smallest piece of flotsam with her name or her port of embarkation.

The U-boat captain leafed through the pages of his merchant ship identification book, but there were hundreds of tankers and so many of them looked the same.

After circling the scene for a while, the submarine submerged. The captain hoped that another ship would spot the smoke and come to investigate. He made an entry in the U-boat's log: "Sunk 7,000-ton tanker with two torpedoes. No wreckage for identification. Ship disintegrated. No survivors."[1]

Later, a report was received by the U.S. Navy Department in Washington, D.C.:

S.S. *Astral*. Did not arrive on ETA [estimated time of arrival]. No word received. Overdue, presume lost.[2]

The U-boat's victim could well have been the *Astral*, one of many ships that left ports during World War II and never came back, as though they had sailed off that mythical shelf of the world so much dreaded by medieval sailors.

The *Astral* had been bound for a neutral country, and her destination was probably known to the Germans. Unarmed, she carried a crew of thirty-five under Captain Chris Alsager and was considered to be one of the finest ships in the big tanker fleet of the Socony-Vacuum Oil Company.

What befell the *Astral*? A German or Italian submarine might have sunk the tanker despite her neutral markings. A torpedo smashing into the tanks containing gasoline might have caused complete destruction of ship and crew. There was a chance that some of the ship's survivors were taken on board a submarine that never returned to port.

Enemy naval records obtained after the war revealed no word about the *Astral* or an American ship sunk in this part of the North Atlantic at the time.

The *Astral* could have met a violent end through a shipboard accident—a sudden spark or fire that destroyed ship and crew in a blast so sudden and complete that the radio operator had no chance to send out the ship's position or SOS.

The U.S. Maritime Commission later gave the *Astral* this all too common epitaph: "Presumed to have been lost with all hands through enemy action."

Not long after dawn on 4 June 1942, the Standard Oil Company's tanker *L. J. Drake* hoisted her lines at the Aruba refineries and left harbor in company with the steamer *C. C. Stillman,* another Standard Oil ship that sailed under the Panamanian flag. Although submarines were having a Roman holiday in Caribbean waters at this time, the fuel-laden vessels sailed without a navy escort. The *Drake* mounted a large stern gun in charge of a U.S. Navy cox'n and five Naval Armed Guard gunners.

Her captain was Peter Nielsen. On board were forty-one men, including the navy gunners. She carried almost 73,000 barrels of fuel, including a large amount of highly volatile gasoline, in her tanks.

Being the faster ship by a knot or so, the *Stillman* gradually drew ahead of the *Drake.* By nightfall, the *Drake* had dropped over the horizon and was lost to view from the *Stillman*'s lookouts.

At 1900 on 5 June, the *Stillman* received several coded messages warning her that one or more enemy submarines were in the vicinity and advising her to change course. The same message was probably received by the *Drake.*

That night at 2115, when the *Stillman* was sixty miles south-west of Puerto Rico, she was hit by a torpedo. Thirty minutes later, a second torpedo hit, and the *Stillman* sank quickly by the stern. Flames from burning oil lit up the pitch-black sky. They might have warned the plodding tanker, far astern, but what good would the warning have done? The *Drake* could not have run away from a submarine at a speed of nine or ten knots. Her captain and crew could only hold to their course and hope that the blackness of the night would protect them.

The *Drake* never arrived at her destination. Beside her name in official war records are written these words: "Lost with all hands."

In September 1942, the 17,000-ton tanker *Esso Williamsburg*, then little more than a year old, was en route from Aruba to Iceland with navy fuel. She did not arrive at her destination, and only the barest conjecture can propose an answer to her fate. Most likely, the *Williamsburg* ran into a U-boat wolf pack and was sunk so quickly that the crew could not get off the ship.

There were many other mysteries of the sea during World War II—a long list of U.S. merchant ships that left port and never returned, with no clues to explain what happened to them.

The *Major Wheeler* was last seen on 31 January 1942. The steamer *LaSalle* was never seen after leaving Mobile in 1942. Her Armed Guard officer was Lt. Carl F. Zeidler, who had resigned as mayor of Milwaukee for service with the U.S. Navy.

The freighter *Margaret* of the Bull Line left Puerto Rico for New York on 8 April 1942. She never arrived, and no trace of her was ever found.

The Liberty ship *Robert Gray* sailed from New York on 16 March 1943. On the night of 13 April, she straggled from her convoy on the North Atlantic run between Halifax and England. Nothing more was heard from her.

The *Ville D'Arlan* sailed from New York and joined the list of unreported ships. Many more names can be added to this melancholy list, including the *Atlantic Sun, James J. McKay, Wichita, John Winthrop, Tillie Lykes, James G. Blaine,* and *Edward B. Dudley,* but these are only a few.[3]

Several ships were listed as complete casualties, but their survivors came back "from the dead" at the end of the war. Among these were the tankers *Connecticut* and *Stanvac Calcutta* (see chapter 12), the freighter *Sawokla,* and the Liberty ship *Jonathan Sturges.* All of these ships had been sunk without trace and their crews captured by submarines or surface raiders before they could send out radio messages.

The tanker *Connecticut* of the Texas Oil Co. left Port Arthur, Texas, on 31 March 1942 for Bombay, India, and Karachi, India (now Pakistan). In her tanks were 82,000 barrels of high octane gasoline, a lethal load. She was commanded by Captain Thomas Peterson, with a merchant crew of forty-two and eleven navy gunners under Ens. Robert Wakefield.

When the *Connecticut* did not arrive at either port within a reasonable time and when no sightings or radio messages had been reported, the big ship was listed as missing with all hands. That is how she was carried on the casualty list of merchant vessels until September 1945, when American troops liberated captured seamen from Japanese prison camps in Southeast Asia and the home islands. They found several crewmen from this long-lost tanker in one of the latter camps.

On 8 April 1942 off Trinidad, a favorite spot for lurking U-boats to bag unescorted tankers and freighters, their ship had been attacked by a surface raider. She escaped by opening a brisk defensive fire and steamed off at full speed. The tanker's reprieve, however, did not last long. At 0210 on 23 April, she was hit by a torpedo, which the crew presumed had come from a submarine.

Peterson ordered the ship abandoned for fear that a second tin fish would turn her into a roaring furnace and make it impossible for anyone to get away. Soon the boats were lowered away, but before they could pull a safe distance from the ship, a second torpedo hit. It ruptured some of the tanks, and flaming gasoline spilled out over the sea. Two lifeboats containing about twenty-four men were engulfed by the flames. The naval gun crew, who had remained on the vessel in the hope of getting a shot at the submarine, were also killed by fire.

About 0300, as the survivors remembered, a ship steamed up, circled the spot, and then faded away in the darkness. She was there long enough, silhouetted in the flames of the burning tanker, for the survivors to identify her as a German surface raider. When she came back some hours later and picked them up, they learned that she was the *Michel* and that one of her motor torpedo boats had sunk them. She carried two of these high-speed small craft on deck.

On 13 May, the *Michel* transferred the *Connecticut*'s survivors to the German supply ship *Speybank*, also known as the blockade runner *Doggerbank*, which took them to Yokohama, Japan. Two of the men died in a labor camp. Less than a dozen finally returned home to tell about the *Connecticut* and her unfortunate crew.

The crew of the *Sawokla* were also unfortunate in their encounter with the *Michel*. After delivering a cargo of trucks and other war supplies to the Persian Gulf in November 1942, the *Sawokla* cleared for the Arabian Sea and then headed down the Indian Ocean. Nothing more was heard or seen of the ship or her crew until VJ-day in 1945, when an American parachute team dropped into Singapore with emergency supplies for Japanese-held prisoners. Opening the gates of Chinghi jail, the paratroopers liberated 14,000 Allied prisoners and found among them a few wan and ragged survivors of the long-lost *Sawokla*.

These men told how their ship had been stopped by the *Michel*, which pounced on them so fast and unexpectedly that they had no time to send out a call for help. The raider had six-inch guns, but the *Sawokla* was unarmed. Firing at the freighter from long range, the raider killed the captain and several of the crew with her first shell, which hit the bridge and almost demolished the wheelhouse.

295

The crew took to the boats at once, but not until more shells had torn into the unprotected ship and killed all but sixteen of the helpless seamen. By the time the *Sawokla* went down, the raider was close aboard. Her motor torpedo boats darted in and out among the wreckage and blasted every bit of flotsam with machine-gun fire until no sizeable evidence of the ship remained.

After being taken on board the raider, the *Sawokla*'s men were kept in close confinement, but they learned that the cruiser was also a supply ship for U-boats. She stopped to service several submarines before heading for France on a long course around the Cape of Good Hope. South of Casablanca, the Germans almost ran into a heavily protected convoy supplying the North

The motorship Sawokla *"disappeared" in November 1942. She was presumed lost with all hands until 1945, when the Allies captured Singapore and liberated prisoners from the Japanese POW camp there. Among them were a few survivors of* Sawokla, *sunk by the German raider* Michal. *(South Street Seaport Museum Library, New York, New York)*

African invasion. Not wanting to be snared by the convoy escort, they turned around and steamed all the way back around the Cape and across the Indian Ocean to Japanese-held Java. There, the German commander tried to unload his prisoners, but he was unsuccessful.

The raider continued on to Singapore, where the men were put ashore and paraded through the streets to filthy, overcrowded Chinghi prison. For three years, they waited out the war before finally returning from the "dead" to report that their ship had not actually joined the ranks of missing ships.

The survivors of the *Jonathan Sturges* also became prisoners but on the other side of the world. At 2217 on 23 February 1943, their ship was plowing along in convoy in the North Atlantic when a torpedo suddenly exploded in her number two hold. Within a minute or so, another torpedo tore into the fireroom, forward of the boilers. The convoy steamed on and left the *Sturges* to her fate. The captain ordered the sinking ship abandoned, and the crew took to the boats.

For more than a year, the *Jonathan Sturges* was listed with the names of ships that had disappeared. Then word came from the Red Cross that some of her crew were alive and prisoners of war in Germany.

What happened after the torpedoes hit the *Sturges* was later related by Joseph Garrido, who spent twenty-six months in a German prison camp.[4]

"I was in the motorboat with ten other men," said Garrido. "The next day we picked up four more on an overturned boat and shortly later we saw the steward all alone in a third boat. We divided all hands between the two boats and tried to stay together. But rough weather separated us the next night. We saw signals from the other boat that night. She was never heard from again!"

The survivors were soaked by rain and continual heavy spray.

"For two weeks," Garrido continued, "we tried to buck easterly winds. And although we were about 400 miles from the coast of Newfoundland we finally had to turn around and sail east."

The survivors of the *Sturges* accomplished one of the longest small-boat voyages of the war. Living on meager rations and in almost constant danger of swamping, the crew had to bail with their hands and caps to keep the boat afloat. On their forty-first day in the lifeboat, when they were about two hundred miles from the coast of England, a German submarine surfaced and came alongside. Speaking in perfect English, the skipper ordered them to come alongside and board his boat as prisoners of war. Although the U-boat crew treated the survivors well, the seamen would rather have been back in the lifeboat. The submarine was homeward bound after patrol, and she played hide and seek with British planes and destroyers in trying to get into Brest.

During several days of interrogation in France, the Germans asked the seamen questions about Liberty ships and various American embarkation ports. Sent to a POW camp near Bremen, Germany, the men of the *Sturges* joined several thousand British merchant seamen in long months of weary waiting before they finally came home.

Many strange tales have come from the experiences of men sailing the wartime seas. Certainly, none is more unusual than Captain William Clendaniel's story.

The captain was pacing the bridge of the *Delisle* as she plodded south through freshening seas about twelve miles off the coast of Newfoundland on 19 October 1943. For many weeks, the ship had been sailing the cold waters of Hudson Bay as she supplied U.S. Army bases and picked up return loads of asphalt and other surplus supplies from airfields in the far north. She had stopped at Belle Isle, Newfoundland, to load six hundred tons of iron ore and was now bound, under escort of armed trawlers, toward Sydney, Nova Scotia, along with seven other ore-laden ships.[5]

At 1830, the ships were proceeding in three columns when the British freighter *Penolver*, which was carrying the convoy commodore, was torpedoed without warning. Deeply laden with iron ore, the ship plunged beneath the waves in less than three minutes.

The convoy had been instructed that should an attack occur, the last ship in line, in this case the *Delisle,* should stop and pick up survivors.

Clendaniel signaled the escort to ask if those orders still held and if he should risk his ship and crew.

The answer was yes, so he ordered the engine stopped. He told the mate to put scramble nets over the side and get a lifeboat over as quickly as possible. Men could be heard calling for help in the pitch-black darkness.

They were still lowering the lifeboat when a torpedo smashed into the starboard side at number two hold, forward. Clendaniel didn't remember much after that. The *Delisle* shivered from the impact. There was a crash of steel when the foremast came down on the navigation bridge. Part of the topmast hit the captain across the shoulders and chest, threw him to the deck, and fell on one of his legs. He was pinned securely to the bridge. Pain stabbed his body, and he lost consciousness.

Clendaniel figured out later that twenty minutes to half an hour must have passed before he came to. His body was wracked by the tortures of fractured and broken bones. When he tried to move, he found that the fallen topmast had him manacled to the deck.

He lay there for several minutes—fighting the pain, trying to remain conscious and evolve a means of escape from the now-deserted wreck.

He called out several times, but there was no answer. He hurt too much to fill his lungs and shout. His body was covered with perspiration, although a cold, mist-laden wind was blowing and, only a short time before, it had felt good to step inside the shelter of the wheelhouse.

Clendaniel tried to throw off the debris that covered him. It seemed to be partly wood, partly canvas—probably a piece of the wheelhouse and some of the canvas windbreak from the bridge.

That was why they had gone off and left him, he decided. He was covered up, and they hadn't seen him in the dark night, black as the inside of a coal bunker. But hell, he thought, who gave the order to abandon ship? Didn't someone think to look for him? The watch on the bridge had known he was standing there.

He heard the deep boom of a ship's whistle in the distance. The convoy, far away now, was making an emergency turn.

A broken door banged against a bulkhead with each roll of the sinking ship.

He mustered his strength and called several times again. It sounded like someone yelling inside an empty hall.

The *Delisle* was listing now.

How would it feel, he wondered, as the ship went under and the cold waves swept the bridge. Twisting in a desperate attempt to throw off the wreckage covering him, a spasm of pain engulfed his body and he lost consciousness again.

He awoke to hear the sound of muffled voices. They were a deck or two below and on the other side of the ship. He heard footsteps on the steel deck plates. In the heavy silence, they sounded like someone pounding on steel.

And then he heard a voice calling for "Blackout . . . blackout!"

"God," he thought, "they've come back for the dog." Tears filled his eyes—tears of pity and tears of gratitude.

Blackout was the ship's mascot. She had given birth to a litter of pups on the way down from Hudson Bay. She was only a mongrel, but the crew treated her like a kennel club queen.

Filling his lungs despite the pain, Clendaniel shouted for help. There was a clatter of shoes on the iron ladder leading up to the bridge from the boat deck. A moment later, Third Mate Alberto Galza was bending over him and throwing aside the debris that half-covered his body.

The mate lit several matches and inspected the skipper's predicament. He felt his body gingerly to see where there might be broken bones.

"We thought you were in the chief's boat," he said. "It's sure lucky we decided to come back and look for the dog."

By the light of a match, the captain could see that Galza was smiling.

"You're lucky, Captain," he said. "This piece of mast fell on your artificial leg. Your other leg is free, just twisted a little bit. If this damn thing had fallen on your good leg, I'd never be able to get you out."

Quickly, for the *Delisle* was listing more heavily now, he set about removing the artificial limb strapped to the captain's thigh. He had worn it since an accident at sea many years before.

After Galza loosed the straps and freed Clendaniel from the artificial limb, he hoisted the heavily built captain onto his back and carried him down two flights of ladders to the main deck. Clendaniel gritted his teeth. The pain felt like a knife jabbing him over and over.

Galza secured a line around Clendaniel and lowered him onto a raft. The crest of a wave doused him with spray as willing hands laid him on the floorboards of the bobbing craft.

A few minutes after they had pushed away from the deserted hulk, the *Delisle* sank. She went down slowly, as though she had fulfilled a mission and was going to join the company of lost ships. Somewhere below in the darkened recess of cabins and passageways, a mongrel dog was guarding her litter of pups.

There were six of them on the raft, which had belonged to the torpedoed *Penolver*. While the wave-swept craft bucked and tossed in heavy seas, they huddled closely together for warmth.

Fortunately, they were picked up after several hours by an armed trawler and taken to St. John, Newfoundland, where the skipper spent many weeks in a hospital.

Several days before he was discharged and packed off on a ship for the States, a Canadian naval officer came into his room with a package.

"It was done up like a Christmas present," Clendaniel said. "Wrapped up in a fancy paper with a ribbon around it."

"Here's a present from one of our fishing vessels," the Canadian officer explained as Clendaniel undid the wrappings. "They figured some sailor might be needing it, so they sent it to naval headquarters."

Inside the package was the last thing in the world Clendaniel expected to see. Scratched, scarred, and a little bit worn from its North Atlantic bath was his artificial leg—back from the sea.

Most sinkings during the war resulted from bombs, mines, and torpedoes, but a few ships succumbed to the oldest foe of the sailorman, the elements—the wind and the waves. The fate of the Liberty ship *William H. Welch*, however, was unique.[6]

Under command of Captain Lee Marshall, the *Welch* had unloaded a war cargo in England. On 25 February 1944, she was steaming north along the coast of Scotland to join a homeward-bound convoy. The weather was not unusual for the time of year in those waters—blustery winds and heavy seas, but nothing that would make a well-found ship go scurrying to port. Then, hour by hour, the weather began to deteriorate into one of the most vicious storms ever seen in that area, with mountainous waves and almost hurricane winds.

Like most ships bound for home after discharging their cargoes, the *Welch* was riding high in ballast, which allowed the winds and waves to exert their full force against hull and deckhouses. It became impossible to maintain steerageway, and Captain Marshall was helpless to keep his vessel from being driven onto a forbidding, rocky shore.

She struck hard against a cliff. With giant foam-crested seas sweeping her decks, the crew were forced to seek refuge on the flying bridge, the highest point above the waves. An SOS had brought several deep-sea tugs and salvage vessels. Although accustomed to stormy weather, they were unable to get near enough to get hawsers to the battered ship, or even shoot lines for a breeches buoy. The waves smashed against the side of the *Welch* with the force of battering rams and swept across the main deck.

Boats and life rafts were carried away, but they would have been useless in the cauldron of breaking seas and swirling foam.

"Soon," according to an official report by the War Shipping Administration, "the waves reared higher, the pilothouse was smashed to pieces and all hands were swept off the ship, which was being broken in two against the rocks. Some of the crew were drowned, and others were hurled to their deaths against the cliff."

Hardy Scots farmers and herders had been alerted and hurried to the scene. They risked their lives to edge as close as possible to the raging surf in an effort to reach the bodies being flung against the rocks. Those they could reach were pulled out of the breaking waves. They made fires and warmed them before laying them on carts and taking them to homes and villages, where they were wrapped in blankets and given hot drinks.

Second Assistant Engineer George L. Smokovitch was plucked from the jagged rocks by two women who risked being drowned themselves. They carried him to a hamlet "over a narrow, winding, rutted road along a snow-covered mountain and ice-covered lochs. For miles, the only sign of life were shivering sheep driven down from the mountains by the deep snow and howling winds."

The men who were dragged from the rocks by the brave Scots soon recovered. Out of a crew of sixty merchant seamen and navy gunners, only twelve survived. Captain Marshall was not one of the survivors.

A strange and unexplained event caused a panic among the crew of the Liberty ship *Henry Wynkoop* on 11 March 1943 while she was steaming eastbound in convoy several hundred miles from Ireland.[7] At 0350, there was a terrific impact near the bow. The vessel heeled over sharply to starboard, as though she had been rammed, but there was no other ship nearby.

"There was a terrific shock, followed by a loud scraping sound," according to the voyage report. "It sounded as though something was bouncing or rolling along the hull . . . a deep, rumbling sound. Afterward, there were patches of oil around the ship and astern as we steamed on."

When the general alarm sounded, some of the crew panicked and lowered a lifeboat so precipitously that it up-ended. Several of the "panic party" were dumped into the water. Altogether, thirty-three of the merchant crew and Armed Guard left the *Wynkoop* without the captain's orders, one of the worst such instances of panic in the annals of the war.

Eight men managed to get back on board. An escorting corvette picked up seventeen of the crew and took them to the *Clyde*. Another five were rescued by a freighter and taken to Liverpool; three were drowned.

Although she was left with a depleted crew, the *Wynkoop* made it to Belfast. Arnold Nilson, the third assistant engineer, took charge of the engine room, with the Armed Guard gunners filling in as firemen and oilers.

Had the ship hit a U-boat or a half-submerged derelict? Navy officials surmised that the *Wynkoop* had collided with a submarine, but German records did not show that a U-boat had been lost in that area at the time.

The *Wynkoop*'s strange adventure remains a mystery of the sea.

In a number of instances during the war, only one man escaped from a torpedoed ship and lived to tell about it. Ordinary seaman William Golobich was one such survivor.

The tanker *Atlantic Sun*, which had survived a torpedoing earlier in the war, had delivered a cargo to Iceland in January 1943 and was homeward bound in convoy. For some reason unexplained in the official report of the sinking, she dropped out of the convoy on 12 February. Three days later, at 0945, she was hit by two torpedoes.

Golobich recalled:

> I ran on deck, and I saw that the ship had broken in two. The forward end was already about fifty yards away with the bow up and sinking. I think there would have been about twenty crewmen and gunners

on that part. I don't know why they weren't trying to launch lifeboats because there were two of them by the deckhouse.

We launched one of the boats aft and twenty-two of us got into it. We pulled away and stood by for about two hours, and when the stern section didn't sink we went back and boarded the ship over the scramble nets. She seemed to be riding OK, what was left of her. We were waiting and wondering what to do next, maybe for two hours or so, when another torpedo hit. The stern part started to go down fast after that.

The boat we had been in broke free from the painter and was swamped as the ship went under. Most of us jumped over the stern, but some didn't want to jump. I guess they couldn't swim. Besides, the water was cold . . . real cold. Somehow the port boat got free when the ship went down, but it was full of water. Eight or nine men were clinging to the grab ropes on the sides. The waves were splashing over us.

I hung on as long as I could. My arms and legs were getting numb and I knew I had to move them, so I let go my hold and started swimming. After about an hour the submarine came up close by. It went on and then came back. I shouted and started to swim toward it. Then all of a sudden everything went blank and I lost consciousness.

When I woke up I was laying on the deck of the sub. They had fished me out of the drink just in time. I passed out again and then I woke up in a bunk. The sub had submerged and it was under way. At that point I really didn't care much what was happening, but later I got some life back in me. They treated me OK.[8]

The U-boat took Golobich to St. Nazaire, France, where she docked 9 March 1943 with the usual welcoming ceremony and a serenade from a navy band. Golobich spent the rest of the war in a prisoner of war camp for merchant seamen.

23
Sailing Alone

THE OUTBREAK OF WAR caught many ships traveling unarmed on the high seas, some heading home, without convoy.
They sailed alone, in a do-or-die dash through waters haunted by
enemy submarines and surface raiders.

The freighter *Honolulan* had delivered a cargo of steel, grain,
and bombers to the Russians in the Persian Gulf. On 22 July
1942, she was pushing along at ten knots off Dakar, Senegal,
on the West Coast of Africa. Tempting submarine bait, she was
sailing alone on an empty sea with no defenses, not even a
popgun.

The author knew several of the men on the *Honolulan*. This
is the story about how they remembered her end.[1]

It was supper time on the 4 to 8 watch. Captain Charles
Bamforth had eaten his dinner hurriedly and was back on the
bridge. He was feeling uncertain about the state of things, but
had seen nothing yet to cause undue alarm.

In the crew's mess room, the men were giving the last rites
to a hearty dinner of potato salad and cold cuts. Seaman Howard

Small, just relieved at the wheel, came in to disclose the "latest information" direct from the bridge.

"We're just south of Dakar," he announced. "Heard the mate give the skipper our position just before I left the wheel."

"South?" someone wanted to know. "How far south? Ten miles or five hundred miles? It makes a big difference."

"Bad waters," one of the others remarked. "Dakar's a sub base and you can bet the Krauts are using it."

Willie Sanderson stirred some more sugar in his coffee and smiled indulgently. "I want to remind you lads what the fortune teller told me in Bombay. She said I'd be leaving this ship the last week in July and you can plainly see that I won't be walkin' down the gangplank for a while—not this week."

"What's the matter, Willie? Haven't you got any more to do than think about fortune tellers? I'll lend you my *Esquire* calendar. Those babes will get your mind off fortune tellers."

"OK, OK. That's what she told me though. 'You will have to leave your ship the last week in July,' the dame said. Don't blame me later that I didn't give you advance notice on my private information."

One of the wipers remarked that fortune tellers were a lot of malarkey. He knew one in Brooklyn, he said. She had to work nights at a Nedicks hot dog stand to make ends meet. "But I wouldn't like to be sunk, anyway," he said, "not after what those guys from the *Bienville* told me in Bombay about what happened when the Japs got them."

Small took an apple from the fruit plate and started out in the alleyway. "Maybe we get it, maybe we don't," he announced, "but I'm sleepin' out on deck on my cot starting tonight even if I get rain-soaked every ten minutes. I want to be three healthy jumps from a lifeboat when a tin fish bites this rust bucket."

"Navy" Brown reached for some more cold cuts. "You guys go on," he said. "I'm hungry. There's no sense wastin' this chow even if we get hit right now."

It was almost like mental telepathy—"Navy" couldn't have uttered a more appropriate pronouncement. At just about that moment, a U-boat skipper was firing a torpedo at the *Honolulan* from under the sea some distance away.

Brown didn't finish his salami and liverwurst. The tin fish bit through the freighter's plating with a jar that broke all the glass and crockery on the mess room table and threw everybody against the bulkhead.

After the first few moments of mental and physical shock, every man in the mess room made a dash for the alleyway. They were all thinking of two things: life jackets and boats. Small remembered seeing Brown leaning against the table as he clutched the remains of his sandwich in one hand. "Torpedo . . . torpedo," he was shouting. "Stay calm. Don't get excited. Get your life jackets and beat it the hell topsides."

The *Honolulan* shook as she recoiled from the impact. An odor of cordite was in the air. The crew felt the blood-tingling thrill of the general alarm as the clanging bells summoned them to emergency stations.

"It's funny," Small recalled, "what some guys think of first when they have to abandon ship. I grabbed a carton of cigarettes myself. Another fellow had an extra pair of shoes. There were even some cans of fruit juice in our boat—that's what one of the messboys thought about when he ran out of the galley. Not a bad idea, either."

Number three boat had been smashed to pieces by the blast, and the remains of it were scattered all over the deck. Its crew divided among the other boats, which were lowered away from the ship without hurry or mishap.

Still on board, however, were Howard Small, Chief Mate Robert Coas, Captain Bamforth, and radio operator "Sparks" Sullivan.

Unhurried by the sinking of the ship, the captain had gone down to the icebox and was coming back on deck with an armload of hams, cheese, and bologna when Small met him on the main deck.

"Well, son," Bamforth said, "we're gonna eat, anyway. No use rowin' around in a boat without havin' your stomach full."

Sparks, still in his shack, was sending out the vessel's position. By this time, the *Honolulan* was down to the main deck.

The Skipper shouted, "Leave her boys, and hurry!"

Number two boat was drifting back toward the ship on a moderate swell to pick them up when they jumped overside. With his arms full of perishable plunder, the captain was standing at the rail ready to drop the provisions into the approaching boat when the second torpedo hit, knocking him onto the deck and scattering his precious delicatessen overside. A few moments later, Bamforth, Coas, and Small jumped clear and were picked up by the lifeboat. Sparks had been determined to stay by his wireless key until the last moment. When he arrived on deck, the old *Honolulan* was already taking water over the boat deck and canting perilously to port.

The bow went down and the stern kicked into the air while Sparks, poised momentarily by the rail, was deciding how best to plunge clear of the side. The ship made up his mind for him. She twisted suddenly in a violent shifting of her cargo and threw him into the sea as though he had been tossed from the back of a bucking bronc. He came to the surface and grabbed onto a raft, but it was still secured to the ship by its painter. As the *Honolulan* surged over on her side, her stack struck a corner of the raft. Missing Sparks by inches, it carried the raft underwater and him with it.

A miracle must have saved him because, about twenty seconds later, the other men saw Sparks shoot to the surface like a shell from a cannon. Apparently, a huge bubble of air from the submerging holds had catapulted him back to the surface. They picked him up. He was breathless and full of sea water but otherwise unharmed.

When the ship plunged over on her side, another unusual event occurred. Something must have fouled the whistle cord, perhaps some tumbling debris, and the old *Honolulan* blew loud and tenaciously as she went under. With the seas engulfing the ship, her alarm bells were still ringing and Old Glory was still

309

flying from the staff on her stern. No doughty cargo carrier could have had a more martial end.

In a few minutes, the submarine surfaced about 250 yards from the lifeboats. Her crew poured out of the conning tower and manned the deck gun and machine guns, which were trained point-blank on the *Honolulan*'s survivors. They thought that everything would be all over in a few seconds. A shot was fired over their heads. They waited breathlessly for the fatal drum of machine-gun fire as one of the Germans put a tommy gun to his shoulder and aimed it at them.

But there were no more shots. The U-boat circled leisurely around them, while her crew took pictures. Coming alongside to interrogate them, the U-boat commander apologized for sinking the ship. He offered them medical assistance, which wasn't needed, and then gave them two cartons of cigarettes. After shouting "Good luck" and "Good trip," the youthful crew of the raider piled below. The commander waved them a last farewell from the conning tower, and the U-boat ran off a short distance before submerging to wait, no doubt, for any ship that might respond to the *Honolulan*'s SOS.

All hands were safe and accounted for except a fireman named McMasters. A check revealed that he was in none of the boats. No one remembered seeing him leave the ship, and they decided that he had gone down with her.

Shortly after dawn the next morning, there occurred what might be called the second "miracle" of the *Honolulan.* The men in the lifeboats heard the roar of aircraft engines and then saw a patrol plane sweeping over the area from the direction of the African coast. The fliers spotted them amid waves that were now tumbling in confusion before a brisk wind. The plane "buzzed" them in recognition before flying off and circling a spot several miles away, where it dropped a smoke bomb. At first, they thought the plane had seen the U-boat, but it came over the boats again to drop a note attached to a float. "You have a man several miles to windward," the note read. "Suggest you hurry."

Beating to windward as fast as all hands could pull, the boats fanned out and headed for the smoking phosphorous bomb dropped by the vigilant fliers. They strained at the oars with every bit of strength they could muster, but it took four hours for the first boat to reach the smoke pot. Its crew found fireman McMasters just as he had decided to let go his hold on a hatch cover and give himself up to the sea and the sharks. He had been adrift for about fifteen hours. Their arrival was not a moment too soon. One shark had already gashed him badly, and they had to beat off the others with boat hooks.

"That was a miracle if there ever was one," Small said. "Another thirty seconds and the sharks would have had him. His strength was all gone . . . he couldn't fight them any longer."

They thought it was a miracle, too, that the plane had spotted McMasters amid the mass of weaving water—a mere speck on such a vast reach of ocean. Hauling their shipmate on board one of the boats, they made a bed of life jackets and tended his wounds the best they could.

"He was tough one," Small said. "He didn't cry or curse or 'goddamn' his luck one bit. Just said 'Hi, boys! Hope you all got off her.'"

On the second day, the plane returned and dropped a note saying that help was on its way, but that particular help never arrived. That night, they saw a bright flash on the horizon as though a ship had been hit in the boilers or the ammunition magazine. Whatever it was, it could have been the vessel sent out to rescue them. A waiting U-boat had probably bagged it.

Returning on the third day, the plane dropped fruit and a pipe, which the men gave to the wounded fireman. Their boats drifted for four more days, as they "feasted" on pemmican stew and beat off avaricious sharks with boat hooks.

On the seventh day, they sighted a distant ship and set off rockets and flares. They yelled and cheered when they saw the vessel change course and head toward them.

The British *Winchester Castle,* bound from Madagascar for New York, picked up the men about an hour later. She stopped just long enough to help them on board, her guns loaded and ready to fire every moment. As soon as the survivors were on deck, she speeded up again. The *Honolulan*'s lifeboats bobbed forlornly in her wake.

Ten days later, after what the castaways called "exceptional hospitality and consideration," they were in the port of New York. Thus ended another chapter in the epic of the war at sea—a happy ending for at least one crew that had sailed alone.

24
The Gallant *Cedar Mills*

S OME OF THE MOST BITTER BATTLES in the war at sea were not fought against the Germans or the Japanese but against the sailor's oldest enemy, the sea itself. Men braved the sea to save ships and fellow seamen as courageously as they battled submarines and bombers. For such a fight against the sea, the U.S. Maritime Commission named the tanker *Cedar Mills* one of the "Gallant Ships" of World War II.

On Thanksgiving Day, 1943, this new tanker left the harbor of Fremantle for Karachi in company with the Dutch freighter *Java* and the French destroyer *Le Triomphant,* which was to act as escort. This "super" destroyer was rated as one of the world's speediest men-of-war.

Because it was more than four thousand miles to Karachi, the *Cedar Mills* was to refuel the destroyer during the voyage. *Le Triomphant* came alongside the *Cedar Mills* on 29 November, and lines were rigged for fueling, but the destroyer suddenly sheered off in a heavy sea and carried away the hose and lines, besides smashing several plates in the tanker's side.

The destroyer was low on fuel, and the *Cedar Mills* took her in tow until calmer weather would permit another try at exchanging oil through the tanker's fire hoses, which were longer than the fuel lines. Using the fire hoses would allow the vessels to stay farther apart during the replenishing operation. Meanwhile, the *Java* proceeded independently.

Two days later, refueling operations were started again, but the hawser parted. While the crews were trying to rig up new lines, a sudden cyclone roared across the Indian Ocean. The *Cedar Mills* was forced to heave to in the face of tremendous seas and howling winds. *Le Triomphant* was soon lost to sight from Captain Morgan Maxey and his men on the tanker.

After the cyclone had blown for more than twenty-four hours, the *Cedar Mills* received an SOS from *Le Triomphant*, followed by direction-finder bearings that enabled Maxey to locate the storm-battered destroyer after a search made under conditions of very poor visibility.

Le Triomphant was listing thirty degrees when the tanker-men finally spotted her through the overcast. Only a few men were on her decks. The rest were down below, bailing out flooded compartments in a desperate attempt to keep the ship afloat. Signals flashed from *Le Triomphant* by a battery lamp reported that the fires were out and the dynamos had stopped for lack of steam.

There was no fresh water to use in the boilers for getting up a new head of steam. The bunker oil was almost gone, with only enough oil left for a few hours of low-pressure steaming. In an attempt to raise enough steam to maneuver for refueling, the destroyer was forced to pump salt water into her boilers.

The youthful Captain Maxey, a veteran of ten years at sea, was faced with a problem that few shipmasters ever have. The falling barometer was foretelling another cyclone. Wind and sea were rising. A valuable ship, with more than two hundred men on board, was at the mercy of the storm. The seas were too high to permit launching of lifeboats. Here was a supreme test for fine judgment and able seamanship.

Steaming back and forth on the weather side of the French destroyer, the tanker dumped oil into the sea in an attempt to keep the huge waves from breaking against *Le Triomphant* and capsizing her.

As darkness wore on, the French captain signaled that he thought his ship could stay afloat through the night. He told Maxey that he would send up green rockets if his vessel started to founder. Fortunately, the destroyer stayed afloat. A night rescue attempt in such weather would have been suicidal.

When daylight came, the destroyer was lying about half a mile off the *Cedar Mills*. She was listing more sharply and sitting deeper in the water. It was quite obvious to those on the tanker that both ship and crew were in dire straits. There was no time to lose in effecting a rescue because, in her present precarious condition, *Le Triomphant* might swamp or capsize.

Captain Maxey asked for volunteers to make a rescue. Every man on board responded, including several army personnel who were passengers, and he selected the hardiest of those not required for other duties. Although the captain reminded them of the dangers, not a man changed his mind.

Two motor lifeboats were maneuvered over the side after a nip-and-tuck race with waves that threatened to smash them against the hull. Each boat stepped its mast so that the captain could keep track of them amid the huge seas that, at times, almost hid the destroyer from those on the tanker as each vessel slid into long, deep swells. One huge wave all but rode over a lifeboat. It swamped the engine and forced the crew to ship their oars. The men regained control and plunged ahead.

The destroyer had signaled that she was out of bread and fresh water, so each boat was loaded with cans of food and water. Most of the men in the lifeboat became seasick from the violent rolling and pitching, but not a man faltered at the oars. The boats crept on toward the battered man-of-war.

Several times, it looked as though they couldn't possibly make it. Disappearing from sight amid the massive combers, they popped up again on a surging crest. The little marker flags whipped defiantly atop the tiny masts and seemed to challenge the ocean: "We will . . . we can . . . we'll do it."

After what seemed like hours of waiting, men on the tanker saw the two lifeboats reach the destroyer's side and the stores hoisted on board. Fine seamanship was needed to keep the surging seas from smashing the lifeboats to bits against the helpless hulk.

The two captains had agreed that only a skeleton crew should be left on *Le Triomphant*. About thirty of the warship's crew came on deck with life jackets and prepared for the grim ordeal of going over to the *Cedar Mills*. The sea was too dangerous for the French crew to climb down into the bobbing boats, so they jumped from the careening deck into the sea. All of them were safely fished into the lifeboats.

The crowded little craft then inched back to the tanker, where the process was repeated in reverse. The French sailors, jumping overboard from the lifeboats, were grabbed by strong hands and pulled onto the tanker's wave-swept deck. The *Cedar Mills* was so deep in the water that every wave washed over the rail. She had so little freeboard that her crew, by hanging onto the lifelines, could reach out to the French sailors as they struggled to the tanker's side. When several of *Le Triomphant*'s crew were about to be carried beyond the *Cedar Mills* by receding swells, the tankermen tied lines around their waists and jumped into the sea to haul them back to the ship.

It took most of the day to make the trip between the two vessels. Not wanting to risk using the boats at night, when they could be easily swamped in the raging gale, Captain Maxey signaled *Le Triomphant* that he would stand by and resume rescue operations at daylight.

The French sailors were given a hot meal and all the coffee they could drink. Crewmen outfitted them with dry clothes and provided bunks.

Seas were still running high when daylight came, but they were moderating. Lifeboats were swung out under more favorable conditions. A total of ninety-one men and officers, along with the vessel's money and confidential papers, were transferred from the destroyer that day.

When most of the crew had been rescued from the careening warship, the two skippers decided that an attempt should be made to save her. The storm had abated enough to make this feasible, but it would require tremendous physical effort on the part of the volunteers who remained aboard *Le Triomphant*.

A messenger line was shot from the *Cedar Mills* by Lyle gun, but the tanker had no towing hawser capable of such a strain. The French sailors had to break out their anchor chain for use as a tow rope—a job of almost heroic proportions. The destroyer had no steam with which to operate the anchor windlass and haul the heavy iron links from the chain locker below decks in the bow of the listing ship. Straining until they all but dropped in their tracks from sheer exhaustion—their labors made all the more difficult by trying to work on a sharply angled deck—the French crew hauled the chain on deck, foot by foot and link by link. Once it was on deck, they had to flake it out very carefully so that it would not buckle when the *Cedar Mills* began hauling in on it.

Many tedious hours passed before the task was accomplished and the two vessels linked. When this was finally done, the *Cedar Mills* got under way at a turtlelike speed of three knots.

Captain Maxey now had to decide whether to break radio silence and request help. He decided on sending an SOS, although if a raider did find them (Japanese submarines and surface raiders were operating in that part of the world), both ships would be easy victims. After the call was sent out, a directive was received from Colombo for the ships to proceed to Addu Atoll.

Wallowing at the end of the makeshift towline, the destroyer was still without water and hot food. The *Cedar Mills* crew fashioned watertight cases so that milk, bread, and other necessities could be floated to the warship. As soon as the cases were pulled on board and emptied, they were hauled back to the tanker, where the cooks filled them up again and the provisioning process was repeated.

After five days of patient plodding, in which an alert lookout was kept for submarines and raiders, the *Cedar Mills* sighted the low-lying strand of Addu Atoll. Within a few hours, the tanker and her tow rendezvoused with the British cruiser *Frobisher,* thus ending another chapter in the age-old story of men against the sea.[1]

For his skill in helping to save one of the finest ships in the Free French Navy and in bringing every one of her crew safely to shore, Captain Maxey was decorated by the U.S. Maritime Commission.

In honor of her crew of merchant seamen and Naval Armed Guard gunners, the *Cedar Mills* was named a "Gallant Ship" of the U.S. Merchant Marine.

25
Ship of Glory

HUNDREDS WHO SAILED THE SHIPS in World War II deserve to be called "heroes in dungarees," but no men deserve the accolade more than the crew of the *Henry Bacon*.

Cold seas clawed at this Liberty ship as she labored from Murmansk toward Scotland in February 1945. All hands were tense, waiting, listening. Gunners at the 20-millimeters huddled behind the gun tubs, their shoulders hunched against a bitter wind that lashed the decks with a cold, hard-driven spray.

For Captain Alfred Carini, there had been no sleep for forty-five hours. He sipped black coffee as he paced the bridge. He glanced apprehensively toward the coast of Norway, which lay unseen beyond the white-edged combers and the dull gray overcast.

Carini had reason to be worried.

After leaving the White Sea a week before, the *Henry Bacon*'s convoy had been battered by terrific storms. The plodding ships were so badly scattered by a series of gales that the escort spent two days rounding them up and forming them into a fleet again.

As the assembled ships continued southward, the *Henry Bacon* had trouble with her steering engine and was forced to drop out of the convoy on 22 February to make repairs. The fleet was soon lost to sight across a misty horizon serrated by endless tumbling seas. The *Bacon*'s men knew the utter loneliness of being helplessly adrift in waters haunted by enemy planes and submarines.[1]

The repairs took several hours. When the pistons were pounding again and the ship resumed her course, a black moonless night shrouded the storm-swept sea. The other ships were nowhere to be seen. The convoy still had not been spotted after a few hours. Carini decided they must have passed it in the dark. None of the ships, of course, were showing any lights.

He decided to turn back over their course for just one hour and attempt a rendezvous. The *Bacon* turned and steamed north. When this produced no results, Carini faced a weighty decision.

Should he continue on alone, hoping to find the convoy? Should he strike out for the coast of Scotland and forget the convoy? Or should he chance a radio message to the convoy and ask its position? If the convoy commodore replied, the *Bacon* could rejoin her companions and enjoy the antiaircraft protection of the shepherding destroyers. On the other hand, a radio message would be dangerous. There was always a chance that it would be picked up by enemy planes, ships, or submarines, or by bases on the coast of Norway.

Carini chose the latter course of action. Perhaps he was swayed in his decision by the presence of nineteen Norwegian refugees on board the *Bacon*. These men, women, and children had fled to Russia during the Nazi invasion and, along with many others, were being sent to England as passengers on returning freighters. Perhaps he also thought the heavy seas and the overcast were in their favor and would discourage an enemy air attack.

Carini gave the radio operator a coded message—a lame duck asking to come back to the flock. It was soon being tapped out on the keys in the wireless shack. Minutes went by. There was no reply. The captain debated whether to send the message again. An hour went by. Two hours. The convoy commodore, he thought, might have dispatched a destroyer to find them. The bridge watch huddled behind the canvas windbreaks and tried to peer beyond the mist and flying scud, with the hope of spotting a destroyer or a frigate coming their way.

The radio operator tuned his receiver to the frequency on which a message would come in, but he heard no talk from other ships.

The Armed Guard officer, Lt. Sippola, called each of his gun stations on the intercommunications phone.

"Bow gun!"

"On watch, sir."

"Number two gun!"

"Ready here, sir."

Ten guns reported back to the bridge. All were ready for action.

The lookouts straining for some sight of the convoy, swept the horizon with their binoculars. An excited call came over the phones from the man in the crow's nest high above the deck.

"Engines," he said. "Airplanes! Sounds like a lot of them. Over to the east . . . off the port quarter."

Carini hurried over to the wing of the bridge. He took off his woolen watch cap and listened. They were engines, sure enough. Even against the whine of the wind, he could hear them—deep, resonant drumming, like the distant beating of some tribal war dance.

Lookouts searched the sky with their binoculars, but they couldn't see anything beyond the low, gray overcast that hung about them in all directions.

Carini ran into the wheelhouse and pressed the button for the general alarm. The wild clanging of the bells called all hands to battle stations. Men off watch tumbled out of bunks and grabbed helmets, life jackets, and extra clothing for the wintry blasts of the open deck. The steward mustered his cooks and messmen, and they broke out bandages, splints, and anesthetics;

covered the wardroom tables with blankets; and prepared for battle casualties.

Below decks in the engine room, the black gang on watch listened to the alarm bells and wondered what was happening. All they could do was listen and wait.

Gunners jerked the canvas covers off the guns and none too soon. The muted drum of the aircraft engines burst into a roar, and a big, black bomber broke out of the overcast close abeam on the port side. Gunners whirled their Oerlikons to meet it. The crew of the three-inch/50 on the bow slammed a shell into the breech.

There were more planes now—Junker 88s. They broke through the cloudy mist right off the port quarter, no more than thirty feet above the wave tops.

No order from the Armed Guard officer on the bridge was needed. Every gun that could bear went into instant action. Fiery streams of steel, brightened by the red flame of tracer shells, streamed from the Oerlikons. Oblivious of the deafening whomp, whomp, whomp of their Oerlikons, the gunners whirled the guns on the targets. The sky was full of bombers.

After the first run, the planes struck at the ship from both sides. This gave the bow gun a chance to fire, and the boom of the three-inch/50 joined the sharp din of the Oerlikons. The clouds were pocked with shell bursts. No range corrections were needed—it was point-blank fire.

Carini counted twenty-three planes.

Twenty-three bombers against one ship! This would have been heavy odds even for a cruiser or battleship. Mighty aircraft carriers had been sunk by fewer planes than this. There was no one that the *Henry Bacon* could call for help.

A bomber dropped a torpedo not more than five hundred yards away on the port quarter.

"Hard aport," Carini yelled to the man at the wheel. The helmsman spun the wheel hard over, and the torpedo sliced past the stern an arm's length beyond the rudder.

The three-inch/50 boomed out again as another Junker started a torpedo run several hundred yards off the bow. At point-blank range, the shell blew the bomber to bits. It disintegrated in a yellow ball of fire and flying fragments. Flaming pieces of wing and fuselage sizzled and steamed when they fell into the sea near the bow.

Another Junker nosed into a wall of 20-millimeter shells. The plane was sliced in two, with the pilot's compartment doing cartwheels over and over until it smashed into the sea. Black smoke rolled up to mark the grave.

But only persistence was needed for so many planes to succeed against one ship. A torpedo hit the *Henry Bacon* in number three hold on the starboard side, forward. The vessel shuddered and a fifty-foot column of water shot up high above the bulwarks. The spray was still falling along the deck when the second torpedo hit.

Carini gave the order to abandon ship. If he waited any longer, a third tin fish might find its target and the ship would plunge to the bottom before the boats could be launched.

"Refugees first," he called to the mate. "Get the passengers on the boat deck as fast as you can. Tell them to bring lots of clothes."

The deep-throated whistle sounded the call of abandon ship in long, mournful blasts. Before the echoes had died out against the lead-colored clouds, the last of the German bombers were winging their way toward Norwegian bases, two hundred miles to the east.

These planes, it was learned later, were ready to return home after a futile hunt for the convoy when they came upon the *Henry Bacon*. The fighting freighter had kept them in action longer than expected. Their gas was getting low, and they could ill afford to circle around and watch this American bulldog settle beneath the seas. As they disappeared into the clouds, the *Bacon's* gunners had the satisfaction of seeing one of the Junkers hugging the wave tops as black smoke poured from an engine.

Carini stood on the freighter's bridge with a speaking trumpet.

"Passengers first," he called out. "Get the women and children away in the first boat. Put some men in that boat who can handle an oar!"

"Load up and lower away."

The *Bacon* carried four lifeboats and four rafts, but men on a raft wouldn't have much chance of surviving in winter seas.

Crewmen filled the second boat, and it was lowered away. This was ticklish work. A boat lowered into the trough of a wave could be caught up on the crest of another comber and sent careening into the vessel's side.

The second boat could not possibly hold them all, but only the boats on the lee side could be lowered. There was no clamor for places, no panic. When the boat was safely overside, Third Mate Joseph Scott counted heads. There was room for a few more.

"I can take six," he shouted to the men above. "Six more— and hurry."

Several merchant crewmen and navy gunners climbed down the scramble nets and jumped into the boat as it rose on the crest of a wave.

The *Henry Bacon* was settling now. The wave tops lapped around the bulwarks.

Bos'n Holcomb Lemmon, survivors said later, was making heroic efforts to help his shipmates over the side into rafts trailing from painters alongside.

One of the men assigned to the third mate's boat was Chief Engineer Donald Haviland. He had taken a seat in the boat when he looked up at Captain Carini and his shipmates who were left on the freighter's deck.

A young navy gunner was staring down at the boat crews pushing away from the sinking hulk. The boy couldn't have been more than seventeen years old.

Haviland looked at the lad for a moment and then stood up at his place in the boat. "Put me alongside the ship," he said to the third mate. "Let that kid take my place. It won't matter so much if I don't get back."

"Hey, you," he shouted to the gunner as the boat bobbed alongside. "Come down here. Make it snappy."

The chief engineer climbed back up the scramble nets to the freighter's deck, while the sailor scurried overside and took the proffered seat in the boat.

The lifeboats pulled away. The *Henry Bacon* was settling lower and lower, and they didn't want to be sucked under with her when she made her final plunge. A raft with several men on it bobbed amid the seas some distance away. The wind and waves were taking the lifeboats farther away from the ship. No amount of pulling on the oars could have brought them back.

Those in the boats saw Haviland and the bos'n and two or three sailors busy on the foredeck. They were probably making a raft out of dunnage—something to cling to when the ship went under.

From the bridge, Captain Carini waved to the boats drifting off amid the mist and scud.

The last that the survivors saw of their ship was her battle ensign, snapping proudly at the gaff, as the *Henry Bacon* slowly sank beneath the sea. Carini and Haviland went down with her.

When convoy escorts finally arrived to pick up the lifeboats, the gallant ship had gone. There were only a few boards and crates to mark her grave. The *Henry Bacon* had written another glorious chapter in the annals of the Merchant Marine.

Appendix A
Major Casualties: American Personnel on Troopships Sunk in World War II

Ten ships were sunk with a loss of life of 50 or more American troops on each ship.

Some 1,015 men were lost on the British *Rohna,* which was sunk by enemy planes off Algiers, 26 November 1943. The troopship sank in thirty minutes.

The next worst disaster was the sinking of the Belgian troopship *Leopoldville* off Cherbourg, 24 December 1944. More than 750 American soldiers were drowned.

The largest loss of life on an American ship was in the sinking of the *Paul Hamilton* off Algiers, 20 April 1944. More than 500 men were lost.

The torpedoing of the *Dorchester* near Greenland, 3 February 1943, resulted in the loss of 404 men, and 86 were lost when the *Henry Mallory* was torpedoed off Greenland, 7 February 1943.

When the *H. G. Blasdel* was mined in the English Channel, 29 June 1944, 76 men drowned or were killed in the explosion.

The torpedoing of the *William B. Woods* off Palermo, 9 March 1944, took the lives of 51 men.

The torpedoing of the troopship *Cherokee* off Boston, 15 June 1942, took the lives of 20 men.

Thousands of troops were carried to the Mediterranean theater of operations on Liberty ships, in which one hold had been fitted with bunks for about 500 troops. Fast liners converted to troopships and crossing the Atlantic without convoy carried the majority of American and Canadian troops to England.

Source: U.S. Maritime Commission

Appendix B
United States–Flag Merchant
Ships Sunk from War Causes
1 November 1940–5 May 1945

Name of Vessel	Date*	Area
1940		
City of Rayville	8 November	Pacific
1941		
Robin Moor	21 May	Caribbean
Steel Seafarer	7 September	Red Sea and Indian Ocean
Lehigh	19 October	Approaches to Mediterranean
Astral	November	Undetermined
Turecamo Boys	17 November	Northwest Atlantic
Sagadahoc	3 December	Approaches to Mediterranean
Nisqually	8	Pacific
Lahaina	12	Pacific
Vincent	12	Pacific
Manini	17	Pacific
Prusa	19	Pacific
Emidio	20	Pacific
Montebello	23	Pacific
Capillo	31	Pacific
1942		
Malama	1 January	Pacific
Ruth Alexander	2	Pacific

1942 (*continued*)

Allan Jackson	18	Northwest Atlantic
City of Atlanta	19	Northwest Atlantic
Frances Salman	20	Northwest Atlantic
Norvana	21	Northwest Atlantic
Venore	23	Northwest Atlantic
Francis E. Powell	26	Northwest Atlantic
Florence Luckenbach	29	Red Sea and Indian Ocean
Rochester	30	Northwest Atlantic
W. L. Steed	2 February	Northwest Atlantic
India Arrow	4	Northwest Atlantic
China Arrow	5	Northwest Atlantic
Major Wheeler	5	Northwest Atlantic
Azalea City	16	Northwest Atlantic
West Ivis	16	Caribbean
Lake Osweya	19	Northwest Atlantic
Mauna Loa	19	Pacific
Pan Massachusetts	19	Northwest Atlantic
Delplata	20	Caribbean
J. N. Pew	21	Caribbean
Republic	21	Northwest Atlantic
Cities Service Empire	22	Northwest Atlantic
Lihue	22	Caribbean
W. D. Anderson	22	Northwest Atlantic
West Zeda	22	Caribbean
Norlavore	24	Northwest Atlantic
Marore	26	Northwest Atlantic
R. P. Resor	27	Northwest Atlantic
Oregon	28	Caribbean
P. A. F. No. 11	March	Pacific
Steel Age	March	South Atlantic
Mary	3 March	Caribbean
Albert F. Paul	4	Northwest Atlantic
Collamer	5	Northwest Atlantic
Mariana	6	Northwest Atlantic
Barbara	7	Caribbean
Cordonia	7	Caribbean

Gulftrade	10	Northwest Atlantic
Carib Sea	11	Northwest Atlantic
Olga	12	Caribbean
Texan	12	Caribbean
John D. Gill	13	Northwest Atlantic
Number Four	13	Pacific
Number Two	13	Pacific
Lemuel Burrows	14	Northwest Atlantic
Ario	15	Northwest Atlantic
Alkaliner	16	Gulf of Mexico
Australia	16	Northwest Atlantic
Muskogee	17	Northwest Atlantic
E. M. Clark	18	Northwest Atlantic
Papoose	18	Northwest Atlantic
W. E. Hutton	18	Northwest Atlantic
Liberator	19	Northwest Atlantic
Oakmar	21	Northwest Atlantic
Naeco	23	Northwest Atlantic
Dixie Arrow	26	Northwest Atlantic
Carolyn	27	Northwest Atlantic
Effingham	28	Northeast Atlantic
City of New York	30	Northwest Atlantic
Allegheny	31	Northwest Atlantic
Barnegat	31	Northwest Atlantic
Menominee	31	Northwest Atlantic
T. C. McCobb	31	Caribbean
Tiger	31	Northwest Atlantic
David H. Atwater	2 April	Northwest Atlantic
Otho	2	Northwest Atlantic
Byron D. Benson	3	Northwest Atlantic
West Irmo	3	Approaches to Mediterranean
Comol Rico	4	Caribbean
Catahoula	5	Caribbean
Bienville	6	Red Sea and Indian Ocean
Exmoor	6	Red Sea and Indian Ocean
Selma City	6	Red Sea and Indian Ocean
Washingtonian	6	Red Sea and Indian Ocean

1942 (*continued*)

Atlas	9	Northwest Atlantic
Esparta	9	Northwest Atlantic
Eugene V. R. Thayer	9	South Atlantic
GulfAmerica	10	Northwest Atlantic
Malchace	10	Northwest Atlantic
Tamaulipas	10	Northwest Atlantic
Delvalle	12	Caribbean
Esso Boston	12	Caribbean
Leslie	12	Northwest Atlantic
Margaret	15	Northwest Atlantic
Robin Hood	15	Northwest Atlantic
Alcoa Guide	16	Northwest Atlantic
Steelmaker	19	Northwest Atlantic
Connecticut	20	South Atlantic
West Imboden	20	Northwest Atlantic
Pipestone County	21	Northwest Atlantic
San Jacinto	22	Northwest Atlantic
Lammot Du Pont	23	Northwest Atlantic
Alcoa Partner	26	Caribbean
Mobiloil	29	Northwest Atlantic
Federal	30	Caribbean
Eastern Sword	4 May	Caribbean
Joseph M. Cudahy	4	Gulf of Mexico
Munger T. Ball	4	Gulf of Mexico
Norlindo	4	Gulf of Mexico
Tuscaloosa City	4	Caribbean
Afoundria	5	Caribbean
John Adams	5	Pacific
Alcoa Puritan	6	Gulf of Mexico
Green Island	6	Caribbean
Halsey	6	Northwest Atlantic
Laida	6	Pacific
Ohioan	8	Northwest Atlantic
Esso Houston	12	Caribbean
Norlantic	12	Caribbean
Virginia	12	Gulf of Mexico

David McKelvy	13	Gulf of Mexico
GulfPenn	13	Gulf of Mexico
Nicarao	15	Northwest Atlantic
GulfOil	16	Gulf of Mexico
Ruth Lykes	16	Caribbean
Challenger	17	Caribbean
Foam	17	Northwest Atlantic
Isabela	18	Caribbean
Mercury Sun	18	Caribbean
Quaker City	18	Caribbean
William J. Salman	18	Caribbean
Halo	19	Gulf of Mexico
Heredia	19	Gulf of Mexico
Ogontz	19	Gulf of Mexico
Clare	20	Caribbean
Elizabeth	20	Caribbean
George Calvert	20	Caribbean
Plow City	21	Northwest Atlantic
Samuel Q. Brown	23	Caribbean
Beatrice	24	Caribbean
Alcoa Carrier	26	Caribbean
Carrabulle	26	Gulf of Mexico
Alamar	27	Northeast Atlantic
City of Joliet	27	Northeast Atlantic
Mormacsul	27	Northeast Atlantic
Syros	27	Northeast Atlantic
Alcoa Pilgrim	28	Caribbean
New Jersey	28	Caribbean
Alcoa Shipper	30	Northwest Atlantic
L. J. Drake	June	Caribbean
Tillie Lykes	June	Caribbean
Hampton Roads	1 June	Gulf of Mexico
Knoxville City	1	Caribbean
West Notus	1	Northwest Atlantic
City of Alma	2	Caribbean
Illinois	2	Caribbean
Aeolus	3	Northwest Atlantic

1942 (*continued*)

Ben and Josephine	3	Northwest Atlantic
M. F. Elliott	3	Caribbean
Steel Worker	3	Northwest Atlantic
Velma Lykes	4	Caribbean
Delfina	5	Caribbean
Melvin H. Baker	5	South Atlantic
George Clymer	6	South Atlantic
Coast Trader	7	Pacific
Edith	7	Caribbean
Suwied	7	Caribbean
Franklin K. Lane	8	Caribbean
Hagan	10	Caribbean
American	11	Caribbean
F. W. Abrams	11	Northwest Atlantic
Cities Service Toledo	12	Gulf of Mexico
Sixaola	12	Caribbean
Solon Turman	13	Caribbean
Scottsburg	14	Caribbean
Lebore	14	Caribbean
Cherokee	15	Northwest Atlantic
Kahuku	15	Caribbean
West Hardaway	15	Caribbean
Arkansan	16	Caribbean
Chant	16	Mediterranean–Black Sea
Millinocket	17	Caribbean
Santore	17	Northwest Atlantic
Seattle Spirit	18	Northwest Atlantic
Cheerio	19	Caribbean
Alcoa Cadet	21	Northeast Atlantic
West Ira	21	Caribbean
E. J. Sadler	22	Caribbean
Rawleigh Warner	23	Gulf of Mexico
John R. Williams	24	Northwest Atlantic
Manuela	24	Northwest Atlantic
Polybius	26	Caribbean
Express	27	Red Sea and Indian Ocean

Potlatch	27	Caribbean
Raphael Semmes	28	Northwest Atlantic
Ruth	28	Caribbean
Sam Houston	28	Caribbean
Sea Thrush	28	Caribbean
Wm. Rockefeller	28	Northwest Atlantic
Thomas McKean	29	Caribbean
City of Birmingham	30	Northwest Atlantic
Edward Luckenbach	1 July	Gulf of Mexico
Warrior	1	Caribbean
Alexander Macomb	3	Northwest Atlantic
Norlandia	3	Caribbean
Christopher Newport	4	Northeast Atlantic
William Hooper	4	Northeast Atlantic
Carlton	5	Northeast Atlantic
Daniel Morgan	5	Northeast Atlantic
Fairfield City	5	Northeast Atlantic
Heffron	5	Northeast Atlantic
Honomu	5	Northeast Atlantic
Hybert	5	Northeast Atlantic
John Randolph	5	Northeast Atlantic
Massmar	5	Northeast Atlantic
Pan Kraft	5	Northeast Atlantic
Peter Kerr	5	Northeast Atlantic
Washington	5	Northeast Atlantic
John Witherspoon	6	Northeast Atlantic
Pan Atlantic	6	Northeast Atlantic
Alcoa Ranger	7	Northeast Atlantic
Olopana	7	Northeast Atlantic
J. A. Moffett, Jr.	8	Gulf of Mexico
Benjamin Brewster	9	Gulf of Mexico
Hoosier	9	Northeast Atlantic
Santa Rita	9	Northwest Atlantic
Andrew Jackson	12	Caribbean
Tachira	12	Caribbean
Oneida	13	Caribbean
R. W. Gallagher	13	Gulf of Mexico

1942 (*continued*)

Arcata	14	Pacific
Fairport	16	Northwest Atlantic
Gertrude	16	Gulf of Mexico
William F. Humphrey	16	South Atlantic
Keshena	19	Northwest Atlantic
Coast Farmer	21	Pacific
William Dawes	21	Pacific
Honolulan	22	Approaches to Mediterranean
Chilore	24	Northwest Atlantic
Onondaga	24	Caribbean
Stella Lykes	27	Caribbean
Ebb	28	Northwest Atlantic
Cranford	29	Caribbean
Robert E. Lee	30	Gulf of Mexico
Wawaloam	6 August	Northwest Atlantic
Kaimoku	8	Northwest Atlantic
Almeria Lykes	13	Mediterranean–Black Sea
California	13	Caribbean
Cripple Creek	13	Approaches to Mediterranean
Delmundo	13	Caribbean
R. M. Parker, Jr.	13	Gulf of Mexico
Santa Elisa	13	Mediterranean–Black Sea
Balladier	15	Northwest Atlantic
Louisiana	17	Caribbean
John Hancock	18	Caribbean
West Celina	19	Caribbean
Arlyn	27	Northwest Atlantic
Chatham	27	Northwest Atlantic
Topa Topa	29	Caribbean
Jack Carnes	30	Northwest Atlantic
Star of Oregon	30	Caribbean
West Lashaway	30	Caribbean
Wichita	September	Undetermined
Patrick J. Hurley	12 September	Caribbean
John Penn	13	Northeast Atlantic
Mary Luckenbach	13	Northeast Atlantic

Oliver Ellsworth	13	Northeast Atlantic
Oregonian	13	Northeast Atlantic
Wacosta	13	Northeast Atlantic
American Leader	15	South Atlantic
Commercial Trader	16	Caribbean
Mae	17	Caribbean
Kentucky	18	Northeast Atlantic
Silver Sword	20	Northeast Atlantic
John Winthrop	21	Northwest Atlantic
Bellingham	22	Northeast Atlantic
Paul Luckenbach	22	Red Sea and Indian Ocean
Pennmar	23	Northwest Atlantic
Antinous	24	Caribbean
Esso Williamsburg	24	Northwest Atlantic
Losmar	24	Red Sea and Indian Ocean
Wesl Chetac	24	Caribbean
Stephen Hopkins	27	South Atlantic
Alcoa Mariner	28	Caribbean
La Salle	October	Undetermined
Alcoa Transport	2 October	Caribbean
Caribstar	4	Caribbean
Robert H. Colley	4	Northwest Atlantic
Larry Doheny	5	Pacific
William A. McKenney	5	Caribbean
Chickasaw City	7	South Atlantic
John Carter Rose	8	Caribbean
Swiftsure	8	South Atlantic
Coloradan	9	South Atlantic
Examelia	9	South Atlantic
Camden	10	Pacific
Steel Scientist	11	Caribbean
Angelina	18	Northwest Atlantic
Steel Navigator	19	Northwest Atlantic
Reuben Tipton	23	Caribbean
President Coolidge	25	Pacific
Anne Hutchinson	26	South Atlantic
Gurney E. Newlin	27	Northwest Atlantic

1942 (*continued*)

Pan New York	29	Northeast Atlantic
West Kebar	29	Caribbean
Sawokla	November	Undetermined
George Thacher	1 November	South Atlantic
East Indian	3	South Atlantic
Hahira	3	Northwest Atlantic
William Clark	4	Northeast Atlantic
Meton	5	Caribbean
Nathaniel Hawthorne	7	Caribbean
West Humhaw	8	Approaches to Mediterranean
Marcus Whitman	9	South Atlantic
Excello	13	South Atlantic
Star of Scotland	13	South Atlantic
Parismina	18	Northwest Atlantic
Yaka	18	Northwest Atlantic
Pierce Butler	20	South Atlantic
Alcoa Pathfinder	23	South Atlantic
Caddo	23	Northwest Atlantic
Jeremiah Wadsworth	27	South Atlantic
Alaskan	28	Caribbean
James McKay	December	Northwest Atlantic
Coamo	9	Undetermined
Alcoa Rambler	14	South Atlantic
Thomas B. Schall	14	Caribbean

1943

Arthur Middleton	1 January	Mediterranean–Black Sea
Birmingham City	9	Caribbean
Broad Arrow	9	Caribbean
Collingsworth	9	Caribbean
Minotaur	9	Caribbean
Louise Lykes	10	Northeast Atlantic
Benjamin Smith	23	Approaches to Mediterranean
Brilliant	25	Northwest Atlantic
City of Flint	25	Approaches to Mediterranean

Cape Decision	27	Caribbean
Charles C. Pinckney	27	Approaches to Mediterranean
Julia Ward Howe	27	Approaches to Mediterranean
Samuel Gompers	29	Pacific
Atlantic Sun	February	Northwest Atlantic
Jeremiah Van Rensselaer	2 February	Northwest Atlantic
Dorchester	3	Northwest Atlantic
Greylock	3	Northeast Atlantic
West Portal	5	Northwest Atlantic
Henry R. Mallory	7	Northwest Atlantic
Robert E. Hopkins	7	Northwest Atlantic
Roger B. Taney	9	South Atlantic
Starr King	10	Pacific
Deer Lodge	17	South Atlantic
Rosario	21	Northeast Atlantic
Chattanooga City	22	Northwest Atlantic
Expositor	22	Northwest Atlantic
Esso Baton Rouge	23	Approaches to Mediterranean
Hastings	23	Northwest Atlantic
Jonathan Sturges	23	Northwest Atlantic
Nathanael Greene	23	Mediterranean–Black Sea
Wade Hampton	28	Northwest Atlantic
Fitz John Porter	1 March	South Atlantic
Meriwether Lewis	2	Northwest Atlantic
Harvey W. Scott	3	South Atlantic
Stag Hound	4	South Atlantic
Executive	5	Northeast Atlantic
James B. Stephens	8	South Atlantic
James K. Polk	9	Caribbean
Malantic	9	Northeast Atlantic
Puerto Rican	9	Northeast Atlantic
Thomas Ruffin	9	Caribbean
Andrea F. Luckenbach	10	Northwest Atlantic
James Sprunt	10	Caribbean
Richard Bland	10	Northeast Atlantic
Richard D. Spaight	10	South Atlantic
Virginia Sinclair	10	Caribbean

1943 (*continued*)

William C. Gorgas	11	Northwest Atlantic
Cities Service Missouri	13	Caribbean
Keystone	13	Approaches to Mediterranean
Benjamin Harrison	16	Approaches to Mediterranean
Harry Luckenbach	17	Northwest Atlantic
Irenee DuPont	17	Northwest Atlantic
James Oglethorpe	17	Northwest Atlantic
Molly Pitcher	17	Approaches to Mediterranean
William Eustis	17	Northwest Atlantic
Walter Q. Gresham	18	Northwest Atlantic
Mathew Luckenbach	19	Northeast Atlantic
William Pierce Frye	29	Northeast Atlantic
Edward B. Dudley	April	Northwest Atlantic
Gulfstate	3 April	Gulf of Mexico
Sunoil	5	Northwest Atlantic
John Sevier	6	Caribbean
James W. Denver	11	Approaches to Mediterranean
Robert Gray	13	Undetermined
Michigan	20	Mediterranean–Black Sea
John Drayton	21	South Atlantic
Santa Catalina	24	Northwest Atlantic
Lydia M. Child	27	Pacific
McKeesport	29	Northwest Atlantic
Phoebe A. Hearst	30	Pacific
West Madaket	5 May	Northwest Atlantic
West Maximus	5	Northwest Atlantic
Samuel Jordan Kirkwood	6	South Atlantic
Pat Harrison	8	Approaches to Mediterranean
Nickeliner	13	Caribbean
William K. Vanderbilt	16	Pacific
H. M. Storey	17	Pacific
Agwimonte	28	South Atlantic
John Worthington	28	South Atlantic
Flora MacDonald	30	Approaches to Mediterranean
Montanan	3 June	Red Sea and Indian Ocean
William King	6	South Atlantic

Esso Gettysburg	10	Northwest Atlantic
Henry Knox	19	Red Sea and Indian Ocean
Sebastian Cermeno	27	Red Sea and Indian Ocean
Samuel Heintzelman	July	Red Sea and Indian Ocean
Bloody Marsh	2 July	Northwest Atlantic
Elihu B. Washburne	3	South Atlantic
Maltran	5	Caribbean
James Robertson	7	South Atlantic
William Boyce Thompson	7	South Atlantic
Eldena	8	Caribbean
Thomas Sinnickson	8	South Atlantic
Alice F. Palmer	10	Red Sea and Indian Ocean
African Star	12	South Atlantic
Robert Rowan	12	Mediterranean–Black Sea
Timothy Pickering	13	Mediterranean–Black Sea
Robert Bacon	14	Red Sea and Indian Ocean
Richard Caswell	16	South Atlantic
Harrison Gray Otis	4 August	Approaches to Mediterranean
Francis W. Pettygrove	13	Mediterranean–Black Sea
John Bell	26	Mediterranean–Black Sea
Richard Henderson	26	Mediterranean–Black Sea
Bushrod Washington	15 September	Mediterranean–Black Sea
Frederick Douglass	20	Northwest Atlantic
Theodore Dwight Weld	20	Northwest Atlantic
Cornelia P. Spencer	21	Red Sea and Indian Ocean
William W. Gerhard	21	Mediterranean–Black Sea
Richard Olney	22	Mediterranean–Black Sea
Steel Voyager	23	Northwest Atlantic
Elias Howe	24	Red Sea and Indian Ocean
Metapan	1 October	Mediterranean–Black Sea
Yorkmar	9	Northeast Atlantic
John H. Couch	11	Pacific
James Russell Lowell	15	Mediterranean–Black Sea
Delisle	19	Northwest Atlantic
Tivives	21	Mediterranean–Black Sea
Santa Elena	6 November	Mediterranean–Black Sea
Cape San Juan	11	Pacific

1943 (continued)

Elizabeth Kellogg	23	Caribbean
Melville E. Stone	24	Caribbean
John Bascom	2 December	Mediterranean–Black Sea
John Harvey	2	Mediterranean–Black Sea
John L. Motley	2	Mediterranean–Black Sea
Joseph Wheeler	2	Mediterranean–Black Sea
Samuel J. Tilden	2	Mediterranean–Black Sea
Touchet	3	Gulf of Mexico
McDowell	16	Caribbean
Jose Navarro	26	Caribbean

1944

Sumner I. Kimball	January	Northwest Atlantic
Albert Gallatin	2 January	Red Sea and Indian Ocean
William S. Rosecrans	6	Mediterranean–Black Sea
Daniel Webster	10	Mediterranean–Black Sea
Andrew G. Curtin	25	Northeast Atlantic
Penelope Barker	25	Northeast Atlantic
Walter Camp	25	Red Sea and Indian Ocean
Samuel Huntington	29	Mediterranean–Black Sea
Edward Bates	1 February	Mediterranean–Black Sea
Elihu Yale	15	Mediterranean–Black Sea
George Cleeve	22	Mediterranean–Black Sea
Peter Skene Ogden	22	Mediterranean–Black Sea
E. G. Seubert	23	Red Sea and Indian Ocean
William S. Thayer	4 March	Northeast Atlantic
Daniel Chester French	6	Mediterranean–Black Sea
Clark Mills	9	Mediterranean–Black Sea
William B. Woods	10	Mediterranean–Black Sea
Virginia Dare	12	Mediterranean–Black Sea
H. D. Collier	13	Red Sea and Indian Ocean
Maiden Creek	17	Mediterranean–Black Sea
Seakay	17	Northeast Atlantic
John A. Poor	19	Red Sea and Indian Ocean
Richard Hovey	29	Red Sea and Indian Ocean

Meyer London	16 April	Mediterranean–Black Sea
Pan Pennsylvania	16	Northwest Atlantic
Thomas G. Masaryk	16	Mediterranean–Black Sea
James Guthrie	17	Mediterranean–Black Sea
Paul Hamilton	20	Mediterranean–Black Sea
Charles Morgan	10 June	Northeast Atlantic
Charles W. Eliot	28	Northeast Atlantic
H. G. Blasdel	29	Northeast Atlantic
James A. Farrell	29	Northeast Atlantic
John A. Treutlen	29	Northeast Altantic
Exmouth	July	Undetermined
Jean Nicolet	2 July	Red Sea and Indian Ocean
Esso Harrisburg	6	Caribbean
William Gaston	24	South Atlantic
Robin Goodfellow	28	South Atlantic
William L. Marcy	7 August	Northeast Atlantic
Ezra Weston	8	Northeast Atlantic
John Barry	28	Red Sea and Indian Ocean
Jacksonville	30	Northeast Atlantic
Edward H. Crockett	29 September	Northeast Atlantic
John A. Johnson	29 October	Pacific
Fort Lee	2 November	Red Sea and Indian Ocean
Lee S. Overman	12	Northeast Atlantic
Gus W. Darnell	23	Pacific
William D. Burnham	23	Northeast Atlantic
Francis Asbury	3 December	Northeast Atlantic
Antoine Saugrain	5	Pacific
Dan Beard	10	Northeast Atlantic
William S. Ladd	10	Pacific
Steel Traveler	18	Northeast Atlantic
Robert J. Walker	25	Pacific
Hobart Baker	28	Pacific
James H. Breasted	28	Pacific
John Burke	28	Pacific
Arthur Sewall	29	Northeast Atlantic
Black Hawk	29	Northeast Atlantic

1945

Lewis L. Dyche	4 January	Pacific
Jonas Lie	9	Northeast Atlantic
Martin Van Buren	14	Northwest Atlantic
Henry B. Plant	6 February	Northeast Atlantic
Peter Silvester	6	Red Sea and Indian Ocean
Horace Gray	14	Northeast Atlantic
Thomas Scott	17	Northeast Atlantic
Henry Bacon	23	Northeast Atlantic
Hashaba	26	Northeast Atlantic
Robert L. Vann	1 March	Northeast Atlantic
Thomas Donaldson	20	Northeast Atlantic
Horace Bushnell	20	Northeast Atlantic
James Eagan Layne	21	Northeast Atlantic
John R. Park	21	Northeast Atlantic
Charles D. McIver	23	Northeast Atlantic
Oklahoma	28	Caribbean
Hobbs Victory	6 April	Pacific
Logan Victory	6	Pacific
Cyrus H. McCormick	18	Northeast Atlantic
Swiftscout	18	Northwest Atlantic
Canada Victory	27	Pacific
Black Point	5 May	Northwest Atlantic

*Exact dates of some sinkings are unknown. In other instances, the dates in this listing differ slightly from those given in the text. Such discrepancies usually resulted from delayed transmittals to the War Shipping Administration; the dates posted were sometimes the dates of receipt of the information, rather than the actual dates of the sinkings.

Source: U.S. War Shipping Administration.

Appendix C
Blockships Used to Form Breakwater on Normandy Beachhead: 1944

Name of Vessel	Date Sunk
Artemas Ward	8 June
Benjamin Contee	8 June
Courageous	8 June
David O. Saylor	8 June
Galveston	8 June
George S. Wasson	8 June
George W. Childs	8 June
James Iredell	8 June
James W. Marshall	8 June
Matt W. Ransom	8 June
Victory Sword	8 June
Vitruvius	8 June
West Cheswald	8 June
West Grama	8 June
West Honaker	8 June
West Nohno	8 June
Wilscox	8 June
West Nilus	7 July
Pennsylvanian	August
Lena Luckenbach	4 August
Kentuckian	12 August
Alcoa Leader	13 August
Kofresi	14 August

Robin Gray	18 August
Sahale	24 August
Exford	26 August
Illinoian	28 August

Source: U.S. War Shipping Administration

Notes

Chapter 1. Prelude to War

1. See Joseph Gainard's biography, *Yankee Skipper*, for his account of the *City of Flint*'s capture by the Germans. Detailed accounts and interviews with crewmen appeared in *The New York Times*, 28 January 1940; *New York Herald Tribune*, 23 and 25 October 1939 and 28 January 1940; and news magazines of the time.
2. Felix Riesenberg, *Standard Seamanship for the Merchant Service*, 2d ed., New York: D. Van Nostrand Co., 1936, refers to the code book as a fixture on the bridge of every merchant ship. Some texts on seamanship refer to it as *The Code Book of Signals*. William B. Hayler, ed., *The American Merchant Seaman's Manual*, 9th ed., Centreville, Md.: Cornell Maritime Press, 1980, calls it *The Code Book*, giving the International Code of Signals.
3. Gainard, *Yankee Skipper*.
4. The *Robin Moor* incident was covered extensively in newspapers and news magazines. See, for example, *The New York Times*, 14, 17, and 21 June 1941; and *New York Herald Tribune*, 10 and 13 June and 3 November 1941.

Chapter 2. The Ships and Men of the Merchant Marine

1. Lane et al., *Ships for Victory*, give a detailed history of the World War II shipbuilding program. In his personal library, the author has a collection of U.S. Maritime Commission news releases about the shipbuilding program. The author also was privileged to have an extensive interview with Adm. Emory S. Land, head of the

Maritime Commission during World War II. Also, see Land, *Winning the War with Ships*.

2. The Maritime Commission was dissolved in 1950. After various changes within the Department of Commerce, maritime affairs were put under the U.S. Maritime Administration, which is now a part of the Department of Transportation.

3. On many foreign-flag ships, the pay was far below the scale on American vessels, and living conditions were inferior to those on American ships. For these reasons, foreign seamen, who faced the same dangers as Americans, were attracted to leaving their own ships and obtaining jobs under the American flag.

4. Records on the Armed Guard are to be found in the War Shipping Administration files, National Archives, and in the Historical Division, Navy Department.

5. A full account of the use of nets can be consulted in the files of the Coordinator of Ship Defense Installations, National Archives.

CHAPTER 3. U-BOAT LANE

1. For interviews with survivors, see *The Seafarers Log*, 26 January 1942; and *The New York Times* and *New York Herald Tribune*, various stories published in several issues following the sinking.

2. German historians of the sea war prefer the spelling Dönitz. American and British historians generally use Doenitz.

3. Account of the *Allan Jackson* is from interviews with survivors that appeared in *The New York Times*, *New York Herald Tribune*, *Time* magazine, and *Life* magazine.

4. See *The Seafarers Log*, 2 January 1942; and *The New York Times* and *New York Herald Tribune*, 27 January 1942.

5. Account of the *Carib Sea* is from the ship's master, Nicholas Manolis, interview with author. Also, see Manolis, *We at Sea*. After the war, Manolis was an executive with a New York steamship company.

6. Account of the *Esparta* is from Voyage Report, *Esparta*, National Archives.

CHAPTER 4. CARIBBEAN CARNIVAL

1. Voyage Report, *Atenas*, National Archives.

2. Voyage Report and news accounts in the file, *Jack*, National Archives.

3. Account by Captain David is from Voyage Report, *Suwied*, National Archives.
4. Robert Burton, conversations with author when both were with the Seafarers International Union.
5. Rohwer and Hummelchen; *Chronology of the War at Sea.*
6. Account of the *Lindenhall* is from Voyage Reports of the ships in this convoy, National Archives.
7. Voyage Report, *Pompoon*, National Archives.
8. Account of the *James Sprunt* is from Voyage Report, *James Sprunt*, National Archives.
9. Voyage Report, *James Smith*, National Archives.
10. "Black gang" is an old Merchant Marine term for the men, especially firemen and coal passers, who worked below in the days of coal-burning ships. They often looked like they had just come out of a coal mine.

CHAPTER 5. BATTLE OF THE NORTH ATLANTIC: PHASE I

1. Winston Churchill, *The Second World War*, vol. 5, *Closing the Ring*, Boston: Houghton-Mifflin Co., 1951, 6.
2. Account of the *Lammot Du Pont* is from Roger Gilman, interview with author.
3. Account of the *Angelina* and her survivors is from Voyage Report, *Angelina*, National Archives; War Shipping Administration, news releases; and Gustave Alm, interview with author.
4. Account of the *Maiden Creek* is from Voyage Report, *Maiden Creek*, National Archives; and Per Lykkc, interview with author.
5. Lykke, interview.

CHAPTER 6. SEA ROADS TO RUSSIA

1. The logistics of supplying the Russians are detailed in Jones, *Roads to Russia.*
2. *Life* magazine, 13 October 1941.
3. "Channel fever" is an old sailors' expression for the burning desire to get ashore after many days or weeks at sea.
4. Voyage Report, *Expositor*, National Archives.
5. Voyage Report, *Michigan*, National Archives.

6. Voyage Report, *Eldena*, National Archives.
7. Account of the *Puerto Rican* is from Voyage Report, Puerto Rican, National Archives; U.S. Maritime Commission, news release; and Morison, *U.S. Naval Operations in World War II*, vol. 1.

CHAPTER 7. CONVOY PQ-17

1. A number of books have been written about this convoy. For authoritative accounts, see Roskill, *War at Sea*, vol. 1; and Morison, *U.S. Naval Operations in World War II*, vol. 1. Also, see Schofield, *Russian Convoys*.
2. See Morison, *U.S. Naval Operations in World War II*, vol. 1; and Roskill, *War at Sea*, vol. 1, for analyses of this momentous and fatal decision.
3. John Thevik, conversations with author, when they were shipmates on the *William B. Giles*, 1943.
4. Account of the *Bellingham* is from Voyage Report, *Bellingham*, National Archives.
5. Thevik, conversations.
6. Voyage Report, *Daniel Morgan*, National Archives.
7. Voyage Report, *Hoosier*, National Archives.
8. Thevik, conversations.
9. Ibid.

CHAPTER 8. CONVOY PQ-18

1. For accounts of PQ-18, see Roskill, *War at Sea*, vol. 1; Morison, *U.S. Naval Operations in World War II*, vol. 1; Schofield, *Russian Convoys*; and other books on the sea war; also articles from *The Seafarers Log*.
2. Al Bernstein, conversations with author. Bernstein kept a diary of his voyage on the *Scoharie* and took many photos of the air attacks on PQ-18.
3. James Harrington, interview in *The Seafarers Log*.
4. Voyage Report, *St. Olaf*, National Archives.
5. Voyage Report, *Scoharie*, National Archives.
6. Bernstein, conversations.
7. Voyage Report, *Nathanael Greene*, National Archives.

8. Voyage Report, *Wacosta,* National Archives.
9. Richard Hocken, interview with author.
10. Voyage Report, *Kentucky,* National Archives.

CHAPTER 9. BATTLE OF THE NORTH ATLANTIC: PHASE II

1. Detailed accounts of the *Dorchester* and *Mallory* sinkings, along with survivor interviews, are in Voyage Reports of the respective ships, National Archives.
2. Voyage Report, *Henry R. Mallory,* National Archives.
3. Reports Made by Cadets to the United States Merchant Marine Academy, U.S. Maritime Commission file, National Archives.
4. Voyage Report, *Pan Maine,* National Archives.
5. *Battle of the Atlantic,* London: His Majesty's Stationery Office, 1946.

CHAPTER 10. FIGHTING FLEETS

1. Voyage Report, *Colin,* National Archives.
2. Account of the collision is from Voyage Reports, *El Coston* and *Murfreesboro,* National Archives.
3. From 1944 on, the ships in convoys often numbered between 80 and 100, or more. A convoy from London to New York in August 1944 consisted of 146 ships and arrived without any contacts with submarines. By this time, of course, the U-boats were on the defensive, and more ships and planes were available for convoy protection.
4. Thevik, conversations.
5. Reports Made by Cadets.
6. Account of the *Liberty Glo* is from Voyage Report, *Liberty Glo,* National Archives.

CHAPTER 11. BATTLES OF THE CENTRAL AND SOUTH ATLANTIC

1. Account of the *American Leader* is from Muggenthaler, *German Raiders of World War II.*

2. Account of the *Cape Sable* is from Cadet William J. DeRemer, post-voyage report to Superintendent, National Merchant Marine Academy, U.S. Maritime Commission file, National Archives.
3. Voyage Report, *John Carter Rose*, National Archives.
4. Voyage Report, *East Indian*, National Archives.
5. The story of the *Star of Scotland* is mainly from Constantin Flink, conversations with author and correspondence that followed. The author also had an opportunity to talk with other survivors of the ship.
6. Voyage Report, *Deer Lodge*, National Archives.
7. Voyage Report, *William B. Giles*, National Archives.
8. Voyage Report, *William M. Meredith*, National Archives.

CHAPTER 12. "WE WON'T SURRENDER WITHOUT A FIGHT"

1. Account of this engagement is from Voyage Report, *Stanvac Calcutta*, National Archives; and *Compass* magazine, house organ of Socony Mobil Oil Co., September–October 1960.
2. After the *Stier* was sunk, Ben Hassan was taken on board the *Stier*'s companion, the supply ship *Tennenfels*, and eventually reached France, where he was hospitalized for several months. Upon his recovery, he spent the duration of the European war in Marlag und Milag, a POW camp for merchant seamen in Germany. Of the *Stanvac Calcutta*'s crew of fifty-one, fourteen were killed and fourteen wounded in the battle. Several more crewmen died in Japanese prison camps.

CHAPTER 13. THE STARK COURAGE OF A VALIANT CREW

1. Account of the *Stephen Hopkins* is from Voyage Report, *Stephen Hopkins*, National Archives; George D. Cronk, interview in *San Francisco News*, 9 March 1943; interviews with other survivors in various newspapers, including *West Coast Sailors*, March 1943, and *San Francisco News*, 9 March 1943; and War Shipping Administration, news releases.
2. Roskill, *War at Sea*, vol. 2.

CHAPTER 14. BOATS AWAY

1. Voyage Report, *T. C. McCobb*, National Archives.
2. The story of the *Prusa*'s survivors is from G. H. Boy, correspondence with author; various newspaper accounts; and Voyage Report, *Prusa*, National Archives.
3. "Nantucket sleigh ride" is a whalers' term for the wild ride that usually occurred when a harpooned whale was not mortally wounded (see Glossary).
4. The story of the *W. L. Steed* and Ralph Mazzucco's personal account are from *Ships of the Esso Fleet in World War II*, Standard Oil Company of New Jersey, 1946. Used by permission of Exxon Corporation.
5. Ibid.
6. *Ships of the Esso Fleet.*
7. Account of the *Taney* is from Voyage Report, *Taney*, National Archives; and Donald Zubrod, postwar conversations with author. Following the war, Zubrod was a steamship company executive in New York City.
8. Zubrod, postwar conversations.
9. Ibid.
10. Ibid.
11. Account of the *James W. Denver*'s lifeboat was given to the author by Dolar Stone and other survivors after their return from Germany. Information on the ship's sinking and the voyage of the lifeboats is also in Voyage Report, *James W. Denver*, National Archives.

CHAPTER 15. THE MAN WHO REFUSED TO DIE

1. Account of the *Wade Hampton* is from Rexford Dickey, conversations with author, when Dickey was a port agent for the Seafarers International Union in Baltimore, Md.; and Worsham Chandler, conversations with author on board the *William B. Giles*, when Chandler was chief engineer and author was purser. Also, see Voyage Report, *Wade Hampton*, National Archives.

CHAPTER 16. THE TANKERMEN

1. War Shipping Administration, news release, 17 December 1944.
2. Further account of the sinking of the *Jacksonville* is from Captain Lester Carroll of the tanker *Champoeg*, part of the same convoy as the *Jacksonville*.
3. Account of the *Dixie Arrow* is from War Shipping Administration, news releases, National Archives; also, *The New York Times* and *New York Herald Tribune*, news stories that appeared immediately following the sinking.
4. Paul Myers, quoted in *The New York Times*.
5. U.S. Maritime Commission, news release.
6. U.S. Maritime Commission, news release.
7. Account of the *Yamhill* is from War Shipping Administration, news releases; and Voyage Report, *Yamhill*, National Archives.
8. The story of the *Brilliant* is in Voyage Report, *Brilliant*, and War Shipping Administration, news releases, both in National Archives. This account is from John Bunker, "The Brilliant and the Brave," U.S. Naval Institute *Proceedings*, October 1958, and is used by permission of the editor.
9. U.S. Maritime Commission, news release.

CHAPTER 17. WAR IN THE NARROW SEA

1. Account of R. E. Barrera is from Voyage Report, *O'Henry*, National Archives.
2. Ibid.
3. E. J. Stull, extract and other quotations are from Voyage Report, *Samuel Parker*, National Archives.
4. The author was a member of the crew of the *Jonathan Grout* during the invasion of Sicily, 10 July 1943.
5. According to Morison, *U.S. Naval Operations in World War II*, vol. 9, some 1,600 British paratroops in gliders towed by 134 planes were to land at various points in the British sector. Hundreds of men were lost when 47 gliders landed prematurely in the sea or were shot down.
6. Voyage Report, *Colin Kelly*, National Archives.
7. Morison, *U.S. Naval Operations in World War II*, vol. 9, praises the

work of American merchant ships in the Eastern (British) sector of the Sicily invasion. Also, he quotes from British Admiral of the Fleet Sir Andrew Cunningham, who commended "the fine spirit, discipline and calm determination of the many officers and men of the Allied Merchant Navies."

8. Voyage Report, *Hugh Williamson,* National Archives.
9. Voyage Report, *John Howard Payne,* National Archives.
10. Voyage Report, *John Banvard,* National Archives.
11. Ibid.
12. Ibid.
13. Voyage Report, *Lawton B. Evans,* National Archives.
14. Ibid.
15. Voyage Report, *Elihu Yale,* National Archives.
16. Voyage Report, *Ann Bradstreet,* National Archives.
17. Ibid.
18. Ibid.
19. Voyage Report, *William T. Barry,* National Archives.
20. Ibid.
21. Ibid.
22. Voyage Report, *Athelchief,* National Archives.
23. Voyage Report, *William Meredith,* National Archives.

CHAPTER 18. WHEN THE STUKAS BLASTED BARI

1. Account of the action at Bari is from U.S. Navy and War Shipping Administration files on the ships involved, National Archives.

CHAPTER 19. THE INDIAN OCEAN WAR

1. Account of the *Bienville* is from Robert Spearing, conversations with author, when Spearing was port captain in New York for the Waterman Steamship Company. Because the ship had no Armed Guard, there is no voyage report.
2. Reports Made by Cadets.
3. Voyage Report, *William King,* National Archives.
4. Account of the *Henry Knox* is from Maurice Price, interview with author; War Shipping Administration, news releases; and Voyage Report, *Henry Knox,* National Archives.

5. This quotation and others throughout the account of the *Henry Knox* are from Price, interview, unless otherwise noted.
6. U.S. Navy Department, report summarizing accounts by survivors, 14 August 1943.
7. Voyage Report, *Richard Stockton*, National Archives.
8. Account of the *Nicolet* is from *West Coast Sailors*, publication of the Sailors Union of the Pacific, 10 November 1944 and 2 February 1945; and Voyage Report, *Nicolet*, National Archives.
9. Account of the *John Barry* and her treasure is from Voyage Report, *John Barry*, National Archives; and U.S. Maritime Administration, news releases.

CHAPTER 20. THE LONG HAUL

1. Japanese submarine attacks on the West Coast are chronicled in the *Los Angeles Times, San Diego Union, San Francisco Chronicle, The New York Times,* and other newspapers of that period.
2. Account of the *Coast Farmer* is from Voyage Report, *Coast Farmer*, National Archives.
3. Morison, *U.S. Naval Operations in World War II,* vol. 12, details the initiation of kamikaze attacks and the havoc resulting from them.
4. Voyage Report, *Adoniram Judson*, National Archives.
5. Voyage Report, *Floyd Spencer*, National Archives.
6. Voyage Report, *Francisco Morazon*, National Archives.
7. Ibid.
8. Voyage Report, *Uriah M. Rose*, National Archives.
9. Voyage Report, *Hobbs* Victory, National Archives.
10. For U.S. Navy losses at Okinawa, see Morison, *U.S. Naval Operations in World War II,* vol. 12.
11. War Shipping Administration, news release, 14 October 1945.

CHAPTER 21. THE GREAT INVASION

1. Generally, this chapter is based on voyage reports in ships' files, National Archives; and news coverage in *The New York Times* and *New York Herald Tribune.*
2. Voyage Report, *Cyrus McCormick*, National Archives.
3. Voyage Report, *Collis P. Huntington,* National Archives.

4. Voyage Report, *Park Benjamin*, National Archives.
5. Voyage Report, *John Merrick*, National Archives.
6. Voyage Report, *Casamir Pulaski*, National Archives.

CHAPTER 22. LOST SHIPS AND OTHER STRANGE TALES

1. This incident is based on author's conversations with wartime submarine officers.
2. Each ship gave the War Shipping Administration an ETA (estimated time of arrival) for her next port of call before leaving on a voyage. When no word was received from the vessel after a reasonable period of time and she had not been reported by other ships, she was declared "overdue and presumed lost." The War Shipping Administration could then notify the next of kin and process death benefits for the crewmen.
3. Many British and other foreign-flag vessels were also lost without trace.
4. Joseph Garrido, interview with author.
5. Account of the *Delisle* is from William Clendaniel, interview with author; U.S. Maritime Commission, news releases; and Voyage Report, *Delisle*, National Archives.
6. The story of the *William H. Welch* is from War Shipping Administration, news releases.
7. Account of the *Henry Wynkoop* is from Voyage Report, *Henry Wynkoop*, National Archives.
8. Voyage Report, *Atlantic Sun*, National Archives.

CHAPTER 23. SAILING ALONE

1. This account is given as several crewmen told it to the author many years ago—in sailor's lingo, rather than in the formal wording of an official report.

CHAPTER 24. THE GALLANT *CEDAR MILLS*

1. A detailed account of the rescue of the *Le Triomphant*, prepared for the War Shipping Administration by Captain Morgan Maxey, is in Voyage Report, *Cedar Mills*, National Archives. Several lengthy

news releases were also issued by the War Shipping Administration and the U.S. Navy Department.

CHAPTER 25. SHIP OF GLORY

1. The story of the *Henry Bacon* is from Voyage Report, *Henry Bacon*, National Archives; and War Shipping Administration, news releases.

Bibliography

Gainard, Joseph A. *Yankee Skipper.* New York: Frederick Stoker Co., 1940.

Gannon, Michael. *Operation Drumbeat.* New York: Harper & Row, 1990.

Hickey, Des, and Gus Smith. *Operation Avalanche, the Salerno Landings, 1943.* New York; McGraw-Hill, 1984.

Jones, Robert Huhn. *The Roads to Russia.* Norman: University of Oklahoma Press, 1969.

Keegan, John. *The Price of Admiralty.* London: Arrow Books, 1990.

Land, Emory S. *Winning the War with Ships.* New York: Robert McBride Company, 1958.

Lane, Frederic C., and Associates. *Ships for Victory.* Baltimore: The Johns Hopkins Press, 1951.

Macintyre, Donald. *The Naval War against Hitler.* New York: Charles Scribner's Sons, 1971.

Manolis, Nicholas. *We at Sea.* New York: Anatolin Press, 1949.

Masters, John M., Jr. *Bloody Winter.* New York: D. Van Nostrand, 1967.

Middlebrook, Martin. *Convoy.* New York: William Morrow and Company, 1976.

Morison, Samuel Eliot. *History of United States Naval Operations in World War II.* 15 vols. Boston: Little, Brown, 1962.

Muggenthaler, August K. *German Raiders of World War II.* Englewood, N.J.: Prentice-Hall, 1977.

Pack, S. W. C. *Operation Husky, the Invasion of Sicily.* New York: Hippocrene Books, 1977.

Rayner, D. A. *Escort, the Battle of the Atlantic.* London: William Kimber, 1955.

Robertson, Terence. *Escort Commander.* Garden City, N.Y.: Nelson Doubleday, 1979.

Rohwer, J., and G. Hummelchen. 2 vols. *Chronology of the War at Sea,*
    New York: Arco Publishing Company, 1972.
Roskill, S. W. *The War at Sea.* 5 vols. London: Her Majesty's Stationery
    Office, 1956.
Schofield, B. B. *The Russian Convoys.* London: Pan Books, 1971.
Schofield, B. B., and Martin, L. F. *The Rescue Ships.* London: Wm.
    Blackwood and Sons, 1968.

Newspapers published by maritime unions:

West Coast Sailors, Sailors Union of the Pacific, San Francisco
S.I.U. Log, Seafarers International Union, Brooklyn, New York,
and Washington, D.C.
N.M.U. Pilot, National Maritime Union, New York

Index

About the Author

From 1942 to 1945 John Bunker served as a merchant seaman in the Atlantic, Pacific, Middle East, and Mediterranean theaters. He later worked as a reporter for the *Christian Science Monitor* and *San Diego Tribune* while continuing to pursue his interests in maritime affairs and the history of the labor movement in America. He is the author of *Liberty Ships: The Ugly Ducklings of WWII*, in addition to a history of the Seafarer's International Union and other works. He lives in West Palm Beach, Florida.

The **Naval Institute Press** is the book-publishing arm of the U.S. Naval Institute, a private, nonprofit society for sea service professionals and others who share an interest in naval and maritime affairs. Established in 1873 at the U.S. Naval Academy in Annapolis, Maryland, where its offices remain, today the Naval Institute has more than 100,000 members worldwide.

Members of the Naval Institute receive the influential monthly magazine *Proceedings* and discounts on fine nautical prints and on ship and aircraft photos. They also have access to the transcripts of the Institute's Oral History Program and get discounted admission to any of the Institute-sponsored seminars offered around the country.

The Naval Institute also publishes *Naval History* magazine. This colorful bimonthly is filled with entertaining and thought-provoking articles, first-person reminiscences, and dramatic art and photography. Members receive a discount on *Naval History* subscriptions.

The Naval Institute's book-publishing program, begun in 1898 with basic guides to naval practices, has broadened its scope in recent years to include books of more general interest. Now the Naval Institute Press publishes more than seventy titles each year, ranging from how-to books on boating and navigation to battle histories, biographies, ship and aircraft guides, and novels. Institute members receive discounts on the Press's nearly 400 books in print.

For a free catalog describing Naval Institute Press books currently available, and for further information about subscribing to *Naval History* magazine or about joining the U.S. Naval Institute, please write to:

Membership & Communications Department
U.S. NAVAL INSTITUTE
118 Maryland Avenue
Annapolis, Maryland 21402-5035

Or call, toll-free, (800) 233-USNI.